SYSTEMS OF REHEARSAL

Stanislavsky, Brecht, Grotowski and Brook

Shomit Mitter

London and New York

First published 1992
by Routledge
11 New Fetter Lane, London EC4P 4EE

Simultaneously published in the USA and Canada
by Routledge Inc.
29 West 35th Street, New York, NY 10001

Reprinted 1993

© 1992 Shomit Mitter

Typeset in 10 on 12 point Garamond by
Computerset, Harmondsworth, Middlesex
Printed in Great Britain by
Clays Ltd, St Ives plc

British Library Cataloguing in Publication Data
A catalogue record for this book is available from the British Library.

Library of Congress Cataloging in Publication Data
Mitter, Shomit
Systems of rehearsal : Stanislavsky, Brecht, Grotowski and
Brook / Shomit Mitter.
p. cm.
Includes bibliographical references and index.
1. Theater rehearsals. 2. Acting. 3. Theater – Production and
direction. I. Title.
PN2071.R45M57 1992 92–43
792.028–dc20

ISBN 0–415–06783–9
0–415–06784–7 (pbk)

To M
in spite of whose every effort
this book is at last complete

CONTENTS

ACKNOWLEDGEMENTS

This book is largely a product of my experience of theatre workshop under Khalid Tyabji and Barry John. A large number of the exercises discussed here are those which they first introduced to me and encouraged me to explore. To Khalid I owe as well the idea of the trip to Orissa, and to Vijay Tankha the initiative which took me to Peter Brook's workshop in Bhopal. I would like to thank Mr Brook for his warmth and openness in allowing me to join his workshop, and Nina Soufy at the Centre International de Recherches Théâtrales in Paris for sending me unpublished material which I would not normally have been able to obtain. I am grateful to Gautam Dasgupta at *Performing Arts Journal*, Richard Schechner at New York University and Judie Christie at Centre for Performance Research for giving me access to their libraries and film archives. I owe thanks to Bobby Banerji for translating some manuscripts I was thus able to acquire, and to Bobby Coe, Sheila Barkham and the duty advisers at the University of London Computer Centre for helping to produce this book.

Many of the ideas here are products of discussions with Paul Smith and Arjun Mahey whose understanding and guidance have been instrumental in developing my ability to express with some clarity the thoughts that have been with me for some time. The expansion of these ideas into a properly schematic form was made possible by Peter Holland to whom I am immensely grateful. I owe thanks as well to David Williams and Jean Chothia for their advice and encouragement, and to KK who first introduced me to the theatre and to the books which I still consult as they have become increasingly representative of my particular areas of interest.

For financial support I owe thanks to King's College, Cambridge, the Judith Wilson Fund, the Le Bas Foundation and the Gilchrist Educational Trust.

Most of all, I would like to thank Tony Singh whose imagination and generosity have been a source of great inspiration for me.

INTRODUCTION

I had lived through a happy moment in my artistic life. I had
received a true gift from Apollo. Were there no technical means of
conscious entry into the paradise of art? When technique reaches
the possibility of realising this hope, our stage craftsmanship will
become a true art. But where and how is one to seek those roads
into the secret sources of inspiration?[1]

(Konstantin Stanislavsky)

He believed that the only directing method to give results was a
fusion of several different methods . . .[2]

(J.C. Trewin on Peter Brook)

There is a curious asymmetry in contemporary theatre studies. On the
one hand theatre historians admit that drama criticism must include
analyses of performance. They argue that, as theatre is a compound
entity comprising both speech and action, criticism must find ways of
addressing theatre's non-verbal elements. On the other hand they
continue for the most part to discuss only those features of the theatre
event that are dictated by the author's text. This is largely because scripts
can be reproduced and are therefore easier to study than performance
which is ephemeral. The indignation of champions of performance
criticism such as Beckerman and Styan has thus tended to obscure the
irony implicit in their position: that while they agree that significance in
drama is a function of both language and gesture, their analyses
elucidate only the texts with which the directors they study are concerned. Productions of *Macbeth* by Reinhardt, Craig and Irving are still
discussed in ways that tell us less about these directors than about
Macbeth. The demand for a method of studying theatre on the basis of its
immediacy is met with all that constitutes the denial of that immediacy –

1

the mechanical and indiscriminate application of the critical methods of literature to theatre.

In an effort to develop a more appropriate means of addressing the distinctive attributes of the theatre, this book takes as its subject the process of rehearsal. Working on the assumption that actors and directors have methods specific to their craft that are independently valuable, it examines three schools of theatre workshop that have proliferated recently. It compares the rehearsal techniques used by Peter Brook at various points in his career with those developed by Stanislavsky, Brecht and Grotowski. The book assesses the extent of Brook's debt to these systems of rehearsal, methods which assist actors to capture, through carefully structured means, the elusive advantages of inspiration.

This study complements existing work on rehearsal technique in three ways. First, whereas books like Viola Spolin's *Improvisation for the Theatre* are sometimes misleading in that they list techniques devoid of the purposive contexts that make them meaningful, I have tried to locate exercises within the larger patterns of which they are products so as to render them properly intelligible. Far too often I have seen young directors using methods drawn from manuals without realizing that these are sterile unless deployed in tandem with certain complementary routines. By elucidating the structures which books like Ms Spolin's make available only in part, I hope I have been able to facilitate more coherent and ambitious sweeps of work.

Second, whereas books like David Selbourne's *The Making of A Midsummer Night's Dream* merely document theatre practice, I have attempted to *model* these experiments so that it becomes easier to relate them to the theories they are designed to realize. I find that rehearsal logs, however accurate and sensitive, tend to be far too embroiled in the day-to-day details of workshop to give a sufficiently substantial account of the principles and aspirations that underlie the work they discuss. A strictly linear narrative of a particular production can tell us what a director does but not, in the long term, to what end. I have therefore tried to rationalize the information provided by these first-hand accounts, to structure it analytically rather than chronologically. My intention is to ask what ambitions these directors have had for their theatres, what problems these have entailed for their actors and what solutions they have been able to offer in workshop. I hope that, as a result, I have been able to approach the larger issue as to what theatre can achieve – not with the dull generality that afflicts universalizing answers to such questions but with the authority that stems from studying specific, dissimilar and profoundly practical projects.

Third, whereas books like Stanislavsky's *An Actor Prepares* and Grotowski's *Towards a Poor Theatre* set out systems of theatre with an attractive semblance of completeness, the element of comparison here provides the advantage of perspective. Manifestos and autobiographical assessments have the virtue of consistency, the product of the refraction of a number of concepts through the filter of a single authoritative sensibility. But they also lack, for the same reason, a multiplicity of opinions and interpretations that characterizes a healthy understanding of ideas. However judiciously written, personal declarations do eventually argue for certain points of view. Whether or not one finds these positions intrinsically interesting, one almost always misses in them the vitality that comes from the interplay of convictions and attitudes. My intention in structuring the book as a series of comparisons has been to redress the balance by having each position comment critically on every other. Whereas each section of this book presents a fairly straightforward exegesis, the juxtapositions, both within and across chapters, are designed to generate a critical counterpoint through the incongruities they reveal.

In the early stages of the work, I was prepared to let these contrasts stand, to let the variations speak for themselves. I was satisfied that the mapping of resonances between the paradigms I had selected would be enlightening enough to furnish material for a book. However, in the course of writing I gradually became aware of an improbable and therefore interesting contrast: whereas the similarities and differences between Stanislavsky, Brecht and Grotowski seemed in keeping with the expectations of common sense, the comparisons between Brook and each of these directors showed a disproportionate convergence. I had not anticipated the extraordinary extent to which Brook would concur with his predecessors as he engaged for a period their approaches. I came to acknowledge that, in spite of my suspicion of lofty critical judgements, there did lurk a conclusion in this extraordinary correlation: Brook seemed to me more a mimic than an inventor. Brook appeared an admirably astute assimilator, a singularly canny user of other people's ideas and techniques; but he was not 'original' if by that we mean one capable of transforming beyond recognition the pre-existing pool of concepts to which we are all inevitably and naturally exposed.

I was aware that such a view could appear to be repudiated by the virtuosity of some of his productions – the obvious freshness of his 1970

3

A Midsummer Night's Dream, for example. However, I was not prepared to relinquish my conviction that there is a price to be paid for emulation, however spirited, skilful or shrewd. I felt that Brook's ability to present his borrowings with vigour and refinement should not obliterate our sense of the place individuality must have in the assessment of theatre directors. The fact that there is no dearth of such brilliance in Brook seemed not to contradict the contention that he does not have a distinctive legacy to hand down to future generations, a consolidated bequest that can outlast the impermanent incandescence of each of his productions taken independently. Whereas critics, however aware of history, must applaud the inventiveness of specific productions, the theatre historian must consider whether these flashes of vitality in fact cohere to comprise a contribution of lasting substance.

It seemed to me to be of some interest, for instance, that Kenneth Tynan should interpret as a mark of originality Brook's infinitely transitional identity as a theatre director:

Theatre Quarterly: You couldn't really associate him with any 'school' of theatre.

Kenneth Tynan: Nor could you accuse him of imitating anybody. He was one of the only English directors of my time whose career was, in a sense, a search for antecedents: . . . his ideas were spun out his own intuition.[3]

Where the critic sees a multitude of varying impressions that seem to constitute independence, the theatre historian can reveal the extent to which each phase of this work is in fact derivative and therefore less remarkable. That Brook contributes very substantially to each of the areas he undertakes to explore is scant praise: from directors of his stature one expects not startling modifications of given paradigms but the institution of personal and therefore unique approaches.

However, it did occur to me that the fact that Brook showed an affinity with such radically different directors was in itself quite extraordinary. I began to feel that his ability to absorb the influence of vastly dissimilar theatres could only be seen as an achievement. There was as well an inescapable correspondence between Brook's appropriation of styles and his dissatisfaction with what he saw as the insular individualism of contemporary western theatre. Brook had long argued against formal consistency in the theatre; he wanted performances that could fluctuate deftly between conventions. He felt that if theatre was to reflect the manner in which life makes discordant elements cohere, it must tell its stories in as many ways as possible – for each style gives access to certain truths but inevitably excludes others. Brook's work in *Le Mahabharata* seemed to confirm this view, for in it Brook was able to present this heterogeneity in a single work. By using a host of different styles in what was nevertheless a coherent body of theatre, Brook was able finally to generate an authentic image of life's plurality. By making irreconcilable elements coexist, the production also illuminated Brook's inordinately misunderstood apprenticeship amidst a plethora of methods and codes. Far from being a covertly adopted substitute for inspiration, Brook's imitations suddenly seemed deliberate. It was a *virtue* to cast around widely for styles – and to have had the insight to recognize it as such was unmistakably original.

The book, as you read it, remains the product of each of these impulses: to elucidate, to impeach, and eventually to champion. These tendencies do not neutralize one another – for Brook's work does eventually find that unity of indiscriminate amalgamation, the hallmark we most admire in Shakespeare. Stanislavsky, Brecht and Grotowski share a certain sharpness of definition which is a mark both of the commendable uniqueness of their inclinations and of the ultimately unavoidable limits of their creativity. In contrast, Brook has an inimitable lack of individuality, a second-hand genius of formidable synoptic power.

1

TO BE:
Konstantin Stanislavsky and Peter Brook

The actor must dig inside himself for responses, but at the same time must be open to outside stimuli. Acting was the marriage of these two processes.[1]

(Albert Hunt paraphrasing Peter Brook in rehearsal)

Actually in each physical act there is an inner psychological motive which impels physical action, as in every psychological inner action there is also a physical action, which expresses its psychic nature.

The union of these two actions results in organic action on the stage.[2]

(Konstantin Stanislavsky)

STANISLAVSKY: TO BE

On 5 September 1869, the six-year-old Konstantin Alexeyev ('Stanislavsky' was a stage name) made his first stage appearance as Winter in a tableau vivant depicting the four seasons. He had been instructed to pretend to tend a fire represented by a candle placed behind some logs. As the curtain rose little Kostya, ashamed at having to make believe, actually prodded the candle which fell over and set fire to the cotton wool with which the stage was covered. The fire was put out but Kostya was unceremoniously carried to the nursery where he was severely scolded and cried bitterly. In his autobiography, Stanislavsky recalls being terribly embarrassed at having to beguile the audience; the act of actually overturning the candle was, in contrast, 'completely natural and logical'.[3] The lessons of this early experience are carefully noted: 'the discomfort of unreasonable presence on the stage, and the inner truth of reasoned presence and action on it', writes Stanislavsky,

6

'control me on the stage even at the present day'.[4] An action is meaningful only if it is real, and reality is a function of reason.

Over sixty years after his incendiary début, Stanislavsky, thinly disguised as the drama teacher Tortsov in *An Actor Prepares*, has another young Kostya (also an autobiographical figure) attempt to light a fire on stage. Kostya makes the mistake of asking for matches:

> 'The fireplace is made of paper. Did you intend to burn down the theatre?'
>
> 'I was just going to pretend,' I explained . . . .
>
> 'To pretend to light a fire, pretended matches are sufficient . . . .What needs to burn is your imagination . . . . [L]et me see what you would do *if* my supposed facts were true . . . . *[I]f* acts as a lever to lift us out of the world of actuality into the realm of imagination.'[5]

Truth on stage is what the actor construes as real.

Both Kostyas face the same problem: they are obliged simultaneously to display their fidelity to two embarrassingly incompatible orders of reality. On the one hand they must imbue with truth the 'fires' their characters tend. On the other hand, sincerity demands that it also be conceded that the fires do not in fact exist.

In the case of little Kostya, this gap is bridged accidentally. As the cotton wool on the stage catches fire, the actor's response can be real because the fire is real. The elder Kostya, unable to allow actuality to intercede on his behalf, must resort to more subtle means. The solution offered to him is that of Tortsov's 'magic if':

> It is as though he says to himself: 'I know that everything by which I am surrounded on the stage . . . is all make-believe. But if it were real . . . this is how I would act . . .'. And from the instant that his soul is aware of the magic phrase 'if it were,' the actual world around him ceases to interest him, he is carried off to another plane, to a life created by his imagination.[6]

The expedient works in two stages. First, Stanislavsky emphasizes that the actor must acknowledge that the objects with which he is surrounded are only stage properties, fictional objects in a constructed world. This is a concession to actuality, a recognition of the literal truth of the situation on stage. The actor thus disarms the audience by establishing that everything is 'clear, honest and above-board'.[7] His concern is with truth, not artifice.

However, having made this gesture, Stanislavsky immediately goes on to dismiss all this as 'crude' and 'having no significance'.[8] What he is really interested in, we now gather, is the truth of the *imaginary* situation on stage – the truth of the world of the character. The concession to actuality is just a stratagem, a means of ensuring that the subsequent flight of the actor's imagination into the circumstances of the drama does not explicitly refute the inescapable fact that the character is only a fabrication. Thus Stanislavsky gives the impression of having resolved the contradiction between the truths of actuality and contrivance by satisfying within the parameters of a single prompt their otherwise disparate claims. In fact the opposition is not resolved at all. The argument secures the release of the imagination not by orchestrating a union of truths but by obliterating the claims of one of the two positions through an elaborate and beguiling pretence of taking account of it. By acknowledging the claims of actuality, the 'magic if' denies it grounds on which to disturb the still waters of imagined truths. By then interpreting its ascendency as axiomatic, Stanislavsky's actor may now construe as real what is blatantly unreal. Through a devastating combination of censorship and propaganda, the actor may make belief.

The ability of the 'if' to rid the imagination of the claims of actuality is concomitant with its ability to rid the actor-character of the burden of acknowledging the presence of the actor-self. Just as 'if' ignores actuality by pretending to take account of it, so also it suppresses the actor's everyday self by viewing the character initially as 'other'. Once that is done the actor can work solely in the world of the character without fear of being interrupted awkwardly by actuality. Thus the actor, by using 'if' in the first instance ('If I was the character I would . . .'), can eventually work 'without dividing his creative problems into "I" and "if I"'.[9] Having set into motion the machinery of its mischief, the 'if' is withdrawn from what is then a pristine and unfettered condition of authentic, non-literal being. From a convenient but uncomfortable apprenticeship under 'if I', the actor graduates to the authority and energy of 'I'.

Thus the value of 'if' is that it allows you to 'achieve a complete merging of yourself and the character of your part'.[10] This is for Stanislavsky the highest condition to which an actor can aspire – a temporary but total transformation into a received order of being. As Stanislavsky wrote of one of his earliest successes as an actor in the role of Rostanov in Dostoevsky's *The Village of Stepanchikovo*, 'I live the life of Rostanov, I think his thoughts, I cease to be myself. I become another man, a man like Rostanov.'[11] At the very end of his career, in a rehearsal

8

of *Tartuffe*, Stanislavsky still holds that 'Art begins when there is no role, when there is only the "I"'.[12] The product of the sublimation of 'if I' into 'I' is a state of unperturbed veracity-in-fiction, 'to be'.

There is of course an irony about using the 'magic if' to generate the condition 'I am' in this way: the ability of the 'if' to neutralize the mutually exclusive opposition between fiction and actuality is contingent upon the resolution of yet another conflict of irreconcilables – the actor's credulity and the fact that the 'I am' is inescapably a product of contrivance. If the actor's sense of truth is an essential prerequisite for an action to be deemed real on stage, then the actor's growing awareness of the strategic underpinning of the 'if' is likely eventually to erode that truth. Veracity cannot reliably be sustained by a device as fundamentally opposed to it as subterfuge.

Stanislavsky's solution to the problem is to invoke a secondary inversion designed to disarm the 'if'. Just as the 'if' muzzles actuality by recognizing it, so also the 'I' now undermines the 'if' in the very act of using it. For instance, when Stanislavsky declares that 'the actor's belief in his own action places him on the path of truth',[13] a subtle shift of emphasis is implied. There is something about the conviction with which Stanislavsky speaks of the 'path to truth' that suggests that for him the actor's belief is not after all a matter of expediency, merely a means to an end, that of convincing the audience of the truth of something that is 'actually' untrue. There is as well a further sense in which the actor, through his belief, *creates* reality in the theatre. In his biography of Stanislavsky, David Magarshack observes that for Stanislavsky 'the actor had to believe in what he did or said on stage and that truth on the stage was merely what the actor believed in'.[14] The absence of the audience in Magarshack's equation suggests too that the relationship between truth and belief is not causal as much as symbiotic. Trivially, an action is true because the actor believes in it; far more importantly, the actor is able to believe in the action because it is true. Stage truth displaces actuality by becoming it.

The impulse to realism in Stanislavsky then seems not entirely to have been based on a desire to imitate reality. Rather, it seems to be born of an overwhelming urge to *engender* nature, to *beget* an order of reality which we cannot possess in life, a reality which we desire precisely because it is 'other'. In all great art the life of the human spirit is realized, but in the theatre a person can become that reality, literally embody it. This, for Stanislavsky, is the essence of theatre – to become another. 'Anybody can imitate an image', he writes, 'but only a true talent can *become* an image.'[15] Of his success as Rostanov, Stanislavsky concludes, 'then I had talent, for in this role (although it was almost the only one) I had become Rostanov, while in my other roles I merely copied and imitated the necessary image'.[16] Stage art for Stanislavsky is not mimesis, it is metamorphosis. The aim is not merely to convince but to create. The subject is not life but its transcendence.

An implication of the notion that stage reality is a product not of imitation but of creation is that actors must really feel the emotions and sensations of the characters they depict. The actors' belief, generated by their imagined sense of reality in a situation, is not in itself sufficient guarantee of their capacity to evoke 'life' on the stage. Their work must be founded on the pulse of their emotions which alone can signal the obliteration of the gulf which divides character from actor. Imagination implies an otherness which is precisely what art frees us of. Merely to imagine is to imitate, whereas to feel is to become.

Stanislavsky's insistence that actors should feel what they portray creates a problem in that there is no reason to suppose that their emotions should on demand coincide with those of their characters. The profound difficulty of the actor's task arises out of this obligation to create in a manner that is true to both personality and text – the one aspect of which is familiar but to be transcended, the other 'other' and to be embodied. This is the challenge of the actor's situation:

> How does it happen that one artist creates a character under circumstances given him by another artist?[17]

STANISLAVSKY: TO FIND THE FACE CONSTRUCTED IN THE MIND

In *Creating a Role*, Stanislavsky maintains that 'in the language of the actor *to know* is synonymous with *to feel*'.[18] Only by feeling something can actors be satisfied that they are intimate with it with a fullness that approaches the required condition of being that thing. In the alchemy of drawing reality from representation, the actor's problem is therefore primarily that of knowledge. If to know is to feel and to feel is utterly to be, then to know is, by logical extension, to be. To know more about a character is to experience it more fully and eventually seamlessly to become it. Stanislavsky's answer to the question, 'What is the actor to do about the portions of the play which do not evoke the miracle of instant intuitive comprehension?' is that 'All such portions must be studied to disclose what materials they possess to incite him to ardour.'[19] In the slippage between the terms 'ardour' and 'comprehension' lies the assumption that the one really is the other. The chapter ends with a section entitled 'The Appraisal of the Facts'. The phrase is explained: 'to appraise the facts is to take all the alien life created by the playwright and make it one's own'.[20] Awareness and possession are one.

Most people who have some experience of teaching would probably agree that students best understand the things they have previously had reason to question. A question sets up a framework of contextual interest to which the answer may be referred so that, through its discovered relationship with its relevance, it is better retained in the memory. One of Stanislavsky's methods of provoking his actors into exploring in sufficient detail the 'other' world of the play involves setting them a series of questions about their characters which, when researched and answered, establish what he calls the 'given circumstances' of the drama. In a rehearsal of Tolstoy's *Czar Fyodor*:

> Now, let us talk it over. . . . What does it mean for each of you to prepare himself for the conspiracy against Boris and Fyodor? First, you must know the life of that period in Russia well. . . . For tomorrow's rehearsal each of you must prepare answers to the following questions: . . .
> 1. Who am I? How old am I? My profession? Members of my family? . . .
> 2. Where do I live in Moscow? (You must be able to draw the plan of your apartment and the furniture in the rooms.)
> 3. How did I spend yesterday? . . .[21]

In a rehearsal of Katayev's *The Embezzlers*:

> 'You are a cashier, aren't you? What do you have in your office?'
> 'Money . . .'
> 'Well, yes, money. But what else? Tell me in more detail. You say "money". Good, how much? What kind? How is it folded? Where is it kept? What kind of table do you have in your office? What kind of chair, how many electric lights?'[22]

The questions are designed to reveal to the actors their ignorance about a way of life so that the answers, when supplied, contain more than the sum of the information they carry. In the wake of the actors' manifest ignorance, they have a personal focus which facts gleaned to no particular end generally lack. Thus the knowledge finally accumulated is imbued with the spirit not of revelation but of recognition. Feeling is the product of a privately perceived pattern of cerebral involvement with a play. In order to be, the actor must feel, and in order to feel, the actor must move from the self to the play via the mind.

11

Whereas an investigation into the 'given circumstances' of a play anchors a character in a knowable past, the analysis of the text in terms of 'units and objectives' locates a character in the context of an intended future. This second major component of Stanislavsky's approach to the problem of characterization involves dividing the given text into sections of time bounded by internally related action. These segments are then labelled in a manner which crystallizes the essence of each unit and discovers its fundamental objective. To ensure that such dissection does not lose in stasis what it gains in terms of insight and lucidity, Stanislavsky recommends that these objectives be expressed as verbs:

> 'Now, tell me . . . give me one word, a verb, which will intensify your line of action.'
> 'To please the Governor.'. . .
> 'To *win* his heart. . . . This is your task: to obtain an invitation. Well, sir, how will you act?'[23]

As in the 'given circumstances' exercise, the actor's impulse to action is a product of analysis and deduction. A cerebral mastery of the temporal imperative in a drama provides the key to the manner of its spatial execution.

In order to ensure that these locally apprehended sources of thrust do not neutralize one another for lack of proper alignment, the tasks thus devised are projected over an extended logical sequence. This leads through the course of the play to a 'superobjective', the *raison d'être* of the character. This is the character's final goal and shaping influence, the aim that runs through the play and dictates the manner in which the role as a whole is to be played. The result is a coherently consecutive file of events:

> Develop, above all, the scheme of your physical behaviour in each episode and unite them later in a single line of action. This is the infallible way to bring about the embodiment of Gogol's Plushkin.[24]

Discretely discovered packages of impulses are intellectually tailored to dovetail one into the other so as to give the actor a steady bearing and the role its drive and energy.

Units and objectives contribute to the unification of actor and character by transferring what for the character is motive to what in the real world of the actor is justification. In the act of discovering verbs with which to label the characters' dominant preoccupations at given points in a play, the actors also supply themselves with reasons for doing what their characters do. If for example a character's objective in a scene is to win the heart of his beloved, this also justifies for the actor his walk to the sofa to sit near her. Yoked together in a single verb lie two axes of significance bracketed together as indeed the actor must be with his character. The fact that the actor's reasons for performing a certain action are identical with those of his character helps generate the impression that the actor and the character are one. In a rehearsal of Bulgakov's *Molière*, Stanislavsky puts this gambit into practice:

> You have a letter in your hand, and this justifies your entering straight from the market. . . . I will direct you for awhile and you justify whatever I say to you.[25]

Within the space of five lines the word 'justify' is used twice, referring in the first instance to the character and in the second to the actor. In both cases the person is addressed as 'you'. Thus Stanislavsky exploits the ambiguity set up by the symbiotic relationship between objectives and justification by semantically consolidating the conclusion that the actor now is the character. If an enquiry into the given circumstances of the drama is an exercise in making the facts of the play familiar enough to seem personal, an analysis of objectives is an exercise in making the logic of the play (literally) one's own.

Significantly, both the 'given circumstances' exercise and the study of objectives are, at different points in the Stanislavsky corpus, construed as being the most productive starting points for work on a production. In Toporkov's accounts of Stanislavsky in rehearsal, the words 'first' and 'beginning' consistently attach to the notion of the analysis of plays in terms of units and objectives: the process by which 'the actor defines for himself the logic of the separate links of the unbroken line of conflict . . . is the beginning of the work on a part'.[26] On the other hand, in *My Life in Art*, Stanislavsky asserts that the 'quality which the poet Pushkin calls "given circumstances". . . is the very first thing which must be made clear in a play, because without it, it is hard to speak of the play's inner nature'.[27] To the extent that motives may be located in the given circumstances which they cannot of their own accord create, the latter may be seen as having the more justifiable claim to being the most useful starting point for work on a role. Be that as it may, these parallel claims to precedence are significant in so far as they show that the distinguishing feature of the system as a whole is that it consistently advocates a cerebral approach to characterization. Since both techniques involve a move from mind to body, and both are credited with being the point at which the work on inhabiting a character must begin, it follows that for

Stanislavsky, analysis precedes action. In *An Actor Prepares* Tortsov urges his students to 'Begin by thinking about the inner side of a role':[28]

> An actor is under the obligation to live his part inwardly, and then to give his experience an external embodiment. I ask you to note especially that the dependence of the body on the soul is particularly important in our school of art.[29]

For Stanislavsky, conception precedes enactment. The mind determines a course of action which it is the responsibility of the body meticulously to follow.

On 8 March 1909, Stanislavsky delivered a paper at a theatrical conference in which he divided the process of creating a character into six stages. In the first stage the actors get to know the author's work. In the second stage they search for the psychological material needed to represent their characters. In the third stage they create imaginary models of their characters. Only in the fourth stage are these images realized in the body. The lecture is, to steal a phrase Tortsov uses in the analysis of a successful improvisation, 'an admirable example of the part of the *mind* in initiating the creative process'.[30] The most attractive thing about the sequence is that it is supposedly effortless: 'From the intuition of feelings I went to the outer image', writes Stanislavsky in *My Life in Art*, 'for it flowed naturally from the inner image'.[31] The work of the mind not only precedes that in the body but organically generates in the body the conditions required to realise the conception it has created.

*

Coherent, logical and internally consistent, the system thus developed seemed perfectly poised to revolutionize Moscow Art Theatre acting with higher levels of conviction and authenticity. However, instead of the relaxation and freedom Stanislavsky had imagined would be the products of his system, his rehearsals were now characterized by unprecedented levels of tension. Performances suddenly became strained and stilted. In Stanislavsky's first production after writing his so-called system – Knut Hamsun's *Drama of Life* – the actors seemed, by his own admission, to have 'moved backwards and not forwards'.[32] The actors reacted to their failure by resisting the system but Stanislavsky persisted with it, convinced that the actors were only being lazy. Unfortunately for Stanislavsky, his next production, Andreyev's *Life of Man*, fared no better as a lure for the actors' acceptance. Stanislavsky's credibility suffered further as his own acting noticeably deteriorated in this period. In the last twenty-three years of his life he did not appear in a single new part. During rehearsals of the 1917 production of *The Village of Stepanchikovo*, Nemirovich-Danchenko took Stanislavsky's role away from him and gave it to a younger actor. The role was that of Rostanov. It was the character which, when he had played it in 1891, had led Stanislavsky passionately to declare, we remember, 'I live the life of Rostanov, I think his thoughts, I cease to be myself.'[33]

*

Daisetz Suzuki, a writer on Zen Buddhism, maintains that 'man is a thinking reed but his greatest works are done when he is not calculating or thinking'.[34] The methods of Zen Buddhism begin with the assumption that enlightenment comes only with the obliteration of conscious purpose. If one lets the unconscious work without conscious interference, the body somehow works more efficiently. If one does not, the body becomes tense and even the most normal motor functions become difficult. The worst dancers look at their feet while dancing, the worst drivers are not able to talk while driving. Theatre is not immune to such self-consciousness. Most actors know that the more one thinks about what one is doing, the more difficult it is to do it. The more clearly one works out what one is going to do on stage, the worse the result. A conscious awareness of the image that is required leads actors to imitate it rather than to live through the experience of which that image should naturally be the creative result. This suggests that the failure of the Stanislavsky system is likely to have been a result of its cerebral approach to characterization. By recommending that actors consciously imbibe the psychology of their characters, Stanislavsky may be seen as having created a situation in which his actors were more likely to experience self-consciousness than transformation into character.

Ironically, Stanislavsky would actually agree with Suzuki that there is in creativity a certain unconscious activity. In *An Actor Prepares*, Stanislavsky writes,

> when an actor is profoundly absorbed by some profoundly moving objective, so that he throws his whole being passionately into its execution, he reaches a state that we call *inspiration*. In it almost everything he does is subconscious and he has no conscious realisation of how he accomplishes his purpose.[35]

However, unlike painters or composers, actors cannot wait for these unsolicited promptings to vitalize their work. Actors are bound by pre-set performance hours during which there is no certainty that inspiration will occur. Stanislavsky's system is therefore intended to be a body of work which actors can use as a safeguard against the failure of spontaneous inspiration. The naturally present subconscious impulse is still Stanislavsky's objective but, if it cannot be relied upon always to be forthcoming, Stanislavsky must explore how to generate favourable conditions for its emergence. In an article he wrote for the *Encyclopaedia Britannica*, Stanislavsky declared that his system was the product of his 'search for . . . ways leading from the conscious to the subconscious'.[36] This was the rationale of the cerebral system: when the subconscious is not compliantly operative, the conscious mind must intervene. The system is merely a fail safe, a lure for what is truly creative.

What Stanislavsky did not see – and what is emphatically explicit in Suzuki – is that it is a necessary condition of the unfettered operation of the subconscious that conscious awareness be actively suppressed during the creative act. Stanislavsky's error, it turns out, was to assume commonsensically that the only alternative to the workings of the subconscious was that of the conscious mind. Hence the emphasis in the system on intellectual approaches – on researching background and defining motivation. Curiously absent from Stanislavsky's work is any hint as to why logic is the most effective substitute for inspiration. It appears that he took this very much for granted: when in *An Actor Prepares* Kostya asks why reason is the most suitable alternative to intuition, Tortsov merely says that 'it seems entirely normal'[37] – which is disturbing precisely because it is *not* evasive.

It is ironic that Stanislavsky should have had Kostya anticipate his later failure without being able to communicate his misgivings with sufficient urgency. Perhaps if Stanislavsky had questioned more deeply the assumption that to be is to know, he would have realized with Suzuki that to know is really to set the object of knowledge against the knower – for knowledge itself implies a dichotomy and can therefore never be the thing itself. The 'I' of 'I am' is not the 'I' of 'I know' and in the gulf between the two lies the system actor's vexation. Late in his career, looking back on the incipient stages of the implementation of his system, Stanislavsky confessed that he 'used to stuff the heads of the actors with all sorts of lectures about the epoch, the history, and the life of the character in the play, as a result of which they used to go on stage with a head full to bursting and were not able to act anything'.[38] Knowledge and being mutually exclude, rather than reinforce, one another.

Stanislavsky thus faced the problem that while the subconscious could not be relied upon to surface spontaneously in performance, the conscious mind could not be used in rehearsal because it inhibited the actors. Some radically original approach had to be discovered to lead the actor out of this dilemma. Some new technique had to be found which would enable actors to control what they were doing without upsetting what was for them the naturally relaxed way of working.

STANISLAVSKY: TO FIND THE MIND'S CONSTRUCTION IN THE FACE

Stanislavsky declared that his system was based on experience, that the techniques he had advocated in it were based on his analysis of the reasons for his success as a practising actor. His failure as an actor after the formalization of his system could then mean one of two things: that his claim to have worked from experience to theory was in fact unfounded, which is unlikely; or that, while writing, he had grossly misinterpreted the cause of his success.

As a young actor, Stanislavsky's favoured technique was to enter a role by physically imitating a person who resembled the character he was playing. If he had to play an old man he would begin by imitating an elderly person he knew. The interesting thing about this technique was that by doing this he found he was able to assimilate not merely the external mannerisms of old age but something of the internal condition as well. Stanislavsky noticed to his surprise that his mastery of outward features always led to an associated emotional state. Following his success in Ibsen's *An Enemy of the People*, Stanislavsky recalled that he 'had only to assume the manners and habits of Stockman, on stage or off, and in my soul there was born the feelings and the perceptions'[39] of the character. In the final stages of his work on Sotanville in Molière's *Georges Dandin*, the catalyst in the process of the transformation of self into character was not gait but make-up:

> I accidentally received a gift from the lap of the gods. One feature in my make-up gave a living and comic expression to my face and something turned within me. . . . All that I did not believe suddenly found my trust. Who can explain this unexplainable, sudden and magical creative motion![40]

On the basis of these experiences Stanislavsky concluded somewhat uncertainly that 'sometimes it is possible to arrive at the inner charac- teristics of a part by way of its outer characteristics'.[41] Contrary to the opinions posited years later in his theoretical writings on the subject, Stanislavsky had in practice intuitively engaged a system in which the body rather than the mind is autonomously responsible for the authentic portrayal of character. When the gap between the self and the role is bridged physically rather than intellectually, the emotions seem to follow of their own accord. It follows that the conscious mind is not the only alternative to subconscious inspiration in the creation of character: the body too has its purposes, mysterious though these may be.

The only detailed account of the process is in *Building a Character* where Kostya 'becomes' the critic as his make-up and costume irresistibly create within him that particular mode of being. At first Kostya does not have the slightest inkling as to whom he will attempt to represent. As the make-up man begins to transform his face, Kostya discovers the incipient stages of an identity:

> I trembled, my heart pounded, I did away with my eyebrows, powdered myself at random. . . . I glanced in the mirror and did not recognise myself. Since I had looked into it the last time a fresh transformation had taken place in me.
> 'It is he, it is he', I exclaimed . . .[42]

Recognition succeeds creation: the conception of the character becomes available to Kostya only after he has created it.

Surprises continue to occur as impulses precede understanding: as Kostya speaks, he is amazed at the brazen, unpleasant tone of his voice: 'Here to my complete surprise I let out a shrill squeak instead of a guffaw. I was quite taken aback myself, it was so unexpected.'[43] Kostya's bewilderment is an indication both of the authenticity of the transformation and of the fact that he is not cerebrally in control of it. It is the expression too of the lasting astonishment of the elder Stanislavsky who, in the period now of his theorizing upon his practice, is manifestly unable to draw out the full significance of this correlation. Tortsov generalizes from Kostya's example merely that 'characterisation is the mask which hides the actor-individual. Protected by it he can lay bare his soul.'[44] The theory accounts for the suppression of the actor-self but does not sufficiently explain the concurrent, and far more interesting, movement into character.

What Stanislavsky is unable explicitly to articulate in the system is that actors are able to 'hide' behind masks because, when wearing a mask with an established expression, they cannot *look* intimidated or embarrassed and therefore do not *feel* those things. What takes place is not the deliberate concealment of an existing identity but the involuntary obliteration of that identity through the physical incapacity of the body to express it. Actors lose their self-consciousness not because they are aware of being protected by the mask. They do so because, when their faces are concealed, they no longer possess the practical means by which to be 'themselves'. By the same measure, the soul, far from being 'laid bare', is possessed to feel only and precisely what the mask reflects. As it does so, the actor 'recognizes' the character and thereby confirms his/her sense of its 'rightness' – as though it conformed to some previously imagined pattern. It follows that, if at all there is an element of certainty about the transition between self and character, it occurs only when the work on the body precedes that in the mind. Indeed, analysis is not merely irrelevant but actively antithetical to the processes by which the muscles can, directly, accurately and almost infallibly, influence the emotions. As Nikolai Gorchakov observes,

> the concrete agency of movement or gesture tears the actor away from himself and brings him into a different reality. This is the reality of the character's spirit along with his psychology. . . . [T]he character of a person *is* his system of movements.[45]

It is as if posture is an objective correlative of a person's state of being. The route to a character's heart lies through the execution of its actions.

*

Working somatically, that is directly from the body to the emotions, has a number of advantages. First, it rids the actors of self-consciousness both through the manifest inability of the masked body physically to express embarrassment and because the mask transforms the self *before* the self has the opportunity to take account of that change. As the actors cannot consciously choose their state of being, the question of their rejecting it does not occur. They merely know the condition, and knowing accept, for the altered self retains the crucial coincidence of being and looking.

Second, whereas feelings can be elusive, the body is palpable and therefore easier to handle. Actors tend to be more comfortable dealing with physical actions than with feelings because actions inspire faith through their actuality. The tangibility of physical experience has an autonomous integrity which helps actors to believe in it. As Stanislavsky observes,

> An actor on the stage need only sense the smallest modicum of organic physical truth in his action or general state and instantly his emotions will respond to his inner faith in the genuineness of what his body is doing. In our case it is incomparably easier to call

19

forth real truth and faith in it in the region of our physical than of our spiritual nature.[46]

If having to submit to the unknown is frightening, it is a comfort to be able to do so in the benignly stable company of straightforward physical manipulation.

Third, material cues, being solid, also have the advantage of being more easily fixed to recur. Where the actor's task is not merely to generate feelings but to retain them over extended runs, the body has the advantage of being far more easily disciplined to respond than feelings which are capricious:

> We cannot set feeling; we can only set physical action. . . . [I]f your feelings dry up, there is no cause for alarm; simply return to physical actions and these will restore your lost feelings.[47]

Whereas the dictates of logic and continuity are fragile, the products of conscious contrivance merely, somatic work inspires confidence because it is always concretely recoverable in performance. When characters have to be played repeatedly, the plastic approach to emotion is more reliable than the machinations of psychological subterfuge.

Lastly, somatic work has the advantage that it can create experience where there is none to be remembered. In so far as belief is usually a function of experience, a product of recognition rather than revelation, it is theoretically required that actors accumulate in the normal course of their lives an enormous range of attitudes and feelings. This is of course impossible – actors are required typically to play roles of greater amplitude and diversity than they can be expected naturally to have experienced. It is then vital that directors have at their disposal solid and unerring means of introducing actors to concerns with which they are unfamiliar.

All characters have feelings with which actors can identify because they directly echo aspects of their own personalities. Here the function of the director is merely to help actors locate the relevant personal experiences which, when invoked, may be expected autonomously to animate the transition between self and character. In playing Chatski's return to Russia after a long absence in Griboyedov's *Woe from Wit*, Stanislavsky must 'compare it to analogous facts in my own life, familiar to me through my own experience'.[48] The memory of a deeply felt emotion can sometimes coax that feeling back into existence. Thereafter it may, through the privileged access feelings have to being, use its prerogative to sharpen the actors' sense of honesty while in character.

The principal problems in the art of characterization occur, however, when features in roles are not as easy to locate within the usually more limited world of the actor. The task of the director is then to generate those experiences in workshop so that they may subsequently be used in performance. Here the cerebral approach founders as it cannot reasonably create and then construe as real what it does not already know in some measure. By contrast somatic work, relying as it does upon external prompts, can engender novel dimensions of engagement and experience.

The need to create 'real' experiences in rehearsal justifies for Stanislavsky the deliberate and sometimes manipulative deception of actors. In Gorchakov there is an account of how, in a rehearsal of Dickens' *The Battle of Life*, Stanislavsky reprimanded an actress so severely that she started to cry; delighted, Stanislavsky exclaimed that those were precisely the tears she needed when playing the scene. In a rehearsal of *The Sisters Gerard*, Stanislavsky designed an improvisation to help the actress Molchanova to enter into the experience of the blind girl she was playing. The lights were turned off and Molchanova was asked to find her way to Stanislavsky through a space crowded with objects. As she began to inch forward, Stanislavsky moved away and instructed the other actors to keep completely silent:

> 'Excuse me,' she said in an odd tone. . . . But no one answered her. . . . 'Konstantin Sergeyevich, have you moved from where you were?' Only silence answered her. . . . Molchanova suddenly stopped in a corner of the room, sobbing terribly. . . . 'Put the lights on now', Stanislavsky said . . . . 'Now you know what blindness is like.'[49]

However naive and suspect this version of blindness, the fact remains that actors put through Molchanova's ordeal are able subsequently to approach their parts with the confidence of knowing them on the basis of their own experience. By having actors really endure what their characters undergo, the gap between self and role is minimised – which is of course precisely what rehearsals are designed to achieve.

*

We have seen that somatic experience is less inhibiting, more concrete, more easily set to recur and can generate the real experiences on which actors can feed their roles. Stanislavsky's untutored approach to character via the body, based on his experience as a young actor, appears therefore to be more effective than the self-conscious perambulations of the imagination recommended by him in his system. The obvious question then is: why did Stanislavsky propose in his writings a method so very different – and indeed so inferior – to the one he had long practised?

There were, one may conjecture, two reasons for Stanislavsky having relinquished the somatic approach in mid-career. First, the method stemmed from what was his rather embarrassing background as an 'insipid copyist'.[50] Its roots lay in a period of his career in which he was successful but of which he was ashamed – for copying was, to his way of thinking, 'sheer imitation, which has nothing to do with creativeness'.[51] Indeed, Stanislavsky consistently uses the idea of imitation as a foil designed to make evident the virtues of the preferred state of 'I am' – in a manner which clearly excludes the possibility of the two ever being causally related. For example, in *An Actor Prepares*, Tortsov exhorts his pupils, 'you must not copy passions or copy types. You must live in the passions and in the types.'[52] By implication, 'the essence of art' for Stanislavsky lies 'not in its external forms but in its spiritual content'.[53] Somatic work is thus relegated to the status of a last resort for immature actors, a failsafe to be used only when the more orthodox cerebral approaches to character are unsuccessful:

> But you must not conclude that the passage from the outward to the inward was our only method. No, even then we understood that it was far from being the best. But what could we do when the more correct inner approaches were still closed to us. . . . Passing from the outward to the inward we were often successful in piercing some of the mysteries. . . .
> But was it right to base our creativeness on accident, . . . on the theory of chance?[54]

Second, although Stanislavsky was aware that the somatic approach did have a link with creativity, he did not consider it to be a valid approach because the processes by which it affected the mind were not properly understood. Looking back on the manner in which he had reached Sotanville through his make-up, Stanislavsky wonders, 'Who can explain this unexplainable, sudden and magical creative motion?'[55] In *Building a Character*, Tortsov's physical impulses to character occur in spite of himself and he finds them difficult to analyse. Of course, not knowing the reason for an effect does not normally prevent people from using those results. But as Stanislavsky had resolved in his system to rid acting of accident, it seemed improper to include within it the agency of a construct that was still incomprehensible. That intelligibility was in fact irrelevant to its operation was itself not fully appreciated – and even if it had been, it too would perhaps have been deemed inappropriate to the purposes of a coherent pedagogical system.

Moreover, by having decided to *write* his system, Stanislavsky had to face the demands language makes upon logic. In so far as a system in print is inevitably a work of explanation, the inexplicable had no place in it. Somatic work, both because it could not be explained and because it was associated in Stanislavsky's mind with the supposedly soulless art of copying, had to be abandoned.

*

Following his discovery that the intellect can inhibit action, that emotions unrelated to physical prompts are fickle, Stanislavsky set about trying to revert to his little understood but manifestly effective somatic approach. This was the beginning of the third phase of his development as an actor and director. In the first stage, as a young actor, Stanislavsky had worked from the body to the mind by copying models for his characters – and he was successful. In the second stage, following the institution of his System, he reversed the process and began to work from the mind to the body – and the result was a crippling self-consciousness. In the third phase, very late in his career, Stanislavsky attempted to work the somatic imperative back into his method of approaching roles. In a rehearsal of *Tartuffe*, his last production, Stanislavsky admitted that when an actor 'begins to reason too much, he is like a horse stamping in place because he lacks the strength to move his load. In order to act without inhibition the actor should not mark time; rather, he should become fascinated with the action.'[56] Appropriately, the actor is now asked to 'start bravely, not to reason, but to act':[57]

> When the actor starts to reason . . . the will is weakened. Don't discuss, just do it.[58]

In his projected work on Gogol's *The Government Inspector*, rehearsals are to be conducted 'without any reading, without any conferences on the play';[59] the actors are to discover emotions in their bodies, for 'in every *physical action*, unless it is purely mechanical, there is concealed some *inner action*, some feelings'.[60] The approach to character through the mind, championed by Stanislavsky after his sojourn in Finland, is firmly rejected:

> Why sit at a table for months and try to force out your dormant feelings? . . . You would do better to go out on the stage and at once engage in action.[61]

In a study of *Othello*, written between 1930 and 1933, Tortsov asks his students to 'execute physical actions, not feel them, because if they are properly carried out the feelings will be generated spontaneously'.[62]

A consistent feature of this change from the cerebral to the physical is that the physical is preferred solely because it is more effective. If one of the reasons for rejecting the physical had been that it was too little understood, its inclusion does not seem to necessitate any obligation to understand thoroughly its basic mode of functioning. This is profoundly ironic, for while the deliberate avoidance of comprehension causes the somatic approach to work most effectively, it also has the regressive effect of blinding Stanislavsky to this very feature – the fact that in somatic work *no* element of rationality is admissible. To anticipate an emotion is, as we have seen, to deny the experience of which that emotion must be the natural result. By implication, the method of physical actions cannot be diluted with the methods of conceptual influx.

However, as a result perhaps of his having adopted the method of physical actions so late in his career – at a stage when he was able neither to relinquish completely the orthodox system to which he claimed to have dedicated his life, nor iron out the teething problems of his new method – Stanislavsky combined what he felt were the advantages of both approaches. The body was used – but compelled to work as the mind does to help actors understand the logic of their emotions:

> [W]e evoke a series of physical actions interlaced with one another. Through them we try to understand the inner reasons that give rise to them, . . . the logic and consistency of feelings in the given circumstances of the play. When we can discover that line, we are aware of the inner meaning of our physical actions.[63]

Logic, consistency, given circumstances, line: the vocabulary here is dangerously close to that of the cerebral system. Rehearsal is still a matter of 'coming to know, that is, to feel, a play'.[64] Where feeling is associated with knowledge, somatic work must fail.

In the last of the three studies which make up *Creating a Role*, that dealing with Gogol's *The Government Inspector*, Tortsov is no more aware of the danger of mixing somatic work with the older psycho-linguistic methods. The body is used – but as an agent of ratiocination: 'I made an analysis', Tortsov declares innocently, 'with my body and soul.'[65] An emphasis on consecutiveness still dogs work which must not be so limited:

You prepare with logic and consistency a simple, accessible line for the physical being of your role, and as a result you suddenly feel inside yourself the life of a human spirit.[66]

To prepare a somatic scenario sequentially is of course to neutralize its ability to generate emotion autonomously. The word 'physical' has crept into the wordstock of the system, but it has not been empowered to effect the overhaul without which it is unworkable.

In Toporkov's account of the work on *Tartuffe*, the somatic imperative is still required to operate within the terms of the logic of human behaviour:

The first step of our rehearsal work might be called 'reconnaissance'; it consisted of analysing the separate scenes.[67]

The physical still succeeds rather than precedes the cerebral – and compromises, to that extent, Stanislavsky's own professed sense of the need to begin with action. An alternative to the self-consciousness implicit in cerebral work has been promised, set up but not fully realized. The pull of the old is still too great. As Stanislavsky declared in his autobiography,

THE SUPERCONSCIOUS THROUGH THE CONSCIOUS!
That is the meaning of the thing to which I have devoted my life since the year 1906, to which I devote my life at present and to which I will devote my life while there is life in me.[68]

It was too much for him to have to relinquish what he felt had been his life's work.

Stanislavsky did not live to see his work on *Tartuffe* completed. The actors put on the play but abandoned the experimental work which, without Stanislavsky's leadership, seemed impossible to develop. What in Stanislavsky remained incomplete and therefore ineffective was refined later by a number of directors. One of those involved in the process of severing the physical method from Stanislavsky's ironically far more widely admired cerebral approach was Peter Brook.

PETER BROOK AND *KING LEAR*

Charles Marowitz's log of Peter Brook's work in 1962 on *King Lear* displays a consistent preoccupation with 'the truthfulness of the emotion'[69] which, when it is lacking, leads to the conclusion that 'the company needs to be trained in feeling'.[70] For Marowitz, Paul Scofield's greatness as an actor in the title role lies in the fact that 'only when fumbling for a line does one glimpse the disparity between the man and the character, and then what one sees is a man winding himself painfully into a Shakespearean fiction'.[71] Similarly, John Kane writes of Peter Brook's rehearsals in 1970 with the Royal Shakespeare Company on *A Midsummer Night's Dream* that they were designed to lead ideally towards 'the fusion of the actor and the text'.[72] It appears that in both productions Brook's actors are required genuinely to feel the dramatized emotions – and thereby to establish that they *are* the characters they play.

However, the manner in which Brook attempts to discover points of contact between actor and character is very different in the two productions. The methods used in *King Lear* derive for the most part from the more cerebral of Stanislavsky's systems, whereas in *A Midsummer Night's Dream*, eight years later, Brook seems to be far more committed to somatic work.

In Marowitz's account of the first reading of *King Lear* at Stratford, Brook declares to the company that 'the work of rehearsals is looking for meaning and then making it meaningful'.[73] The order of activities is important: action is the product of thought; the body executes what the mind has already formulated. Appropriately, Brook arrives at the reading with an interpretation of the play already in place. He says he sees *King Lear* as a play about sight and blindness. The purpose of rehearsals is to give this idea a form: action is to follow analysis.

As rehearsals proceed, there is a further threefold remove between the worlds of thought and action. First, it becomes apparent that Brook's conception is in part a product of the analysis of verbal echoes which only nominally relate diverse aspects of the plot:

> Gloucester who does not see Edmund's villainy, loses his eyes. Edgar who does not see his brother's covetousness, loses his freedom. Lear who does not see the corruption and rancour that seethes within his family and state, loses his senses and ultimately his life.[74]

King Lear becomes a play about sight and blindness through the strategic arrangement of several instances of *metaphorical* blindness ('does not see Edmund's villainy', etc.) around a single instance of actual blinding which then becomes 'the germinal scene in Brook's production'[75] and conditions the interpretation of the play as a whole. Before the actors have voiced a syllable of the text, the production has been structured along lines determined by a semantic association of ideas.

Second, this interpretation is itself inspired by an interpretative text, Jan Kott's essay, '*King Lear*; or *Endgame*'.[76] As its title indicates, Kott's reading of the play ironically contrives to ensure that the ideas preceding the action in Brook's production partially derive from those contained in yet another text – Samuel Beckett's *Endgame*. This then is the third remove of intellection: the action developed in rehearsal is the product not merely of textual analysis, nor even of the study of texts which analyse the script to be played, but further, of texts which inspire the texts which analyse the primary text. Beckett precedes Kott's discussion which influences Brook's analysis which in turn determines the play's non-verbal structure. Action in the Brook production is the offspring of the incestuous complicity of three mutually parasitic worlds of words.

Appropriately, Marowitz's 'Lear Log' begins with a discussion on discussion. *King Lear* is for Brook a 'series of intellectual strands'[77] which demand 'hours of speculation and conjecture'.[78] The first reading of the play is used 'mainly as a study session',[79] and the second and third are devoted to 'readings, stops, analysis and discussion'.[80] At the third reading Brook points out 'the pattern the play makes in space'.[81] Even the spatial element of the production, that which is the medium and legacy of action, is requisitioned by the mind in the name of analysis.

Much of the discussion is geared towards discovering Stanislavskian objectives:

> 'Why,' I asked, 'at the height of his power, obviously still robust and energetic, does Lear decide to apportion out his kingdom and step down?'[82]

It is decided that 'a sub-textual reason has got to be found to set the tone of the opening scene'[83] for, as Brook observes, 'When Paul [Scofield] finds his reasons he will shift from low gear into high. . . . He refuses to *throw himself into* something he does not *feel* and cannot *answer for*.'[84] Notice the links here between being, emotion and analysis: feeling, the touchstone of transformation into character, is contingent upon justification. The route to a character's emotions lies through the self-authenticating filter of a personal standard of logic and motive. Marowitz agrees with Brook: 'When Scofield is sure of his reasons and his text, he is firing on both pistons and Lear soars. When he is not, he falls into a studied, wilful, over-reasonable rendering of the verse'.[85] When the character discovers emotion, it is because the actor is satisfied that there is reason for it; when this ceases to be the case, the actor must go back to the motives arrived at through discussion. Scofield's method is 'to start from the text and work backwards. He is constantly testing the verse to see if the sound corresponds with the emotional intention'.[86] Reason not only precedes action but is also the incontrovertible agent of subsequent referrals and verification. Thus the mind enjoys a self-endorsed guarantee of lasting influence – for it is only to reason that action has recourse in the event of something going wrong. Reason deems that it must itself be both author and critic, plaintiff and judge.

As in Stanislavsky, it is not sufficient that objectives be found for scenes independently of one another for this is likely to set up discontinuities of portrayal and perception. A pattern of internally normalizing motivation must be found and adhered to consistently through the course of a performance:

> After the run Brook talked to the cast about continuity. 'We've spent all our time structuring individual scenes and have necessarily lost sight of the whole. Now we must begin looking at one scene in relation to the next.'[87]

A discussion of Edgar's motives in his spell as Poor Tom centres on the issue of psychological homogeneity: 'Where is the consistency of this transformation?',[88] asks Brook, seeking 'to discover Edgar's place in the scheme of things.'[89] For Brook, 'the play had such a hard inner consistency that everything must be there for a purpose'.[90] One remembers Stanislavsky: 'Everything in life has a logical sequence, hence it should also obtain on the stage'.[91]

The second major segment of Stanislavsky's conceptual approach to characterization was, we remember, that involving the study of the given circumstances of the drama. Like Stanislavsky, Brook believes that the entire corpus of objectively available material on the character – that contained in the drama – is insufficient. The actors need a far more detailed picture of the world in which their characters live. Thus, where it is felt that the text does not supply enough contextual information – as in the case of the relationship between Lear's daughters, for example, or the background of the Albany–Cornwall feud – unscripted dramas of the actors' own making supply the necessary supplementary material. These improvisations provide information – but only along lines already sketched in through discussion. Note the sequence of events in Marowitz's account of Brook's work on the role of the Fool:

> Brook sees the Fool as an inspired zany; . . .
> It struck me that the Fool is also Lear's conscience; . . .
> Difficulties with the Fool stem from the fact that the actor playing the role is a highly-organised individual; . . .

Last night we set him an improvisation with Cordelia in order to establish the Fool's off-stage character. 'He is a worried man and terribly tired of all the desperate foolery that he has to carry on all day long,' the actor explained. In the scene that followed, we saw the Fool with Cordelia as she was preparing for the court occasion which is the first scene of the play.[92]

Brook and Marowitz begin with theoretical insights into the nature of the Fool. The fact that these are incompatible with the inclinations of the actor playing the role necessitates improvisations which generate material to fit an alternative but still rigidly preconceived mould. Even the actor's insight is theoretical, only to be *confirmed* in improvisation. Discussion precedes action. The work of the mind precedes the work of the body.

PETER BROOK AND *A MIDSUMMER NIGHT'S DREAM*

Stanislavsky's success as an actor, combined with the fact that his most-read books posit an analytical system, has led to a popular conflation of the two. Stanislavsky's achievement as an actor and director is popularly seen as a vindication of cerebral work. As a result, when directors and actors break with the cognitive approach to characterisation, they often believe they are breaking with Stanislavsky. Yoshi Oida, who first worked with Brook on *The Tempest* in 1968 (two years before Brook's *A Midsummer Night's Dream*), writes of his search in Shinto training for an alternative to Stanislavskian rationality:

Usually, western theatre education based on the Stanislavsky system, is from the inside. But I am interested in finding certain movements that can, from the outside, change the personality. When I make a laughing sound, without feeling, but just trying Ha . . . Ha . . . Ha . . . then I start to feel good. That is an exterior movement that will change you.[93]

Oida is of course wrong to assume that Stanislavsky was ignorant of somatics. The error notwithstanding, he speaks, perhaps with greater objective understanding than Stanislavsky, of a reversal of everyday assumptions about psychological phenomena discussed much earlier by William James:

Common sense says, we lose our fortune, are sorry and weep; . . . this order of sequence is incorrect. . . . [T]he one mental state is

not immediately induced by the other. . . . [T]he bodily manifestations must first be interposed between, and that the more
rational statement is that we feel sorry because we cry.[94]

Whereas the mind is able merely to conceive of emotions, the body is
able physically to inhabit them.

Like Oida, Joseph Chaikin too worked with Brook between *King
Lear* and *A Midsummer Night's Dream*. Like Oida, Chaikin responded
to the revelation that intellectual analysis is damaging by searching for
somatic stimulants. A participant in a Chaikin chord exercise describes
the immediacy of its influx:

> I hear breathing. . . . It turns into a drone, and I drone too. . . .
> Now it is a humming, and I hum. . . . I can hear it all around me. I
> am within it. I match myself to it. I don't want to alter it but to let it
> alter me.[95]

By influencing the body directly, the sound is able to generate a response
undiminished by the possible relative paucity of the actor's psychological resources. The skill of the director lies in using his experience of such
effects to ensure that this response is formally related to, and may
therefore reasonably be expected to induce, appropriate attributes of
character.

In his book on *The Making of A Midsummer Night's Dream*, David
Selbourne describes Peter Brook conducting a chord in much the same
manner:

> The whole company sat in a circle. Brook asked them to close their
> eyes, sitting close but not touching, and to communicate to each
> other by sound. . . . This sound was heard. . . . Then, in . . . a
> rapidly induced state of trance, others began to 'answer'.
>
> Eventually, Brook stopped it . . . . He told them 'not to control
> the sound intellectually, by mind', but to 'let it govern them'. . . .[96]

To control the sound intellectually is to restrict its effect to that which
the mind already knows – which is of course to defeat the purpose of an
exercise designed to liberate the body. The sound, or any external
impulse, must be allowed to invade and transform beyond preconcep-
tion the performer's state of being. It works as an objective correlative
for a realm of energy which, if self-consciously cultivated, would
anaesthetise expression. All such generalized emotion is anathema to
Brook. Selbourne's book is replete with exclamations from Brook
condemning analysis before action: third week, first day, 'Don't use

logic . . . don't give explanations';[97] fifth week, third day, 'Discover, do not comment.'[98]

Obviously a far cry from the mainly conceptual nature of his work on *King Lear*, Brook, like Oida, sees his conversion to somatics as an abrogation of the influence of Stanislavsky. Brook's professed intention in *A Midsummer Night's Dream* is to approach characterization 'without using a Stanislavskian sense of natural character development'.[99] John Kane and Michael Crawford agree that in this production Brook had decided 'it was no use approaching the parts in Stanislavskian terms'.[100] Brook explains:

> One of the things that had to be maintained very, very strongly was an elimination of the barriers to the play that can come from the sort of rationalising, of intellectualising working habits.[101]

Quite unfairly, Stanislavsky is synonymous with psychology, with pre-conception which hinders proper access to character. As an alternative to this system, Oida, Chaikin and Brook posit an approach based on the ability of the body directly to generate emotional states. The actors must not attempt consciously to feel the character's emotions; these emotions are to be produced by physically inhabiting a condition analogous to that required by the role.

*

Stanislavsky's reputation generated an immense interest in his books. This in turn produced a generation of actors schooled in only those sections of Stanislavsky's work which had a pronounced cerebral orientation. For a director in Brook's position, this meant two things. First, his somatic work, along with that of people like Chaikin and Oida, was likely to be treated as original. Second, it would be enormously difficult to persuade actors, who had been influenced even a little by Stanislavsky, to substitute rationality with action. The cerebral approach was so firmly ingrained that it was likely to take enormous openness on the part of the actors to accept the substitution of a logical system with a method so little amenable to rational analysis. Both factors are present in John Kane's account of the interest of Brook's work on *A Midsummer Night's Dream*:

> What was novel in working with Peter was that he wanted the play to *do things* with us. It was very difficult for us to break down our desire to immediately seize on scenes and characters and start doing things with them. Making them fit a rational concept.

31

Certainly, for people who like to plan everything out for their work – and I am one of those people – I found it very very difficult not to start bending the play *my* way. It was hard to clear my mind – it was a purification – to allow the play almost to drip through your mind and colour *you*, without you colouring the play. This was quite revolutionary.[102]

To take each of the implications of Kane's statement in turn, Brook seems to Kane first to have broken new ground whereas in fact he was only building on the initiative he had received indirectly from Stanislavsky. In 1922 Stanislavsky's pupil Meyerhold, for instance, had observed that 'all psychological states are determined by specific physiological processes. By correctly resolving the nature of his state physically, the actor reaches the point where he experiences the excitation which communicates itself to the spectator and induces him to share in the actor's performance.'[103] In so far as Meyerhold's practical application of these ideas in what he called 'bio-mechanics' was known to Brecht and Brecht was abundantly available to Brook (the connection is treated in chapter 2), it is unlikely that Brook would claim to have re-invented somatics. Brook is ignorant not of somatics but of Stanislavsky's contribution to its development.

Second, Kane notes Brook's awareness of the need to divorce somatic work from cerebral far more explicitly than had been the case under Stanislavsky. In an effort to impress upon his actors the need to pursue bodily work entirely independently of analytical interference, Brook now discusses characterization using a vocabulary with a pronounced somatic orientation. In Stanislavsky, the actor must on the one hand recognize that 'the way to art is in yourself and only in yourself'[104] but, on the other, must affirm that the truths arrived at are 'those of the character you are portraying'.[105] In Brook, the same dichotomy, fundamental to the art of the actor, is couched entirely in terms of physical determinants. On the one hand, the performance must be 'in your rhythm, or in no rhythm at all',[106] but on the other, 'the impulse must come wholly from the outside'.[107] There is therefore 'both a rhythm to be found and a particular actor to find it'.[108] The substitution of terms like 'character' and 'meaning' for 'rhythm' and 'impulse' comprises an attempt to re-align the actors' assumptions about their approach to a role. Talk of 'character' not only reminds actors of the potential duplicity of their situation on stage but disconcertingly provides only the most tenuous and brittle of solutions to the problem. In contrast, the designation of nature as rhythm at once makes concrete the task of generating the role-self and circumvents the fruitless issue of its ambig-

32

uous ontology. Contrary to the spirit of the actors' fears, seeing their problem as an assemblage of rhythms renders their task less daunting: although they must give up the security of reasoning, they undertake merely to perform simple and concrete tasks which lead inevitably into character.

The change in Brook's terminology is symptomatic of a more general shift in his attitude to language in this period. The words of the text are no longer to be treated as abstract signifiers but as concrete agents working through sound and rhythm. It is to these tangible attributes, rather than to semantic significance, that the actors' attention must be directed. If actors find this difficult because their ingrained sense of meaning interferes with their ability to seek out the pre-verbal thrust of the drama, they must be trained not to follow the lines of a text intellectually: '[L]istening to the rhythms of the words, rather than attending to their literal meaning,' says Brook, 'will take one towards a deeper understanding.'[109] Appropriately, at the second rehearsal, Selbourne notes that Brook, contrary to his practice in *King Lear*, 'had not told them "what the play was about"'.[110] Nominal formulations set up rationally apprehended targets in the pursuit of which actors lose their capacity to immerse themselves completely in the mainsprings of impulse and action. A baffled actor, accustomed to using interpretation as a starting point, complains to Brook, 'I don't know what I'm aiming at.' Brook's reply is firm: 'As long as that's true, you'll be all right.'[111]

*

Clearly, to tell actors not to follow the text intellectually is not to guarantee that they will be either able or willing to break an old and comfortable habit. Verbal instructions are themselves intellectual and therefore less persuasive than experience. If Brook is to be truly responsible to his new-found conviction that only action gives access to character, he must also design exercises that school the actors in rhythm. This is the goal of the first stage of his work on *A Midsummer Night's Dream*: before somatic catalysts can be used to induce specific attributes of character, the actors must be weaned off their dependence upon meaning and sensitized to the *sound* of Shakespeare's language:

> We passed sound, gestures and dance steps from one to another trying to amplify or transmit the initial impulse residing in the core of the physical action before passing it on. Then we were handed copies of the Bottom/Pyramus 'Death' speech and asked to read it as if we had never seen it before, as if it had no future or

past. It was then broken up and read by the three of us word and word about in an attempt to fuse us into a single voice.[112]

The exercise draws directly on the methods used by Joseph Chaikin to introduce actors to the autonomously creative capabilities of rhythm:

One actor would begin a simple repeatable gestur-5e using both body and voice, not selecting in advance what the action should express, but playing with it until it touched on a clear condition: that actor then approached a seccond, who tried to copy the forms exactly, thereby being led to their emotional content. . . . Using kinetic impulses to locate inner states, actors were able to discover emotions that had not been in their experience before.[113]

Both exercises begin outside language: the demand for appropriate reactions compels an anxious but heightened responsiveness to sound and movement. This is the period of tuning in, of warming up those parts of the body which may eventually be conditioned to respond to the pre-verbal. Any scepticism as to the ability of action to create emotion is dispelled as imitation palpably leads to feeling. Only after the actors are sufficiently accustomed to discerning states of being in action are they handed the text. Brook's demand that they read it as if it did not belong in any definable intellectual tradition is both the statement of a goal and a hint as to how that goal may be realized: the mind must have no part in determining intonation. Significantly, this verbal nudge in the direction of physical work comes only in the immediate aftermath of somatic training within it. The actors are encouraged to divest themselves of their intellectualizing routines only after they have unsuspectingly had direct experience of a viable and attractive alternative. The speech is then broken up to ensure that no actor imposes a private reading on the text. The actors must be sensitive instead to the rhythms generated by the language in one another. '"Hearing the rhythm in each other's words," . . . will "set up a preparedness for response" . . . [and] will "draw one on to the next stage of understanding meanings"',[114] claims Brook. Meaning is now generated exogenously rather than internally, through somatic imperatives rather than through reasoning. The actors work not through the mind but through the fuller agency of corporeally intelligible experience.

In another version of the exercise, the notion of substituting specula-tion with less fragile agents of influx is carried even further as spatial constructs palpably distil for the actors the import of Brook's subtly suggestive instructions:

34

In rehearsal this produces a number of exercises, an example of which is one that discovers Stanislavskian objectives not through the intellect but through sound:

> Brook asks Egeus to make a sound of rejection and dismissal and for Hermia and Lysander to respond to it. They do so, with what is intended to stand in sound for the innermost pulse of grief and longing. The reading of the words begins immediately after it. They are to speak them, Brook says, 'remembering the sounds which came upon the deepest impulse'. And by this means, Lysander's 'How now, my love! Why is your cheek so pale?' can, at the outset of rehearsal, be freed from what Brook calls the 'generalized sentiment' which has come to afflict the speaking of it.[121]

Just as the use of song sensitizes actors to undiscovered rhythms in the text, the use of sound, as it too precedes sense, is designed to marry the driving force of the text with the actor's own rhythms and inclinations. Whereas a Stanislavskian objective would merely read 'to reject', Egeus' location of the import of rejection in sound draws him away from stock conceptual associations and gives to his intonation a vital freshness. Thus an effective amalgamation of sound and sense is generated and meaning bolstered with naturally expressive cadences which the intellect typically cannot supply.

If the actors are unable to find the required impulses in themselves, the director can make their task a little easier by producing the required rhythms externally and having the actors assimilate them unselfconsciously through action:

> The rhythm is given by the instructor, and – instrument in response to instrument – the actors must improvise within the rhythm as it changes. This is a musical metaphor for the word's impulses. . . . And so they dance, while wooing with sound; wordlessly threaten and attack each other to a rhythm of their own making; a drum speaks to the stick and bells.[122]

Although the initial impulse is given by an instructor, the actors still carry the responsibility of finding a voice within the offered structure. The dictated rhythm is a hint merely: the actors retain the prerogative to modify the prompt in order to satisfy a personal condition.

If however the actors are unable to make the necessary adjustment, the director may utilize the link between rhythm and character far more explicitly:

Brook taps on a drum two differentiated rhythms, which he wants respectively from the mechanicals and the courtiers. As a result, Theseus' 'The wall, methinks, being sensible, should curse again' has the heightened arrogance of a swift and (as if) princely wit, while Pyramus' reply 'No, in truth, sir, he should not', with its heavy round vocables, has more than ever the pedestrian gait of the sturdy Bottom.[123]

Unwilling to make a subjective exploration, the actors absorb almost completely the order of the environment. This is the somatic equivalent of a director making suggestions: whereas cerebral work would involve directors assisting their actors through analysis, Brook's commitment at this stage to body-oriented work has him counselling his actors through rhythms so that the self-consciousness of discussion is avoided. Again, action precedes meaning; rhythm *is* character.

Meaning is a function not merely of temporal elements such as rhythm but also of spatial imperatives such as grouping. Whereas the conceptual approach to characterization would, for instance, have an actor define the notion of kingship and then coax his body to fit the parameters of that definition, somatic work has the director place the actor in a physical situation in which he feels the regal imperative naturally and without conscious interference. 'Oberon (up a ladder and high above the rest of the cast . . .)', Selbourne tells us, was 'now in fuller command of his regal resources than ever'.[124] The experience of being physically above the rest of the cast produces a sensation which the actor has no difficulty in harnessing to signify royalty. Like Stanislavsky, Brook is aware that there is a correspondence between the metaphor of ascendency and its literal import.

Stanislavsky had acknowledged the role set-design could play in generating emotion. In *My Life in Art* he observes that, while watching some actors negotiate the hazards of rocks and boulders on the set of *The Sunken Bell*, it struck him that 'the art of construction . . . helps the actor to reveal his inner nature'.[125] Similarly, Brook uses the set to help generate emotion:

> this is hand-wringing, not heart-felt; not ardour but hard labour, and heavy going. To lighten the load of it, Brook changes the plotting of the lovers' hectic quartet. . . . Instead of standing their ground four-square . . . they will now run up and down ladders. . . . The life of these exchanges is, at the last, *not* to come from the actors' words but from their actions. Rhythm and impulse, unfound in the lines, will be found in the ladders.[126]

The search for the rhythms in the text is in this case literally interchangeable with the act of running up and down the ladders on the set. Brook knows on the basis of experience that the dimensions of the ladders are such that, in having to climb them, the actors' bodies must assume a particular rhythm which matches perfectly the rhythm he requires in the delivery of the lines. The ladders are used as objective correlatives for a segment of the text: through a host of secondary factors such as the intervals between the rungs or the sense of ascent or descent, the ladders can physically provoke the actors into assuming the attitudes Brook requires.

Selbourne comments on the somatic assistance of this sort that while it is an 'expedient and ingenious gesture . . . it is also one imposed upon the actor by the need to find uses for the stage-machine which has been invented, for him, by the director'.[127] There is a hint here of exploitation: it seems to be suggested that to provoke the actors' real emotions into play by means over which they have no control is morally suspect. And indeed, in its most extreme form, somatic work does engineer emotions in a manner that is distinctly manipulative. For instance, on one occasion Brook instructs the off-stage cast to create a disturbance so that the actors on stage have to struggle to make themselves heard:

> Indeed both noise and harassment are intensified to, and beyond, breaking-point. The cast, become a brawling mob, steps up its actions. It is foolery, become tormenting. And, suddenly, this is the goad which at last drives Hermia, in her desperation to survive vocally, to a 'genuinely' despairing impulse. 'Help me, Lysander', as Brook had originally wanted, is audibly drawn from panic feeling rather than from girlish coyness.[128]

In his descriptions of actors breaking into tears or making their bitterness felt as weariness and bewilderment sweep over them, Selbourne criticizes what he sees as an unequal alliance between Brook and the actors based upon a relentless pressure for a surrender of will. Stanislavsky justified the technique by claiming that, if 'to reproduce feelings you must be able to identify them out of your own experience',[129] the director carries the responsibility of creating in rehearsal any experience the actors lack. In so far as the actors' awareness of these purposes is directly antithetical to their capacity to experience the designated emotions, they must be excluded from the process of designing somatic exercises. Brook agrees with Stanislavsky: not only is it the case that 'you can only understand, if you use the right experience of your own to draw from',[130] but ignorance is a necessary precondition

39

of involvement – for understanding only encourages actors to reach directly for effects without living through the concerns which give to the result its value as truth. If one can relinquish the notion that the actor must always be consciously in control (as is of course required in somatic work), then one can come to appreciate how provocation of this sort can be liberating. To manipulate is not always to coerce; it also implies skill of the kind a chiropract may use – where too success is contingent upon submission.

*

Somatic work is not merely a matter of allowing the body to influence the emotions. Finally there must come a point when the distinction between the catalyst and its effect, action and feeling, is obliterated:

> Imagine one hundred blind people listening to you. The fact that you swing on a trapeze, is irrelevant. But the impulse which takes you to the trapeze should be in what you say.[131]

Whereas somatic work of the kind acknowledged by Stanislavsky would merely have movement suggest meaning, Brook acknowledges that, at its best, the somatic agent and the significance it brings to the text are indistinguishable. The actors *must not know* whether they are interpreting the words of the text through action or whether the words are suggesting meanings to them through sound – for in this innocence lies the indication that the actors have achieved the state of 'I am'. Brook's actors must not merely be creatively ignorant of the purpose of each of the exercises; they must thereafter be oblivious even to their achievement, the sublimation of language into meaning. They must be aware only of their existence as themselves within a particular pattern of action. The lines they speak must also exist purely on the basis of that rhythm. If the movement the director has selected is the appropriate catalyst, then the lines and the action will be united kinetically without this congruence seeming extraordinary or unnatural. The actor will then 'become' the character without the slightest embroilment in questions of fidelity to alternative orders of truth. The actors and the lines they speak would simply *be*, harmonized by the movement which for each is truth.

Selbourne's language often reveals how meaning and action may eventually be formally inseparable:

> Brook can be heard telling Puck consciously to tap out a measured rhythm in his great striding. . . . Puck, gigantic, is now an awesome sound and fearful presence, his voice . . . bellying and

lurching among Lysander's terrors . . . . Brook shouts out against him that Lysander must be 'literally driven to the wall' by Puck's sound and striding.[132]

Notice the implicit acknowledgement of the material unity of the actor's art in the notion of Puck being both an awesome sound and a fearful presence, his voice bellying and lurching (spatial metaphors) among Lysander's equally tangible terrors. Trewin comments on this mutually reinforcing reciprocity in performance: 'The more closely we watched the actors' unexpected virtuosity', he observes, 'the more we heard of the play, better spoken than most people had ever known.'[133] In somatic work at its best, language and action – and as a consequence, actor and character – are one.

*

If actors are to re-create meaning afresh each night, as Brook requires, they must experience in each performance the excitement that in rehearsal accompanies the birth of an authentic reading. By implication, the advances made in rehearsal cannot be artificially recaptured in performance. For Brook, 'every form once born is mortal, and its new conception will bear the marks of all the influences that surround it'.[134] The assertion has a bearing both on somatic practice and on the attitudes actors and directors have to their work. In the context of Brook's career as a whole, the two are improbably related. On the one hand, somatic work requires the actor to cultivate a sensitivity not merely to the self but also to the environment. Thus in *The Empty Space*, the actor is called upon to be 'completely involved while distanced – detached without detachment.'[135] If this sounds more like Brecht than Stanislavsky, then it is to Brook's relationship with Brecht that I turn in the next chapter. For, on the other hand, if the actor's growth involves a constant shedding of insight as it is gained, so too for the director this must imply the abrogation of particular modes of being as the agents that breed them begin to suggest other structures.

2

TO BE AND NOT TO BE:
Bertolt Brecht and Peter Brook

The most beautiful of all doubts
Is when the downtrodden and despondent raise their heads
and
Stop believing in the strength
Of their oppressors.

Oh, how laboriously the new truth was fought for!
What sacrifices it cost!
How difficult it was to see
That things were thus and not thus.[1]

(Bertolt Brecht)

No one seriously concerned with the theatre can by-pass Brecht.
Brecht is the key figure of our time, and all theatre work today at
some point starts or returns to his statements and achievement.[2]

(Peter Brook)

BERTOLT BRECHT

Brecht's understanding of Stanislavsky is loaded with images of coer-
cion. For Brecht the Stanislavskian theatre 'systematically compels the
empathy of the spectator'[3] who is then a 'victim of hypnotic experience,
. . . completely "entangled"'[4] in the action. Brecht is clear: this 'forcing
of empathy'[5] must stop – for, he argues, 'how is the spectator to be made
to master life when all that happens masters him?'[6] There is a hint here
of the larger political purpose of which this confrontation with
Stanislavsky is a microcosm. The situation of Stanislavsky's audience is
analogous to that of the proletariat who are the 'passive object of
politics'[7] and must also be freed.

The effect Stanislavskian drama has in common with political oppression is enforced submission. Theatre which naturalizes social reality is oppressive in that it compels assent. By seeking merely to depict the world, the Stanislavskian actor implicitly accepts it: to 'represent' is both to 'present an image of' and to speak 'on behalf of'. By seeming then to give us that world 'as it really is', the Stanislavskian actor induces a corresponding acceptance of that world in the audience. The tyranny of the 'given circumstances' exercise, for example, lies not merely in its power to convince; far more pernicious is its product, tolerance, that which submits to and thereby perpetuates the constraining order. Circumstances that are 'given' are to that extent not subject to question.

Similarly, when Stanislavskian objectives are used to 'justify' the action, justification implies not only motivation but vindication. In seeking to inspire the actor, the Stanislavskian theatre inadvertently demonstrates the correctness of the world as it is experienced. The 'through line of actions' into which these objectives are then arranged has a quite different but equally crippling effect: it effaces the socially constructed and therefore changeable nature of political reality. By immersing the audience in a swift current of objectives and their consequences, it fosters the illusion that the causal sequences it depicts are in some way absolute. A sequence in which a causes b causes c overwhelmingly suggests that, given a (the 'given circumstances'), c is inevitable. This too is something that Brecht wants to avoid: Brecht would like to use theatre to demonstrate that, in any given situation, a larger number of options is available than people normally assume. For Brecht, social reality is neither determined nor always defensible – so whereas Stanislavsky elicits submission, Brecht will seek to inculcate dissent.

The two principal components of Brechtian theatre address directly the political inertia implicit in the two main aspects of Stanislavsky's theatre. First, it seems to Brecht that Stanislavsky's emphasis on the authenticity of the given circumstances contrives to make those conditions far too inconspicuous to be politically subject to question – they become so familiar that it becomes impossible to challenge the social implications of the way they are construed:

> What he [Stanislavsky] cared about was naturalness, and as a result everything in his theatre became far too natural for anyone to pause and go through it thoroughly. You don't normally examine your own house or your own feeding habits, do you?[8]

43

To counteract this Brecht proposes to dislocate the spectator's habitual frames of reference through a critical counterpoint designed to provoke a need for reappraisal. Where the power structures that underlie social situations become invisible when considered natural, Brecht will attempt to make startling what seems obvious, curious what seems self-evident. This is alienation:

> The A-effect consists in turning the object of which one is to be made aware . . . from something ordinary, familiar, immediately accessible, into something peculiar, striking and unexpected. . . . Before familiarity can turn into awareness the familiar must be stripped of its inconspicuousness; we must give up assuming that the object in question needs no explanation.[9]

Brecht's audience is to be induced not to share the reality of the situation presented, but to review it. If as a result the spectator begins generally to adopt an attitude of inquiry, then Brecht's purposes are fulfilled:

> Such things occur. But what would you suggest? . . .
> There's only one solution we know:
> That you should now consider as you go
> What sort of measures you would recommend
> To help good people to a happy end.[10]

The utility of estrangement is not propaganda: it teaches insight.

The second major resource of the Stanislavskian theatre is acceptance as a consequence of causality. This is displaced by that other complex of theatre theory associated with Brecht, the epic. Critical writing on Brecht has tended rather blithely to use 'epic' as a blanket term for all performance practices designed to achieve alienation in the theatre. It is, however, the force of the specifically Aristotelian sense of the term that is relevant here. This involves the dissociation of adjoining segments of a work as though the narrative through them was independent of time. The result is the dislocation of the 'through line' upon which Stanislavsky depends so heavily:

> the individual episodes have to be knotted together in such a way that the knots are easily noticed. The episodes must not succeed one another indistinguishably but must give us a chance to interpose our judgement.[11]

Notice the assumed equivalence of the awareness of these divisions with appraisal. Strategic interruption unmasks causality: the frustration of a sequence of events reveals the nature and momentum of the forces that

44

drive it. Causality thus unveiled is also causality rationalized: in Brecht, cause has material antecedents only, and the location of these factors within history virtually comprises the abolition of determinism. A consequence of the proposition that 'man's fate is man himself'[12] is that man's fate is changeable. If the slavish obedience of Stanislavsky's audience is an image of the servility to which the world is subject, Brechtian subversion would, by virtue of the same correspondence, feed back into society via the spectators' new-found authority.

Brecht's achievement is then the redefinition of the function of theatre in terms of social instrumentality. Brecht admits that the truths sought by Stanislavsky are difficult to discover – and by implication admirable; but, he asks, what is the public to *do* with such a theatre? 'Of what use was the whole box of magic tricks?'[13] The phrase is reminiscent of the 'witchcraft', 'hypnosis' and 'mastery' of empathy – and is, to that extent, a measure of Brecht's political distance from Stanislavsky:

> I wanted to take the principle that it was not just a matter of interpreting the world but of changing it, and apply that to the theatre.[14]

Stanislavsky and Brecht move apart on adjacent rails from unlike premises to appropriately incongruent forms of presentation.

*

We have seen how the two main elements of Brechtian theatre, alienation and the epic, work in tandem to neutralize the two features of the Stanislavskian theatre to which they are addressed – identification and causality. It is as though Brecht's theatre of utility, in its temporal (anti-sequential) capacity, switches off the machine, the world, so that we may at leisure apply the insight granted us by that theatre in its spatial (distancing) aspect.

The spatial and temporal imperatives do, of course, overlap. For instance, although interruption is principally an agent of the 'epic', it could in practice have an alienating effect by disorienting the spectator. Again, the operative agent seems in both cases to be the introduction of a metatextual irritant into what is otherwise a closed and sequentially conservative body of text. By text I mean a body of creative assertion to which attention must explicitly be drawn lest its continuity mask its import. Metatext, comprised too of words and action, is by contrast the agent of the reorientation that makes perspective possible. Text and metatext are distinguished not by the medium of their articulation but by their function. Brecht himself uses the metaphor of metatextuality when he asserts that alienation is 'a technique of taking the human social incidents to be portrayed and *labelling them* as something striking, something that calls for explanation'.[15] The image is that of a scribble in the margin, a note that breaks the force of internal consecutiveness in the text and consequently draws attention to it the more distinctly.

An example of a theatrical equivalent of laterally signifying marginalia is the use of titles and projections:

> The orthodox playwright's objection to the titles is that the . . . text must express everything within its own confines. The corresponding attitude for the spectator is that he should not think about a subject, but within the confines of the subject. . . . [This] is something that the new school of play-writing must reject. *Footnotes*, and the habit of turning back in order to check a point, need to be introduced into play-writing too.
>
> Some exercise in complex seeing is needed – though it is more important to be able to think above the stream than to think in the stream.[16]

To think above the stream is both to think independently of the course advocated (an analogue therefore of Brecht's temporal imperative) and to think *away* from it (a spatially oriented injunction). Thus projections prevent the spectator from identifying with the action either by explictly exhorting the audience not to do so or by subtly insinuating into the metatext an attitude which may contradict the concurrently active text and thereby upset its comfortable momentum.

Similarly music, as metatext, can be used both spatially (in *The Caucasian Chalk Circle* the singer describes the servant girl's rescue of the child as it is mimed on stage) and temporally (Brecht insists that 'the actor ought not to "drop into" song, but should clearly mark it off from the rest of the text'[17]). Both modes offer the music freedom to respond critically to the subject dealt with. It is of course precisely this independence that Brecht requires from his audience. Metatext is both a model for the spectator and a means of assisting with the realisation of the attitude it recommends.

It takes two to create the phenomenon of metatextuality, two to create the tussle between text and commentary that is the hallmark of the Brechtian theatre. Transposed into the world of characterization, this implies the retention of the actor–character gulf that Stanislavsky sought so unreservedly to eliminate:

> A definite distance between the actor and the role had to be built into the manner of playing. The actor had to be able to criticize. In

46

addition to the action of the character, *another action had to be there* so that selection and criticism were possible.[18]

It is not sufficient for Brecht that this 'other' action stem from another character merely: external conflicts between internally consistent 'truths' are of daily occurrence and therefore provoke only the alignment of sympathies, not their alienation. The opposition between text and metatext on the other hand, being internal, provokes the impulse to see in it a continuity. When this is denied, the audience is led to double-take – which is of course the essence of alienation. Just as Brecht's music often seems to belong to the text but then alienates the action by suddenly failing to support it, so also different aspects of the actor's performance, while appearing at first to be consistent, must suddenly fail to complement one another.

The internally antipathetic performance is given when the actor is able not merely to inhabit a role but also to embody explicitly the act of presenting it. In the *Short Organum* there is a wonderfully vivid account of the creation of this dual aspect of characterization:

> the actor appears on the stage in a double role, as Laughton and as Galileo. . . . Laughton is actually there, standing on the stage and showing us what he imagines Galileo to have been. . . . [W]e find a gesture which expresses one-half of his attitude – that of showing – if we make him smoke a cigar and then imagine him laying it down now and again in order to show us some further characteristic attitude of the figure in the play.[19]

In so far as Laughton is required to put down the cigar every time he begins to play Galileo, the smoking of the cigar becomes associated with the actor Laughton and the absence of it with the character Galileo. Gradually the audience begins to recognize two quite distinct personages – the character, and the actor who intermittently plays that character. Thus, in a single gesture, that of smoking, is contained the germ of an additive precept: the demand that 'he who is showing should himself be shown'[20] makes two, actor and role, where Stanislavsky would have just one, the character.

The metatextual image for the dissociation of actor from role is that of the actor standing between the spectator and the text 'like a quotation':[21]

> He is not Lear, Harpagon, Schweik; he shows them . . . [as] when a producer or colleague shows one how to play a particular

passage. It is not his own part, so he is not completely trans-
formed; he *underlines* the technical aspect and retains the attitude
of someone just making suggestions.[22]

Here the director is a model in a dual sense. First, he introduces the
actor to some aspect of character which he feels should be incorporated
into the performance. Second, in doing so he is present simultaneously
as director and character, which is itself significant and an example to be
followed. Interestingly, the fact that this is not disconcerting suggests
that we are not as unfamiliar with dual presence as long years of
schooling in Stanislavsky has led us to believe. What Brecht requires is
that his actors drop Stanislavsky's ultimately quite artificial demand for
consistency and regain on stage the quite commonplace ability to tell a
story and mimic one's characters at once. The actors must appear as
themselves, intermittently impersonating their characters while speaking the playwright's lines.

The term for this kind of acting is 'gestus' which, in John Willett's
translation, is at once 'gesture and gist, attitude and point'[23] – a
compound term which intrinsically harnesses both content and opinion. As the word 'gestus' suggests, the creation of metatext is not merely
a matter of generating a space adjacent to the text; Brecht requires in
addition that it be filled with a critical discussion designed to displace
the concurrently active momentum of the drama. For instance, in
Helene Weigel's portrayal of Mother Courage, we have the simultaneous presentation of both the character's dogmatic blindness and the
actress's exasperation that it should be so:

> how, for example, am I as Courage at the end of the play, when my
> business dealings have cost me the last of my children, to deliver
> the sentence: 'I have to get back to business' unless I am *not*
> personally shattered by the fact that this person I am playing does
> not possess the capacity to learn?[24]

Whereas in Stanislavsky, emotion occurs at the point of greatest resonance between action and character, in Brecht it marks the extent of the
divergence between these worlds. In Stanislavsky the result is identification; in Brecht it is perspective.

As the actor delivers the text underscored by a metatextual gest of
delivery, two effects become possible. First, the presence of the actor in
addition to that of the character makes the audience aware that what
they are watching is only a drama, a scenario which is of human
contriving and therefore changeable. Second, the spectators are encour-

aged, by the force of the actor's example, to form opinions as to the kinds of changes they would like to see in society:

> Because he [the actor] doesn't identify with him [the character] he [the actor] can pick a definite attitude to adopt towards the character whom he portrays, can show what he thinks of him and invite the spectator, who is likewise not asked to identify himself, to criticise the character portrayed.[25]

Just as the identification of actor and character generates a corresponding influx of empathy in the audience, so also the dislocation of actors from their roles offers the audience an opportunity to deconstruct as malleable an orthodox formulation. Through their experience of defamiliarization in the theatre, they learn not to identify as well with the social conditions to which they are subject.

The actors' 'truth' in this situation stems from their acknowledgement that the dramatic text stands in relation to life outside the theatre as metatext does to text. Theatre's 'reality' is now the reality of comment upon life; it is not the thing itself. Whereas Stanislavsky's 'magic if' obliterates the claims of actuality in order to allow the actor a more compelling release into the imagined truths of character, Brecht emphasizes the literal truth – that the stage is a stage and the drama only a drama. Whereas Stanislavsky, in Brecht's view, can only offer us artificial reconstructions of reality, Brecht is determined to 'show things as they are'.[26] The premium is still on 'truth' but the definitions have altered: *'Realist'* now means 'laying bare society's causal network'.[27]

*

It is an essential prerequisite of the vitality of such a theatre that the antithetical positions it presents be held to maximum effect. Alienation is effective only in proportion to the emotional charge it undercuts. As Brecht once remarked to Giorgio Strehler, while the music in his theatre was designed to break the illusion, that illusion had 'first to be created, since an atmosphere could never be destroyed until it had been built up.'[28] Just as metatext depends for its existence upon text, so also estrangement depends upon identification for its effect:

> It is absolutely necessary for us, if we are to progress beyond it, to recognise that complete transformation is a positive, artistic act, a difficult matter, an advance by means of which the identification of the spectator with the actor is made possible. . . . [I]f we leave transformation behind, it will not be a total abandonment.[29]

Criticism must be generated concurrently with passion if the dislocation of assumptions, rather than mere propaganda, is to be achieved.

If alienation cannot exist without emotion, then Stanislavsky is to Brecht an absolute necessity. Brecht acknowledges the connection when, tired of the controversy surrounding the place of emotion in his theatre, he begins to write of a 'dialectical' theatre. That his intention was not to canvass for certain opinions but to achieve a 'truly rending contradiction between experience and portrayal, empathy and demonstration, justification and criticism'[30] had always been implicit in Brecht's writings. It had merely been eclipsed by Brecht's over-exclusive concern with the epic which was, after all, the novel half of the conflict he had posited. In redressing the balance so as once more to emphasize that the most telling theatre is that which is able to sustain the conflict of *equal* opposites, Brecht invokes Stanislavsky:

> this contradiction is dialectical. As a writer I need an actor who can completely empathise and absolutely transform himself into the character. This, indeed, is what Stanislavsky holds to be the first goal of his System. But at the same time and before all else I need an actor who can stand away from his character and criticise it as a representative of society.[31]

The problem Brecht's actors now faced was that they had to learn both how to identify with their characters (as in Stanislavsky) and, intermittently, how to break the spell of identification and reveal that they were in fact merely actors presenting the roles assigned to them.

There is a temporal sequence implicit in the preparation of this dialectic whereby the text must be realized before it is undercut. This is reflected in the three-stage rehearsal programme (significantly entitled 'Building a Character') outlined by Brecht for his company:

> (i) Before you assimilate or lose yourself in your character you must first become aquainted with it. . . .
> (ii) The second phase is that of empathy, the search for the character's truth in the subjective sense . . . becoming one with it. . . .
> (iii) And then there is a third phase in which you try to see the character from the outside, from the standpoint of society.[32]

Brecht does of course acknowledge that in practice the stages overlap, but the pattern is clear: unlike amateur actors who often fail to identify with their characters, Brecht's actors must disavow empathy by transcending it.

If empathy is what Brecht's actors initially require, then it is the 'given circumstances' of the drama to which he must at first refer them:

> Then they attempted to approximate premature aging by actively imagining the background: childhood abuse, hard labour, rapes, disfigurements, having to lick boots of many colours. With the character thus far along, they attached behavioural specifics.[33]

As in Stanislavsky, a character must for Brecht also be satisfactorily motivated as a human being. A tape recording of Brecht in rehearsal makes vividly apparent the extraordinary care he lavished on detailed psychological analyses. The smallest fragments of action are justified so as to ensure plausibility: a farmer is 'genuinely upset because the cheese, which in his opinion cannot taste good, is liked by all'.[34] Grusha's brother is 'angry at his wife, the woman from Kulak, because he is dependent on her'.[35] In Stanislavsky, objectives must to be located in terms of verbs which label specific drives through the satisfaction or frustration of which the action acquires its energy. Similarly in Brecht the analysis of the text is in effect the resolution of projected purposes in the pursuit of which character is revealed:

> She longs for the war but at the same time fears it. She wants to join in but as a peaceable business woman, not in a warlike way. She wants to maintain her family during the war and by means of it. She wants to serve the army and also to keep out of its clutches.[36]

In addition to the microscopic interest of such analyses, Brecht's notes also contain schema which relate more expansively to the development of character through a play. 'Grusha changes slowly', he says, 'under the weight of sacrifices.'[37] In order to ensure that 'rhythms and cadences develop which run through entire scenes',[38] 'linking passages' are created to establish 'the relationship of the episodes, their construction'.[39] This effort to 'pull the inconsistences together'[40] is, of course, the product of the adoption of Stanislavsky's 'through line of action'. Little wonder then that Angelica Hurwicz once observed, on reading Stanislavsky's *An Actor Prepares*, that she discovered in it exercises which she had, under Brecht, made use of for years.[41]

Brecht's attempts initially to ensure that his actors are able to generate a lifelike treatment of the text are not restricted to techniques derived from the orthodox Stanislavsky of the 'middle period'. Like Stanislavsky, Brecht discovered that an actor's consciousness of the psychological state aimed at in performance leads only to self-consciousness. Stanislavsky, we remember, responded to the problem by insisting that his actors put action before language. Similarly Brecht, influenced by Stanislavsky's student Meyerhold, the director from whom he had borrowed as well the idea of using placards in the theatre, declares in rehearsal, 'Don't tell me, show me':[42]

> The actors . . . would suggest a way of doing something, and if they started to explain it, Brecht would say that he wanted no discussions in rehearsal.[43]

Instead, his actors are encouraged to use the body to influence the emotions directly: as Inna observes in *The Resistible Rise of Arturo Ui*,

> Its a funny thing about tobacco. When a man
> Is smoking, he looks calm, And if you imitate
> A calm-looking man and light a cigarette, you
> Get to be calm yourself.[44]

By imitating external attributes, actors can reach internal conditions. Thus, for instance, Brecht recommends in the course of *'On The Caucasian Chalk Circle'*, that 'Actresses playing Grusha should study the beauty of Brueghel's *Mad Margaret*'.[45] If the demeanour of Mad Margaret unwittingly evokes for Brecht an association with the Grusha of his drama, the actress playing that role would profit far more from the spontaneous and unselfconscious access to that conception offered by the painting than by discussion in a discursive medium. Again, Helene Weigel describes a stage in the evolution of the character she plays in *The Mother*:

> The gentleness of Pelagea Vlassova's gait and manner grew out of the idea of giving her a drooping left shoulder.[46]

Emotion follows action. Through the agency of a physiological imperative, Brecht's actor can 'become' the character.

*

Brecht's actors, we remember, have to do more than just get into character: they must be able as well to stand apart from their characters and generate a critical perspective on the action. It follows that the period of the actors' apprenticeship with Stanislavskian acting must be followed by a novel and telling further stage of rehearsal in which alienation both encompasses and transcends identification.

Given the immensity of the Stanislavsky system and the scale of its influence on Brecht, one would expect the actor-training methods developed by Brecht to include, at least in part, an adaptation of

Stanislavsky. Indeed, the encounter with Stanislavsky could itself form a part of the dialectic Brecht wanted his theatre to achieve. The actors could approach the problem of dislocating themselves from their characters by tackling at first the more immediate, concrete and reflexively educative task of breaking with the Stanislavskian rehearsal methods to which they had become accustomed.

Thus for instance, if the 'given circumstances' are established in Stanislavsky by a question-and-answer method, the interrogative form is retained in Brecht – but the questions asked now comprehend not the substance of the drama but its relevance:

1. Who is the sentence of use to?
2. Who does it claim to be of use to?
3. What does it call for?
4. What practical action corresponds to it?[47]

Having found a place for themselves in the world of their characters, the actors must now find a place for that fiction in the real world. There is a twofold alienation here: first, the actors, having become used to finding their way into the orbit of their roles must now adjust to being placed outside them. Second, in so far as the method used here bears some resemblance to that employed in the earlier period, the actors are encouraged to examine critically their technique – and recognize the shift away from Stanislavsky. Whereas the similarly numbered questions posited by Stanislavsky aim to create a context that establishes the reality of the text, Brecht's questions generate a metatext which feeds back into, and possibly alters, the context.

The study of objectives too is subverted as the actors now dislocate the tight causality upon which the Stanislavskian theatre relies for its supposedly hypnotic dynamism: 'with an epic work, as opposed to a dramatic, one can as it were take a pair of scissors and cut it into individual pieces, which remain fully capable of life'.[48] Stanislavskian objectives, having been assembled in terms of a 'through line', are once again sundered so that social determinism, once seen as absolute, is now unmasked as manipulable. Of course, Brecht's refusal to streamline his units of action does not mean that his actors lack orientation. The superobjective in Brecht is superstructure, that vision of a just society which is now the final goal that brings purpose to the manner in which each scene is played. This construct has the advantage that it naturally dislocates the actor from his role – for 'if the actor understands the super-objective he is representing society and stands outside of his character to that extent'.[49] Just as the superobjective governs motive, so too does superstructure; but in the light of the ideology supporting that structure, the objectives generated by the text now attach to the actor, not the character. The actor now 'becomes' the metatext. And once again, Stanislavsky is adopted only to be adapted to the purposes of utility.

In so far as the difficulty of discovering and sustaining the metatext is above all a psychological problem (the influence of Stanislavsky's system is overbearing only because actors treat it as such), one would expect its most drastic solutions to occur in the realm of somatic work. Where the development of a metatext can be self-conscious, the product of socio-political 'discussion', somatic work can be relied upon to effect a dislocation between the actor and the role before the actor has had the opportunity to take account of such a change. Thus, for example, stage design, the material terms of production, that with which the actor is constantly in bodily contact, may in Brecht be provocatively irregular:

> One chair will have short legs, and the height of the accompanying table will also be calculated, so that whoever eats at it has to take a quite specific attitude, and the conversation of these people as they bend more than usual when eating takes on a particular character, which makes the episode clearer. And how many effects are made possible by his [the designer's] doors of the most diverse heights![50]

As in Stanislavsky, design precedes disposition; but in so far as Brecht's plans include inconsistency, their effect is calculated not to enhance but to inhibit the actor's tendency to identify with the character. One can hardly lose oneself in one's character if one has to stoop terribly or stretch awkwardly to do the commonest things. As familiar activities are thus made unfamiliar, the actors also experience in a concrete form something of the astonishment in the face of the natural which comprises the essence of Brechtian alienation. Moreover, as the prompts have a specific location in space, they may deliberately be used intermittently, thus drawing the actor into and out of a psychological position – which is precisely the effect Brecht is looking for. Appropriately, the word 'attitude' recurs as it signals a state less personal, permanent or consistent than that featuring 'emotion'.

Just as space can force an attitude upon the body, so too can time. For instance, Brecht notes that 'slow motion . . . alienates the little sub-incident, emphasises its importance, makes it worthy of notice'.[51] As easily performed actions become difficult as a result of deceleration, the actors are compelled to observe themselves. Conduct becomes deliberate and the actors are dislocated from their roles. Action may, of course, also be speeded up to similar effect: as Brecht observes, 'the nearer the performance gets to being a run-through, the more epic it will be'.[52] As actors hurry through the script with time merely to indicate but not fulfil its action, they are quite unselfconsciously detached from their characters. Brecht recommended to Strehler that run-throughs be conducted not just before performance as is normally the case but at regular intervals throughout the rehearsal period. The actors must not merely learn to be and not be their characters; they must at all times be able to move uninhibitedly between these positions – for defamiliarization is not a position but the result of a transition.

Playing sequences of action slowly or quickly does not exhaust the resources of time somatically to render strange the familiar. One of Brecht's exercises for acting schools involves rhythmical verse-speaking with tap-dance. As significance alters with the emphases dictated by tempo, a multiplicity of meanings is suggested – which is of course a mark of their relativity. This dislocated pattern of delivery may subsequently be retained in performance: by highlighting what the audience, with its realistic assumptions, does not expect to hear emphasized, or splitting with caesuras lines normally delivered undivided, the actors ensure that the text is 'not brought home to the spectator but withdrawn from him'.[53] Meaning is alienated through a technique not entirely dissimilar to the process by which it was previously absorbed. It is as if Brecht were using the Stanislavsky system to help the actor to empathise first with the character and then with that other quite unfamiliar role that has also to be mastered – that of the Brechtian actor, metatext to the character's text.

*

In a performance of *Round Heads and Pointed Heads* in Denmark in 1936, Brecht had his actors carry umbrellas through exaggerated outbursts of elevated and passionate acting in the hope that 'the spectator, having had his attention drawn to the outmoded nature of such conduct . . . [would go] on to notice that lofty speech is bound up with the individual problems of the upper class.'[54] If speaking verse to tap-dancing forces dislocation upon a text in a politically quite neutral manner, this deliberate puncturing of both social and theatrical affectation carries a sting in the tail of somatic alienation. A concern with content has now emerged to complement the hitherto purely formal interest of Brecht's foray into alienation.

In a diary entry of 10 September 1920, Brecht projects an idea for the alienation through parody of that which is mannered both in society (content) and on the stage (form):

> I shall hire two clowns. They will perform in the interval and pretend to be spectators. They will bandy opinions about the play and about members of the audience. Make bets on the outcome. . . . 'That staircase gives off an aura of real tragedy. . . . There's going to be some real crying. . . .' The idea would be to bring reality back to things on the stage.[55]

The action of the clowns effects a three-fold alienation. First, by parodying the text, the clowns embody the metatext that must dislocate the otherwise unchallenged substance of the drama. Second, by ridiculing the manner in which the actors deliver the text, the clowns alienate style as style and not System: emotion and mood are not the only factors that determine the success of a stage production. Third, by satirizing the attitudes of the spectators, the clowns remind them that they are members of a theatre audience merely, not witnesses with God-like perspective at the scene of the events portrayed. As opinions of the kind the audience is likely to have are expressed, the spectators are dislocated from their views and forced to reconsider the purposes of the drama.

When parody is transferred to the rehearsal situation, the full thrust of Brecht's original contribution to acting technique is felt. Brecht's practice scenes for actors mirror the three-stage estrangement of his clowns. First, a parody of *Hamlet* turns out to be just as much a parody of Stanislavsky:

> Hamlet learns that Claudius has created a strip of land in Norway in return for a trade agreement which guarantees the sale of Danish salted herrings to Norway; this *puts him into the right mood* to hear Fortinbras' expedition to Poland and *explains* his change of mood in 'How all occasions do inform against me.'[56]

By altering the given circumstances so as to render them absurd, Brecht produces a travesty not of the text as much as of Stanislavsky's use of context to justify a character's response. The reflexive orientation persists as the connection is made with both motivation and the supposedly inevitable influx into an emotional condition.

Second, and as is often the case in Brecht, the humour of such situations carries the bite of social satire:

> Romeo: What do I know about estates – I'm burning up.
> Tenant: And we are hungry – sir.

Romeo: Stupid! . . . Don't you animals have any feelings?
Tenant: . . . *Are* we animals? Then we must feed.[57]

It is not entirely coincidental that the caricatured Romeo should combine the characteristics most pointedly targeted by Brecht – the extremes of emotional sensitivity and moral insentience. It is as though the two are symbiotic, if not entirely synonymous. As the defamiliarizing hunger of the figure introduced by the improvisation intrudes upon the mawkish suffering of the figure we recognize from the original drama, so also reality infiltrates the politically insular truths of the Stanislavskian 'magic if' and its effects.

Lastly, the alienation of the text:

> The murder scene in *Macbeth* is equated with the pangs of conscience of a concierge's wife who has broken off the head of a china statue belonging to the lady of the house, and finally blames the deed on a passing beggar.[58]

Brecht recommended to Strehler that he play tragic scenes for comic effect in rehearsal so that the actors are at once distanced from the text and compelled to provide a contextualizing commentary on its otherwise universally ingestive design. The subversive energy thus generated is infectious: in seeking to create a metatext, the actors are induced, inadvertantly, to become it.

In a variation on the impulse to travesty, tape recordings of rehearsals are played back to the actors so that they are literally placed outside their roles and can view both the substance of the drama and their manner of playing it with objectivity. Brecht recommends as well that actors should sometimes exchange roles with their partners during rehearsals. If there is a danger of actors clinging to early discoveries and building strictly linear sequences in roles devoid of all dialectic, the process of exchanging parts has the salutary effect of alienating the actors' interpretations and providing them with the alternatives upon which epic theatre depends so crucially. Again, Brecht's exercises for acting schools include the characterization of fellow actors. As student actors play other actors playing their roles, the reality of 'character' is doubly distanced. Characterization is revealed as relative both implicitly (in juxtaposition with other interpretations) and explicitly (by being itself subjected to interpretation).

In *The Caucasian Chalk Circle* a number of songs describe actions as they take place on the stage. For example,

> She rose, she leaned over, she sighed, she lifted the child

She carried if off
She does what the singer says as he describes it
Like booty she took it for herself
Like a thief she sneaked away.[59]

A familiar enough device which, as it is adapted for rehearsal, involves some of Brecht's best-known rehearsal techniques:

> In Scene Three of his [Brecht's] adaption of Lenz's play *Der Hofmeister* (*The Private Tutor*) there occurs the following passage:
> (*Enter Count Wermuth. After a few silent compliments he sits down on the sofa.*)
> Count: Has Your Excellency seen the new dancing master who has arrived from Dresden.
> During rehearsals the actor playing the Count was made to say:
> Then the Count entered. After a few silent compliments he sat down on the sofa and asked whether Madame had seen the new dancing master, who had arrived from Dresden.[60]

As the actor speaks aloud both the character's lines and the stage directions, he needs to use two quite distinct tones of voice. In so far as stage directions are conventionally metatextual, the two tones of voice are in effect those associated with text and metatext. Moreover, in so far as somatic theory suggests that external attributes lead to internal conditions, the use of these cadences perceptibly generates the states of being they represent. The exercise thus introduces actors to the distinction between text and metatext through experience rather than analysis.

Second, the text is paraphrased. This could, if done with calculated insensitivity, generate the subversive energy of parody. As verse becomes prose and prose in turn the actor's native dialect, the emphasis is as much on deflating vanity within the text as on alienating the text itself as text. The metatext now finds a Stanislavskian objective: it must generate a social critique of class conceit.

Third, the past tense is used to dislocate the speaker from the text: the actor can now 'look back' on the events described and thereby both confirm that the events on stage are not taking place for the first time and harness any perspective that may thus be produced.

Lastly, the exercise requires that the actor speak in the third person which, in tandem with the use of the past tense, creates the detachment that Brecht requires. The character is 'out there', not 'in here'. The actor now *is* the metatext.

*

In *The Measures Taken* three 'comrades' report on a trip to China by
acting out not only their roles but those of all others who enter into the
narrative. Played as a rehearsal exercise, the scenario takes us into a
higher stage of Brechtian acting technique. Whereas the exercises
described thus far help actors to *locate* a metatext, this improvisation is
designed to teach actors how in performance to fluctuate between text
and metatext once the metatext has been identified. It is assumed that
the actors are now able to comprehend the complex interplay of
different levels of reality in their work. The purpose of rehearsal is now
to develop the flexibility that would enable actors to move deftly and
critically between these planes. Alienation, we remember, is not a static
condition but the result of a series of transitions.

However, Brecht's objective is not merely to facilitate transitions
between the levels of text but to help actors to hold two levels of text
simultaneously so that transitions are either natural or unnecessary.
Finally, Brecht requires 'an actor who can completely empathize and
. . . *at the same time* . . . can stand away from his character.'[61] The
following is perhaps the most vivid of Brecht's exercises designed to
meet this need:

   (l) Exercises in temperament. Situation: two women calmly fold-
       ing linen. They feign a wild and jealous quarrel for the benefit
       of their husbands; the husbands are in the next room.
   (m)They come to blows as they fold their linen in silence.
   (n) Game (l) turns serious.[62]

At stage (l) the actors are already required to hold two levels of reality
concurrently, but this is made easy for them by the fact that one level is
clearly more 'real' than the other. We know that they are merely *feigning*
the quarrel (itself an 'act' and to that extent a lesson in dislocation – but
we have come a long way from exercises which involve merely the
recognition of metatext). At stage (m) the content of the actors' gestures
is expressed as speech and the speech-text is expressed purely as action.
The actors are thus introduced somatically to the elements of both
inversion and simultaneity in alienation. At stage (n) the test occurs: as
the 'roles' they are playing slowly assume the status of 'reality', two
'truths' emerge in a manner whereby neither takes obvious precedence
over the other. On the one hand a fiction has become reality, but on the
other, that fiction continues to be merely a fiction. The action is and is
not real at once – and both levels must be played with as much
conviction.

The technique, once learnt, is adapted to include a more explicitly political aspect. For instance, one of Brecht's exercises for acting schools requires an actor simultaneously to perform a conjuring trick and show the attitude of the spectators watching it. The bite of the exercise lies in that it requires actors not merely to play two levels of reality at once, but to display as well the gulf of knowledge which comprises the difference between these two positions. It is of course not entirely fortuitous that this mirrors exactly the gulf between actor and spectator which sustains the supposedly coercive 'magic' of the theatre of empathy. By embodying the attitudes of both oppressor and oppressed at once, Brecht's actor defamiliarizes each as relative. The trick is revealed: the illusion which sustains the theatre of empathy is shown up as being of human contrivance.

The theatre of utility is interested not merely in exposing the surprisingly pliable underpinning of propaganda but offering as well if not definite alternatives, at least an attitude that seeks change. Finally the purpose of being able to play and not play a character is to be able to indicate the presence of options where none are apparent:

> When he appears on the stage, besides what he actually is doing he will at all essential points discover, specify, imply what he is not doing; that is to say he will act in such a way that the *alternatives emerge* as clearly as possible, that his acting allows for *other possibilities* to be inferred. . . . The technical term for this procedure is 'fixing the "not . . . but"'.[63]

'Not . . . but' is the structure of a sentence which comprises a simple alienation. For instance, 'it was not red but blue' alienates red and blue in relation to one another. Here red stands for an expectation based on common sense which is betrayed by the revealed presence of the blue. The result is that we double-take as the second term undercuts the security of the first. The purpose of this form of alienation is to reveal that there were always two possibilities, not just one as we had imagined. It is this revelation that lies at the core of Brecht's vision of the theatre. In order to achieve this, the actor must in rehearsal explicitly 'precede each thought expressed in the dialogue or each action with its dialectical opposite, thus enabling him to define the various alternative choices available to his character which he, the actor, may make clear to the audience'.[64] In performance the actual stating of alternatives is suppressed but the consequent awareness that necessity is an illusion may, as in somatic work, find tacit expression in the action. Reality is not absolute as Stanislavsky would have us believe. And to see reality as relative – that is the true measure of our political potential.

Like Stanislavsky, Brecht hopes that the audience will follow the lead of the actor – not, in this case, to identify with and therefore accept as inevitable the course of events portrayed but to see within it choices that were not visible before. There is an optimism about such performances, designed as they are to convince us by their example that alternatives may be found in the seemingly determined fabric of our lives. It is an optimism shared and not shared by Peter Brook.

PETER BROOK

'There is so much of Brecht's work I admire', muses Brook in a retrospective chapter of *The Shifting Point*, 'so much of his work with which I disagree totally.'[65] Never one to be listlessly inexact, Brook has in mind very specific reasons for ·his seemingly idle reminiscence. Antagonistically,

> I did not really agree with his view of the difference between illusion and non-illusion. In his production of *Mother Courage* by the Berliner Ensemble, I found that however much he tried to break any belief in the reality of what happened on stage, the more he did, the more I entered whole-heartedly into the illusion![66]

Two lines later, by way of affirmation,

> Craig, by putting the question: 'How much is it essential to put on stage to convey a forest?' suddenly exploded the myth that it was necessary to show an entire forest, trees, leaves, branches. . . .
> Brecht follows the same line of thinking, but relates it to acting. . . . [I]f you can get that physical side down to a simple outline, . . . then you have more means at your disposal.[67]

Brook appreciates Brecht's economy of presentation but does not believe alienation is possible. Indeed, we shall see that the conditions which sustain Brechtian compactness are the very factors which render defamiliarization unfeasible.

What Brook admires is Brecht's awareness of the advantages of allowing actors to avoid having to abide by every aspect of their characters' behaviour. As there is no attempt in Brecht's theatre to make stage action consistently lifelike, it is possible for an actor to present a situation in the minimum of time merely by reporting the requisite information. Thus for example Pelagea Vlassova is, rapidly and without much ado, 'Pelagea Vlassova, forty-two years old, the widow of a worker and the mother of a worker.'[68] As John Willett marvels, the 'whole problem of explanation and establishing the characters is got over as easily as that'.[69]

One of the advantages of having the option to suggest rather than imitate reality is that, assuming there is a limit to the amount of sensory information a spectator can process at any one time, Brechtian theatre can carry a denser truth than appearance-bound naturalism. In Stanislavskian drama there is a demand for consistency which implies, for instance, that the set must exist with all its paraphernalia throughout a scene. As Brook observes, naturalism requires that images 'stay in the frame long after their need is over. If we have a ten minute scene in a forest, we can never get rid of the trees.'[70] In other words, the information provided by the set continues to be conveyed even after the message has got across. In Brecht, by contrast, the actors can, minutes after having set up a scene, go on to develop some other facet of the production. 'You are in Chicago in 1912'[71] we are told *In the Jungle of the Cities* – and so, as a result, we are. Thereafter the substance of the prompt can be dropped and space made for other orders of information. Thus, whereas naturalism squanders its inevitably limited supply of semiotic energy by reiterating rather than replacing information, Brecht, by permitting inconsistency, can give the audience more in the same amount of time.

Non-naturalistic theatre does not merely present with greater cohesion truths that are available in naturalism. The more telling advantage of Brechtian flexibility is its capacity to beget a quite different *quality* of experience as a function of its ability to depict both the surface and the structure of reality. As Brook puts it, 'What realistic image can show a man sitting in his chair and another life calling him?'[72] As actors can move between identities, mutually exclusive aspects of content can be presented and access had to truths that cannot be reached through the depiction of lifelike externals, however minutely observed. The result is not just a greater concentration of meaning but a completely different, and potentially much fuller, order of experience than is available in naturalism. This is what Brook admires – and in doing so acknowledges something of a debt: for it was Brecht who threw the gauntlet down at the feet of naturalism grown heavy with the veneration accorded to it as the First System.

*

Curiously, the quality of Brecht's drama most admired by Brook leads causally into that to which Brook is least sympathetic. The subconscious capacity by virtue of which an audience sustains a sense of continuity within a fragmented series of images is precisely the faculty which prevents the spectator from being unsettled by any strategic discontinuities in presentation. The irony of Brecht's observation that 'plausible' need not mean 'lifelike' is that this is true only because the spectators almost always continue to fill in for prompts after they have been removed. There is an assemblage in the mind's eye of a compound 'true' action comprised of both present and latent stimuli. The audience continues to 'see' a forest on a bare stage long after the source of this information has been replaced. The disconcerting implication of this for defamiliarization is that it is virtually impossible to achieve the intermittent cessation of illusion through the interjection of metatext. Beyond illusion lies not alienation but obscurity. Thus whereas Brecht would have both density and defamiliarization, Brook knows that the two are mutually exclusive. Metatext is not a sufficiently powerful agent to counteract the persistence of remembered belief upon which presentational drama depends for its density. For Brook, Brecht's strength and failure is his rediscovery of the capacity of audiences to accept incongruities.

Brook's contention that it is fallacious to suppose that in the theatre illusion can be neutralized by interruptions carries a more potent charge as he addresses the problem of mendacity in audiences. In *Tell Me Lies*, Brook's film about Vietnam, a person is murdered on the street but at the windows the onlookers do not move. The need people have to avoid contact with disturbing subjects is of course as true of their responses to the portrayal of horror in art as it is to its occurrence in reality. As Brook observed in the early stages of his work on *US*, 'I suppose I've never got over hearing Alain Resnais' film about concentration camps described as "beautiful".'[73] Habitual blindness of this sort is of course Brecht's theme, yet Brook seems to imply that estrangement is not response enough. In *The Empty Space*, Brook observes that 'alienation is above all an appeal to the spectator to work for himself, and to become, as a result, more and more responsible'.[74] However, where 'the contemporary event touches raw nerves but creates an immediate refusal to listen',[75] where 'we need shields to prevent ourselves from being hurt by a theatrical experience'[76] such a plea, Brook insists, is naive and inadequate. If people seek out ways of warding off contact with disturbing themes, it is futile to rely on their conscience.

There is an assumption in Brecht that blindness is passive, an accidental product of inurement, and that awareness would be welcomed by audiences if only theatres were able to make it attainable. It is as though reform is a function of illumination merely, and insight contingent upon information. Brook is less inclined to believe that it is possible to change things merely by pointing things out to people. Brook is as little attracted to Brecht's view of 1926 that 'reason is fairly comprehensive and to be relied on'[77] as to Galileo's in Brecht's play of 1938: 'Look Sagredo, I believe in Humanity, which means I believe in human reason.'[78] Brook seems rather to be of Sagredo's camp: 'Forty years spent among human beings has again and again brought it home to me that they are not open to reason. . . . Try making one rational statement to them, and back it up with seven proofs, and they'll just laugh at you.'[79]

In the character of Sagredo, Brecht is not merely playing the devil's advocate, foil to the approved view of Galileo. In a note on *Mother Courage*, Brecht admits that 'ever recurring misfortune has forced mankind into a ceremonialization of his defense mechanisms, which of course can never save man from actual fear itself. We must break, in performance, through this ceremonialization of defense.'[80] In 'Theatre for Learning' Brecht acknowledges epic theatre's reliance for its effects upon a pre-existing willingness in the spectator to engage the issues raised in performance. He admits sadly that epic theatre 'can by no means be performed everywhere. Few of the great nations today are inclined to discuss their problems.'[81] Where Brecht, in the face of Fascism and war, acknowledges the limits of alienation as a vehicle of social change, Brook, in the face of yet another genocide, that in Vietnam, must achieve and transcend alienation to 'uncover what we *want* to forget.'[82]

*

Brook's solution to the problem of mendacity, of the spectator's terrible *desire* for blindness, is actively to confront spectators with their self-censorship. This is done by presenting as drama both the political situation in question and, as an equally important aspect of the performance, the audience's struggle to avoid facing the truth. Brook's socially conscious drama, like Brecht's, works through the juxtaposition of incompatibles. But whereas in Brecht the tension posited is that between text and metatext, in Brook the contradictions operate between two alternative texts, one of which draws attention to a situation and the other to the spectators' resistance to it. The intention is to jolt the audience into recognizing that it is to a large extent *their* disingenuousness that lies at the heart of the horror that is the drama's other subject.

There are two quite distinct parts to this shrewdly forthright modification of defamiliarization. First, Brook assumes that metatext is not sufficiently powerful to enforce the alienation of a text and therefore assigns to a second text the antithetical agency traditionally associated with Brechtian metatext. Brook recognizes that there is a difference in status between metatext and text which stems from the relative extent of their realization in the drama: whereas metatextual pointers depend entirely upon the text for their existence, conventional text is autonomously articulate. Whereas metatext, as marginalia, can be marginalized, text, as that which *is*, compels attention. Thus whereas in Brecht there is text (the dramatized assertion of a character who *is*) and metatext (the discursive, contextualizing opinion on those assertions), in Brook there are two fully realized texts within the body of a single work which comment upon each other through the force of their revealed incongruity. If in the Brechtian model the image is that of a play in progress with a commentator to one side drawing attention to the social implications of the action, in Brook there are two significantly incongruous dramas in progress simultaneously. As a result, the dislocation of perspective upon which the principle of alienation relies for its effects, is now potentially practicable.

Second, and far more potently, one of the texts in question is designed explicitly to embody those attributes of the audience which render them unwilling to see the truths offered to them by the drama's other text. To the extent that texts demand attention, the contradiction between them must comprise an effective alienation; if one of the texts, moreover, enacts the very evasiveness that this alienation seeks to combat, the audience is rendered relatively powerless to resist the implication that their situation is potentially hypocritical. Thus *US*, for example, is a compound title encompassing the import of both external and internal texts – the United States and us, the war and Britain's dogged obliviousness to its horror. If Brecht points to (metatext) the exploitation which his audiences will not see, Brook dramatizes (text) both social injustice and the incapacity of his spectators to take sufficient account of it. In the presence of a fully realized and disconcertingly personal example, the audience has little option but to absorb the strategically multi-faceted significance of Brook's drama.

Like Brecht, Brook believes that 'society needs changing – urgently'[83] and that theatre should be devoted to 'making something that has a use'.[84] And, like Brecht, Brook knows that 'For an idea to stick it is not enough to state it';[85] the theatre must work by 'breaking open a series of habits'[86] through a 'healthy double attitude'.[87] However, in Brook this dialectic – and Brook uses the word often – has to be that between 'what is going on *in ourselves* and the world around us'.[88] Brook's subject is therefore as much the gap between the views held by Americans and the Vietnamese as that destructively in operation between the attitudes concealed in the audience and those conceded by them:

> We were not interested in the Theatre of Fact.
> We were interested in a theatre of confrontation. . . . In the case of Vietnam, it is reasonable to say that everyone is concerned, yet no one is concerned. . . . Is it possible then, we ask ourselves, to present for a moment to the spectator this contradiction, *his own* and his society's contradiction?[89]

As in Brecht, *US* uses 'a multitude of contradictory techniques to change direction and to change levels';[90] but if 'Whatever the cost, a man marshals everything at his disposal to skid away from the simple recognition of how things are',[91] Brook must use Brechtian flexibility to include amongst the contraries presented a portrait of its attentive but sightless audience. Only the most rending revelations of guilt can compel responsibility by insinuating themselves into the truth-resistant fabric of our sensibilities.

*

Brook's approach to the task of generating in his spectators an intelligent willingness to take account of the problem of Vietnam creates in rehearsal a three-part difficulty. First, there is the question of creating the reality of the subject matter, the politics of the confrontation between the United States and Vietnam. In order to ensure that both sides of the conflict are properly represented, the actors must be able to enter the sensibility of each of these cultures. This is difficult in proportion to distance:

> How were we to say anything about a peasant culture when none of us knew anything about peasants? Were we simply to ask the actors to imitate Vietnamese peasants rather badly?[92]

Second, as a consequence of Brook's conviction that *US* would be effective only if it was able to portray as well the habitual apathy of the British, there is the problem of creating a self-portrait through unsparingly honest introspection:

We were going to examine our own attitudes, to ask ourselves as totally as possible how the Vietnam War affected *us*.[93]

Third, in an effort to keep the audience from settling into an impenetrable attitude, there is the problem of training the actors to alternate between each of their profiles – of the Vietnam and London, the war and the theatre:

> The actor must dig inside himself for responses, but at the same time must be open to outside stimuli. Acting was the marriage of these two processes.[94]

The three problems correspond to three quite distinct stages in the rehearsal process. As Brook, looking back over the rehearsal period, observes:

> In the first, you opened up as many fields as you could, ranged as widely through our knowledge and ignorance and images as you could. With Grotowski, you explored deeply and intensely a very focussed, tight, personal area of commitment, your own bodily commitment as actors. Now, in the third stage, we shall broaden our scope again. But the intense personal exploration will continue.[95]

If Brecht's actors must be able at once to play and not play their characters, the task facing Brook's actors is to play with complete conviction the two antithetical positions that comprise his drama so that the tension between them may be the more excruciatingly educative. If in Brecht the instructive dialectic is that between text and metatext, in Brook it utilizes two fully realized but embarrassingly incompatible texts, inner and outer, each of which must be infiltrated with full Stanislavskian paraphernalia. Appropriately, the techniques used by Brook in the first two stages of rehearsals of *US* are Stanislavskian; their Brechtian effect is a product of their juxtaposition in the third stage.

*

Brook's debt in *US* to the more orthodox of Stanislavsky's methods is evident in the efforts made by the actors to familiarize themselves with the situation in Vietnam through reading, discussion and the analysis of relevant documents:

> We began to read all we could lay our hands on about Vietnam. By far the most useful documents we found were the records of the Fulbright Committee Hearings on Vietnam and China. There was

a striking phrase by one of the key witnesses, Dr Fairbank: 'Great nations on both sides are pursuing their alternative dreams.' We began to see the war as a collision of dreams.[96]

In the early stages of the work, documentary memorabilia make verbal suggestions: as facts are introduced and sorted, themes suggest themselves semantically. A more substantially interactive introduction into the given circumstances of the drama is sought through contact with a Vietnamese monk who is asked to speak to the cast. In keeping with the tendency of all analytical preparation to perish in desultory dispute, the session ends with a discussion on some erudite points of Buddhist belief and very little theatre work is achieved.

Under the supervision of visiting director Joseph Chaikin, the actors are encouraged to abandon this potentially crippling intellectualism and move 'into another dimension. Previously we had read and talked. Now, the ideas were to be explored collectively by the actors through their bodies.'[97] In an effort to absorb something of the American sensibility, the actors are asked to model themselves on film stars and play out typical situations:

> Frank Sinatra tried to pick up Debbie Reynolds in Central Park. . . .
> The exploration of American myth took the form of more improvizations from movies, an attempt to play out advertisements, and a study of horror comics.[98]

If the academic mapping of a society is inevitably circumspect, subject always to an awareness of what is *not* known, physical impersonation gives Brook's actors access to the heart of the everyday American imagination in a manner that is as disarmingly entertaining as it is educative. A concern with rhythm now takes precedence over meaning:

> One afternoon an American woman . . . came and commented on what she saw. Her comments were not very useful, but while she talked, the actors studied her. It was clear that the whole rhythm of her speech pattern was quite different from anything the actors were at this stage able to produce.[99]

The actors focus not on what the woman says but on how she says it. When the actors do not have live subjects to imitate, remembered rhythms are transmitted through the body as in a standard mirroring exercise:

Those who had been to America continued to invent ordinary scenes. A woman revealed herself by talking to a friend on the telephone. An actress who had not been to America tried to repeat the situation.[100]

Whereas the absorption of a way of life through the mind can be fraught with an inhibiting awareness of complexity, physical imitation provides a concrete and simple discipline through which the sensibility of a society can effectively be imbibed.

Vietnam too is explored somatically in improvizations spanning the whole range of visible culture from the naturalistic details of how rice is cooked and huts swept to lessons in Chinese presentational acting technique:

He showed the actor . . . how to depict the sunset. He showed the wife how to walk and bow. . . .

Chiang Lui came and put their hands and feet in the correct position. . . .

[T]hey all ended the afternoon by working at a basic Chinese exercise. They tried in pairs to imitate the scene from Chinese theatre in which two people travel on a sanpan.[101]

The workout under Chiang Lui makes an instructive contrast with the discussion with the Buddhist monk: the more complex the message, the easier and more effective it is to transmit it through the rigour and discipline of bodily work. The skin is mute and will not voice its protest to being invaded by an alien way of being.

At a later stage, somatic work is used to enter not a society's cultural condition but its impulse and response to conflict. In a very simple but powerful exercise, Brook 'placed the actors in two rows facing each other, and gave each row a note. They sang against each other, going higher and higher up the musical scale, until the sound broke down into rival screams.'[102] The exercise begins as a parody of diplomacy: the actors use song, normally a vehicle of harmony, to generate a situation of discord. The incompatibility between the object of the exercise and the means provided to achieve it compels an unanticipated lapse into screaming. This defamiliarizes for the actors the import of an unstoppable escalation into friction. The exercise is a good example of the natural affinity between somatic work and alienation: the strength they have in common is the use they make of the unexpected.

A more elaborate improvization generates through the body an almost tactile sense of the absurdity of war:

five players felt their way, with paper bags over their heads. . . .
Two carried blue flags, two carried red, and one . . . carried a
stick. The player with the stick hunted for the others. When he
caught anybody, he raised his stick. A referee . . . blew his whistle;
everybody froze; the referee led the victim to the front of the stage;
the lights went off, feed-back screamed through the amplifier, a
girl shrieked – and when the lights came on, the victim, holding a
flag, was lying dead . . . and another player, pushed through a
door at the back, had taken his place. The hunter never knew
whether he had caught a red or a blue.[103]

The scenario reads like a complete dramatic event but to regard it as such is
to miss the import of the actor's *first* encounter with a series of somatic
stimuli which are externally, impersonally, almost ritualistically dictated.
As with all somatic work, it is crucial that the exercise be conducted
without the actors having any previous knowledge of its content. Even as
the improvization is set in motion, the actors' awareness of – and potential
control over – the barrage of impulses to which they are subjected is limited
by the paper bags they wear over their heads. The hunted control neither
their exits nor their entrances; and even the hunter is the victim of the
environment, his 'kills' less a product of design than of accident, of chance
fatal encounters. As the grisly aural consequences of their actions scream
back at the actors, the bewilderment and exhaustion that sweeps over them
is genuine. Not through understanding but through the lack of it, not
through their minds but through their bodies, the actors emerge with some
experience with which to feed their roles. A play is not always play – in
order that it may *be*.

*

In *US*, the actors' attempts to locate points of contact between their own
lives and that of their characters takes on an added poignancy as Brook
insists that the actors are themselves a vital fraction of the meaning of the
drama – not as vehicles of remote complexes of personality but as
inadvertantly active collaborators in the creation of the horror that is
their subject. As the actors repeatedly return to the inhumanity of
Vietnam and attempt to relate it to what they can experience for real in
themselves, they too are revealed as less than humane:

The tortures were sickeningly convincing, and most of us watched
them with fascinated attention. What was revealed was the gap
between what we pretended to feel, and the disturbing impulses
inside. . . . Everybody threw themselves with great gusto into the

business of frightening those who could not see – and afterwards everybody sat around again, telling each other how torture was disgusting. . . .

[I]t was important for each one to confront the germs of cruelty in himself as a first step towards understanding.[104]

As the actors work to establish empathy with their characters, the surprising extent of the rapport achieved reveals too their own concealed mendacity. The exercise does not merely make a connection between the violence in Vietnam and the impulses to violence in the actors' own lives; in doing so it generates an alternative text which is also the drama's subject – the *lies* about Vietnam which are at least as interesting as the 'truth' the actors strive for in their work. As a Stanislavskian exercise in empathy thus becomes a Brechtian exercise in alienation, a second concurrently active text is born. This is the drama about 'us', the text without which the drama about 'U.S.' would lose its capacity irresistibly to infiltrate the spectator's habitual hypocrisy.

In a particularly delicate exercise designed to generate material for Act Two, the actor Mark Jones, playing a character called Mark based on himself, answers questions in his own person in the given circumstances of the play:

'You are in Grosvenor Square,' said Brook to Mark Jones, 'with your petrol-can and your matches. You have come to burn yourself.' Mark started to make preparations. Along came Cannan, working off a clipboard of questions. He stopped Mark in midstream, and probed the reasons for his action. . . .

It was a sustained, John-Whiting-like assault on man's (and Mark's) presumption. . . .[105]

The exercise superficially resembles Stanislavsky's quite standard method of provoking actors into exploring the 'other' world of the play by setting them a series of questions about their characters. In this case, however, the character in Brook's play is the actor himself. Of course it is then ironic that the motivation of the character should have to be eked out in this way, but as disingenuousness is a theme in the drama, the need for these disconcertingly dispassionate questions is itself significant, an important part of the meaning that is alienated by incongruity.

As the exercise develops – and the interrogation must, if it is to be productive, be sustained for two hours or longer – a truth crystallizes which is not the truth of hypocrisy. Left with no room in which to hide his indifference, the actor forges from the resources of his being an attitude which he regards as constructive. The process mirrors the projected development of a conscience in the audience: the questioning implicit in the performance must reveal to the spectators their evasion of responsibility and allow them no space to manouevre but in the direction of a more creative frame of mind. As the actor now begins by representing the audience, the spectators' obligation to follow the actors' lead is all the more inescapable. The actor's vulnerability is his strength – for it translates unmistakably as accountability in the audience.

Mark's response to the question at the heart of the drama, 'If I say I care about Vietnam, how does this influence the way I spend my time?',[106] is to use suicide as a means of drawing attention to the substance and sincerity of his protest. As text to be realized, the projected sacrifice is explored in a further exercise. Kustow's account of the work is extensive but must, if it is to be appreciated, be quoted at length:

Brook: 'I want you to start by searching deeply for the idea of being dead. It's nothing to do with imagination or the idea of having been; just try and get as close as you can to the problem of being nothing, now.'[107]

The slate is wiped clean. That this may be achieved only partially is, in the context of what is to follow, irrelevant. It is sufficient to the purposes of the exercise that nothingness is at this stage an act of will merely.

'Next; you're no longer dead, you're alive. Listen deeply to what, in the quietest sense, is the feeling of being alive. What is the smallest difference between that nothingness, that emptiness, and being alive.'[108]

The inner. Again, that the trance may be incomplete is inconsequential. The condition is a springboard merely; concrete elements follow:

'Now you have just one possibility: you may place beside you one person, . . . the person who is closest to you. . . .

'Now . . . you may have one of your faculties. . . . Test your choice – . . . . can you find complete life in that one choice? Is it better than death? . . .

'Now you have another possibility: you may only bring to life one point of your body. . . .

'Now a new possibility: you can live with your whole body – but only in a small closed room. Seek the things and people you need to live. What is the *least* you need to live?

'Now come out of the room into the outside world. As you put your hand on the doorhandle, decide on the one thing in the outside world that makes you want to go out.'[109]

In carefully constructed stages the movement from inner to outer. The restrictions discipline the impulse outward, compelling the actors to choose and therefore explore minutely, to live through and thereby appreciate fully, the extent of their reliance upon essential externals.

The second stage of the exercise requires the actors to relinquish in stages these indispensible affinities:

> After a break, Brook set up five benches, and did the entire exercise in reverse. . . . Each actor had to take six steps which would lead him to the end of the bench and off. But each step could only be taken after the actor had:
> discarded the world and why it mattered
> discarded the closed room with precious possessions
> discarded the one living point in the body
> discarded the one living faculty
> discarded the one needed person
> discarded the feel of being just alive, accepted death.[110]

The movement from outer to inner, surrendering what has been known intimately, renouncing what has been felt deeply to be of greatest value. 'Most of the actors', Kustow tells us, 'got to step four; Bob Lloyd got to step five and stuck.'[111] We are at the incipient stages of a less callous attitude to the needless loss of life in Vietnam. The fact that the actors are unable to complete the exercise is a vivid indication of the extent to which they now stand in relation to the primary text (that of Vietnam) not as metatext but as text soaked in the sweat of reappraisal.

*

As in Brecht, Brook's use of Stanislavskian techniques of complete ingress into character in the first two stages of rehearsal leads inevitably to the problem of preparing the actor to cut with sufficiently alarming alacrity between the two discretely developed texts that make up the content of the drama:

> We had to be able to . . . make thematic links between these different worlds. It could only be done . . . with actors who could move rapidly backwards and forwards between different styles. But since the training of actors in British theatre is limited, and

largely centred on 'character' acting, the actors had to begin slowly and painfully.[112]

Brook's solution to the problem draws directly upon a technique first developed by Brecht:

> the actors had to learn new and basic techniques. . . . Two actors spent several hours on one Brecht exercise. They went through *Good King Wenceslas*, singing alternate lines – each moving quickly from Sinatra to Caruso and then to Mick Jagger.[113]

The exercise is not merely a matter of switching from one role to another but also of relating each character to the fixed structure of the song. The actors must therefore be able to 'be and not be' their characters in a dual sense. First, they must convincingly embody, and then rapidly relinquish, each personage. Second, even when 'in character', they must be sufficiently outside their portrayals to relate each variant to the unvarying rhythm of the song. So the exercise rehearses two skills at once: to alternate between impersonations, and to experience what it is to be and not be each of those characters in turn.

The flexibility thus developed is eventually brought to bear upon the gulf between the sensibilities that comprise the cross-bred title *US*:

> A group played out a number of New York intellectuals trying to stage a Happening. They never reached the Happening, and in their failure they caught at an image, a group of people struggling with their own ineffectiveness. It was a superficial image. . . . But the limitations were ruthlessly exposed as soon as Brook asked them to turn the scene into an English drawing room on Sunday afternoon.[114]

The exercise has two functions. First, it draws attention to the actors' initial inability to move with adequate agility from one sensibility to another. Second, the transition between satire and self-portrait reminds the actors of the all too easily concealed affinity between societies and the responsibility this entails. Alienation is now a function not merely of learning to be and not be the character. As important is the passage of the actor from the person of the character to a *normative* view of the self. A concern with content now complements the actors' formal skills.

Both purposes, flexibility and the definition of the limits of empathy, underlie Brook's work on a torture scene:

> He used four actors, with the rest sitting round in a group watching. He asked those watching to give their immediate,

74

spontaneous reactions to what they saw, first as if they were watching Americans carrying out the torture, and then as if they were the inhabitants of a bombed village, watching an American airman being tortured.[115]

Attention is drawn as powerfully to the capacity of the actors-as-audience to see the other point of view (twice) as to the ability of the actors-as-performers rapidly to re-align their sympathies. The ability to make rapid transitions between identities is not an end in itself. Among its many effects is a modicum of imaginative sympathy, a vital precondition of peace. In conjunction with the potentially humbling implication of the self in the destructive action that is alienated, defamiliarization now becomes a means of combating dogma, the most prolific source of conflict. By the time real spectators have replaced this audience of actors, the actors will have had some experience of provoking introspection, of revealing the unsuspected extent of collective responsibility, of communal guilt. In the exercise the actors learn what it is to be such an audience – and therefore, all the more profoundly, what it is to play to one.

In Brecht, the transitions between various stages of rehearsal are themselves instructive and may be used reflexively to rehearse the actors' capacity to alienate what they must at first engage completely. So also in Brook, exercises are designed to consolidate the defamiliarizing effects of shifts in the object of rehearsal by combining these in telling sequences of requirements. For example,

> Brook then asked Mark Jones and Robert Lloyd to re-enact the Buddhist burning himself which they had seen in the film *Mondo Cane*. The other actors were asked to stand around in a square and watch. This was repeated a second time, with everyone pointing out details. . . . The third time, the actors were asked to react personally to the event in the most sincere way, and to state their attitude in a sentence, prefaced by their name, details, the place and date.[116]

In the first instance, the actors play an external text so that its import may somatically be absorbed by them. This produces an internal text not merely as all 'truly' played text must be internalized, but in the more prescriptive sense in which this text embodies an example to be followed by the actor-as-character. The exercise then shifts up a gear as this in turn produces a need for a critical reaction designed to effect a defamiliarizing distance between the actor and actor-character. Finally, as the actors are asked to preface their immediate and deeply felt responses with the objective stance and tone of registration, the exercise carries the actors into the third stage – that of moving rapidly between emotion and discipline, being and not being themselves and the characters in their drama.

In practice, flexibility leads very quickly to simultaneity, to the actor's capacity concurrently to embody two or more orders of reality. In all exercises designed to train actors nimbly to adopt and disavow characters in sequence, there comes a point when, after a suitable period of perambulation through preparatory stages in which each of the characters is firmly located, that purpose is explicitly revealed. One must, for instance, allow actors some time in which to prepare to sing the *Good King Wenceslas* song as Sinatra. Once the Sinatra manner is fixed, the actors are given time to prepare the Caruso figure, and so on. Only after the dramatis personae are firmly located does the director reveal to the actors that they must now fling themselves between these unhurriedly constructed positions. From the moment this aspect of the exercise is revealed, the actors, conscious of the task ahead, are inevitably induced to hold both conditions in their minds at once so that they may be realized in action more efficiently.

If this is at first difficult, it may, as in Brecht, be practised in isolation:

> When they played through a Doris Day story, 'Blueberry Pie', they demonstrated the advances in control they had made over the last few weeks. They succeeded in producing moments of pure emotion while being beside themselves with laughter. . . .
>
> The rudiments of an acting style had been created – the actors were now able to move much more flexibly from one mood to another. A language of theatre, based on a bringing together of many different elements, was being tentatively formed.[117]

There is in this passage, from what is after all a Royal Shakespeare Company document, a curiously suggestive ambiguity as to whether the transition from sequential to simultaneous defamiliarization is a novel element in *Brook's* work or a revolution in the theatre *generally*. There is, in the reference to 'an acting style' being 'created', to a 'language of the theatre' being 'formed', just a glimmer of an indication that the force of these terms is not restricted to the evolution of *US* but intended to apply more widely. It would of course be untrue to hold that Brook is the first director in modern times to enable actors at once to be and not be their characters. But it must be conceded that in Brook this is achieved by the fact that his actors are represented in their drama not by their opinions merely as in Brecht, but by their courageous portrayal of their every evasion, hypocrisy and untruth. The actors present a view of the situation in Vietnam, but far more unnervingly they hold up for scrutiny themselves. In this, Brook acknowleges the influence of Grotowski:

> instead of the normal glazed brightness of first-night perfor-mances, you gave the audience something rock-solid, authentic. Remember what Grotowski said about the actor offering himself to the audience? That's what you deeply did last night. . . .[118]

It is to Brook's debt to Grotowski that I turn in the next chapter.

3

LET BE:
Jerzy Grotowski and Peter Brook

Grotowski has emphasised many times that the most important thing for him is searching for answers to the question: how should one live?[1]

(A. Lechika)

The theatre is a search for an expression that is directly concerned with the quality of living.[2]

(Peter Brook)

This act ought to function as a self-revelation. . . . At the moment when the actor . . . discovers himself . . . the actor, that is to say the human being, transcends the phase of incompleteness, to which we are condemned in everyday life. . . . [T]he reaction which he invokes in us contains a peculiar unity of what is individual and what is collective.[3]

(Jerzy Grotowski)

The purpose of theatre is . . . making an event in which a group of fragments are suddenly brought together . . . in a community which, by the natural laws that make every community, gradually breaks up. . . . At certain moments this fragmented world comes together and for a certain time it can rediscover the marvel of organic life. The marvel of being one.[4]

(Peter Brook)

JERZY GROTOWSKI

In Andrei Tarkovsky's *The Sacrifice*, the protagonist Alexander rescues the world from imminent nuclear holocaust by forfeiting his every possession and attachment. Although the affirmation implicit in this act

78

of faith is qualified somewhat by obligatory intimations of insanity, the energy of the film as a whole does posit individual votive action as a viable solution to social ills. However implausible such a remedy may seem to ordinary mortals nurtured on earthly conjectures and civic assurances, belief of this kind has repeatedly found attestation in literature. In particular, the interplay of the three main elements of this phenemenon – social concern, the emphasis on the role of the individual, and recourse to oblation – is a characteristic of virtually all the major plays staged by Jerzy Grotowski. As Zbigniew Osinski recalls,

> *Kordian* led directly to *Akropolis*. . . . [T]hrough its treatment of the hero, who perceived the sense of his existence in saving others . . . even to the point of total self-sacrifice . . . it was another forerunner of *The Tragicall History of Dr. Faustus* and its hero, as well as of *The Constant Prince* (with the element of self-sacrifice stressed in the very title), and of *Apocalypsis Cum Figuris*, with the Simpleton's sacrifice. . . . [T]he protagonists of all Grotowski's productions, from Cain to Simpleton, are variations on the same theme.[5]

Werner Herzog often demands of his actors that they perform in circumstances which resemble to a bizarre and sometimes inhuman extent the conditions in which the real events portrayed originally occurred. For example, Herzog required during the shooting of *Fitzcarraldo* that a real ship be pushed over a mountain in spite of modern cinema's technical ability to render lifelike a lighter and safer replica. *The Wrath of God* too was shot not in some convenient corner of Amazonia but hundreds of miles from the nearest village or road – with all the real risks and terror that such a situation creates. Here the 'given circumstances' need not be imagined: their almost absolute authenticity enables actors to secure the severest realism in characterization merely by playing themselves.

Similarly, in Grotowski's theatre, actors play their characters by playing themselves. As in Herzog's cinema, Grotowski's actors 'must not illustrate but accomplish an act':[6] they must express as fact the fiction of their narratives. In *The Constant Prince*, Ryszard Cieslak *really* suffered the torment inflicted on the Prince, was *literally* scourged in the person of his character. As one reviewer wrote in *Odra*, 'This is not theatre! . . . The actors of 13 Rows flagellate themselves until they have red welts on their backs. . . . Fanaticism worthy of the highest recognition.'[7]

The implication of the juxtaposition of Grotowski's affinities with Tarkovsky and Herzog is that the Laboratory Theatre actors seek in their theatre to make a sacrifice of themselves in an attempt to redeem the society for which they play. If, in the manner of Herzog, Grotowski's actors literally invade the fiction of their characters, and if the principal theme of that fiction is a Tarkovskian preoccupation with salvation through sacrifice, then it follows that it is Grotowski's intention to save *his* society through the *real* sacrificial action of his actors.

*

To the extent that sacrifice for Grotowski is social therapy, his theatre may, in impulse if not in appearance, be said to be political in the manner of Brecht. Just as Brecht intended not to interpret the world but to help alter it, so also Grotowski's is a 'moral and social mission – built on a core of intellectual values, committed to progress, proposing a new secular and rational ethic.'[8] Brecht we remember had substituted didactics with dialectics in an effort to help people query, and thereby perhaps influence, social conditions. So too in Grotowski 'there is no message':[9] theatre attempts rather to 'teach people to think politically, to understand their interests . . . to live like humans and to be masters of their fate'.[10] Like Brecht, Grotowski knows that familiarity dissolves discrimination. 'You try to draw attention',[11] says Grotowski. There could be no better definition of Brechtian alienation.

The acquisition of dialectical technique could of course turn Frankenstein-like upon its maker and render relative the model of which it is the product. As Grotowski invokes a conception of the theatre based upon interrogation, that conception could itself come to be deemed subject to question. The actor, skilled in scepticism, may begin introspectively to mistrust the art of doubt itself. For Grotowski the alienation of stage-action as fiction appears increasingly destructive in that it has the potential to discredit any solutions hinted at in the body of text on the grounds that they are not demonstrably applicable to the real world outside the theatre. Grotowski is aware as well that de-familiarization could, in an age of uncertainty, turn scepticism to cynicism, doubt to despair. For Grotowski, criticism does not always create; an excess of it could cripple.

In *US*, Brook's misgivings about Brechtian alienation resulted in the inclusion of the spectator's mendacity within the scheme of the pre-sented dialectic. Blonski's 1970 portrait of the Laboratory Theatre, as an institution which 'opposes the way of an age which prefers to change conditions rather than attitudes, circumstances rather than souls',[12] suggests that Grotowski's movement away from Brecht was in some ways similar to that of Brook. What Brook and Grotowski shared, on the basis perhaps of their having worked together on *US*, was the conviction that a social problem must somehow be internalized by the spectator before it can be met with a politically constructive response.

However, for Grotowski, even Brook's work is insufficiently possessed of the affirmation that must fuel change. Grotowski is determined to use the theatre not, like Brook, to unsettle the audience, but deeply to inspire the spectator to adopt faith in the feasibility of change. This is done through the demonstrated capacity of his actors genuinely to suffer in the manner of the great redeemers of myth. This is in effect a return, both wary and spirited, to the sources of theatre. We are poised on a curious middle ground between the literal and the symbolic killing of the goat which must purify society. Today, as belief thins and the sacred becomes increasingly suspect, Grotowski must abandon the sophistication of metaphor and embrace instead the force of visible demonstration. His actors must eke out credibility on the indubitable evidence of their suffering, the naive conviction of the real event. Thus the 'action is literal – and not symbolic'[13] in his theatre. Artaud wrote that actors should be like martyrs burnt alive, still signalling to us from their stakes. Grotowski's actors attempt to do just that.

*

In a 1967 article in *Flourish*, Grotowski wrote of Artaud that he 'gave us, in his martyrdom, a shining proof of the theatre as therapy'.[14] As in the case of Herzog's actors, Artaud's bequest is meaningful not by virtue of its occurrence in his theatre but because it is authentic on the level of fact. And, as in Tarkovsky, this experience can forge a link – as reason cannot – between remedy and oblation, succour and sacrifice. If in Greek tragedy the principle by which individual votive offering has the power to heal a society is that of the scapegoat, so too for Grotowski, Artaud had to 'take society's sickness into himself'[15] in order to purify the community through his release. This implies that an analysis of Artaud's ailment would give us some insight into the nature of society's illness: as Grotowski writes of Artaud, 'His chaos was an authentic image of the world.'[16]

Grotowski's article on Artaud is entitled 'He Wasn't Entirely Himself'. The phrase is taken from Artaud's diagnosis of his own condition:

> Artaud defined his condition remarkably in a letter to Jacques Rivière: 'I am not entirely myself.' He was not merely himself, he

was someone else. He grasped half of his own dilemma: how to be oneself. He left the other half untouched: how to be whole, how to be complete.[17]

The statement admits of at least three interpretations. First, Artaud is seen as referring to a gap between his conception and his daily experience of himself, a gulf which could in turn mean two things – that it is the result either of unsound self-knowledge or of deliberate inauthenticity. Second, the 'real' self is measured against its potential for 'wholeness' and found to be wanting. In Grotowski's gloss, wholeness is a state of internal integration, an antidote to the condition in which 'civilisation is sick with schizophrenia, which is a rupture between intelligence and feeling, body and soul.'[18] The generalizing sentiment of Grotowski's references to a 'civilization' in which 'we' suffer suggests, moreover, a third, broader form of schism. Grotowski calls this the 'loss of a 'common sky' of belief'[19] – the external aspect of this internal rift, the breakdown of harmony in society. In Grotowski, the anarchy of fission is ubiquitous.

The analysis of Artaud's suffering thus reveals three fundamental conditions of sickness in society: inauthenticity, deliberate or ignorant, and the fragmentation of both self and society. Grotowski's work may be seen as being concerned in turn with each of these interpretations of Artaud's malady. As each response is found to be wanting, Grotowski shifts laterally between his targets. The result is a lattice of interlocking paths covering an immense terrain. To map it, one must follow one trail at a time, and chart with caution the offshoots which will be our future guides in parallel but perhaps more deeply penetrative passages.

*

Grotowski's answer to the problem at the centre of his explorations, the question 'how should one live?',[20] is that one must have 'the courage to be oneself and not to hide.'[21] It is the objective of Grotowski's theatre 'to destroy social roles'[22] so that actor and spectator alike can 'achieve a true self-realization'.[23] This condition, in which a person simply 'is', avoids tautology by positing the existence of at least two modes of being: a lying exterior and an underlying honesty. In *Towards a Poor Theatre*, the 'struggle with one's own truth' involves an 'effort to peel off the life-mask'.[24] The abrogation of the inauthentic façade results in a state of being in which appearance and substance are one. Herein lies the connection with wholeness: pure being is a condition of unaffected resonance between inner and outer. Self-possession is a condition of concord, of integrity in internal indivisibility.

Grotowski has, in different periods, pursued very different strategies in his attempt to assist the actor to achieve authentic selfhood. At first Grotowski believes, in the manner of the Stanislavsky of the 'middle period', that it is not possible to be something without knowing it. To 'realize' is both to 'apprehend clearly' (know) and to 'convert into fact' (be). If one can only inhabit what one is aware of, and if people are strangers to themselves, then it follows that one can only truly *be* oneself if one *knows* oneself. The specious image of the self must be identified and removed so that its true content can be discovered. The purpose of rehearsal is therefore to encourage actors to use theatre to undertake a creative exploration of the self. The first item on Grotowski's list of the objects of methodical investigation to be conducted at the Laboratory in 1967 reads 'To stimulate a process of self-revelation'.[25] Rehearsal still involves elucidation, but its principal object is now not the character but the self. The interest of this phase of Grotowski's work lies in the manner in which he is able to modify received techniques so as to transform the process of rehearsing a play from that of getting to know the characters and their situation to that of becoming better acquainted with oneself.

In *Self and Others*, R. D. Laing writes that 'All "identities" require an other: some other in and through a relationship with which self-identity is actualised.'[26] The need for a foil is particularly acute when one is oneself the object of one's study for then one typically lacks the means of comparison necessary for self-knowledge. For Grotowski too the presence of another is an essential prerequisite for self-knowledge:

> it is possible to reduce oneself to man-as-he-is; not to his mask, not to the role he plays . . . only to himself. . . . This reduction to the man is possible only in relation to an existence other than himself.[27]

In so far as the 'other' is an agent of contrast, the pressure of its influence implies perspective. When the object under scrutiny is the self, the operation of perspective encourages the subject's avowal of subjectivity: the self comes to be 'out there', not 'in here' and can therefore be studied more easily.

As a vehicle for this dynamic, theatre offers the enormous advantage that it naturally necessitates this relativizing leap of identity. R. D. Laing notes that in psychology the 'other' is 'often discussed under the heading of role'.[28] In the theatre this is literally the case:

> On stage in a theatre we usually play some role. If I am to play King Lear, the difference between myself and Lear is big enough for me to be aware that I am playing someone else. But if I am to be

myself under that tree, a terrifying question arises: which self? The one known to my friends? The one known to my enemies?[29]

It is impossible to view the self directly: the self cannot be both subject and object at once. But the moment the actor attempts to play a role, the self is objectivized. As the actor becomes another, the self can be brought to light as an extrinsic entity. The fact that it is difficult to sustain this state of transcendence helps rather than confounds the process – for in the struggle to match self to character, the actor inevitably learns something about himself. Aspects of character that are easily portrayed suggest that they reflect something of the actor's own engagement with the world. Elements that are more remote define the self by negation: for stage performance makes actors aware not merely of the fact of the difference between themselves and their characters but also, in the effort to embody that otherness, of the particulars of that unlikeness:

If Hamlet is for you a living area, you can also measure yourself up against him; not as against a character, but as a ray of light, falling on your own existence, which illumines you.[30]

As attempts to obliterate dissimilarity heighten relational identity, playing a role can be used critically to elucidate the self.

However, just as the Brechtian actor has first to master Stanislavsky so as the more deeply to disconcert the spectator, so also it is a necessary precondition of the self-revelation sought by Grotowski's actors that they first inhabit their roles in proper Stanislavskian manner. In *Towards a Poor Theatre*, the purpose of the first stage of rehearsal is to 'find the authentic impulses. The goal is to find a meeting place between the text and the actor'.[31] Perhaps a single long quotation from Anthony Abeson's rehearsal log of Grotowski's work on *The Seagull* will provide a glimpse substantial enough to make a case which, as it draws on material discussed in detail in the last two chapters, it would be wearisome to labour:

Nina says to Treplev, 'I was afraid that you might hate me.' Grotowski pointed out that the actor playing Treplev had done nothing to indicate otherwise. Logic dictates that Nina pause at the end of the line, waiting for reassurance, and that Treplev, through some gesture . . . would give it to her. Such logic is the logic of comportment. . . .

Nina says, for apparently no reason, 'let us sit down.' Why, asked Grotowski, does she make that suggestion? The actress had no answer, she had been merely saying the words without a reason. Grotowski explained that it was therefore necessary to find one in comportment, and proceeded to do so.

Treplev, having taken Nina's coat earlier, has allowed it to drape to the floor. Nina . . . wants to rescue her coat. . . . Thus she suddenly crosses to him, and gently takes it, suggesting at the same time that they sit down. Now the line makes sense. . . . It is now a *logical* thing for her to say.[32]

It is not merely the extent of the care lavished on logical justification that is reminiscent of Stanislavsky but also the manner of its ascertainment through questioning. As in Stanislavsky, questions alienate aspects of motivation worthy of greater logical scrutiny than is habitually accorded them.

However, unlike Stanislavsky, Grotowski will in a subsequent stage of rehearsal interrogate actors on the nature not of their characters but of the self – of which too they are routinely ignorant until offered this opportunity through existential displacement to be more vigilant:

Grotowski: 'Sing your name. . . . Evoke this Joseph. Who is he, this stranger? . . . Find the mask of Joseph's face. Is this really Joseph's mask? Yes, this is the essential Joseph. And now it is this essential Joseph, his mask, that sings.'

We notice that the pupil's voice changes, deepens, and becomes unrecognisable.[33]

The use of song reinforces the actor's sense of inhabiting an 'other' realm which is otherwise only semantically present in his invocation of himself by name. This releases the actor from subjectivity: as the actor is identified with the mask, the self becomes an external attribute that can be studied. The alienation of the self is reinforced as Grotowski's questions explicitly expose the actor's inadequate understanding of the various levels of authenticity that comprise his everyday image of himself. Then, in a vivid and unanticipated expression of the success of the exercise, the actor is unable to find his voice. Denied the cover of personality, the actor cannot seek refuge in what is clearly an adjunct of the now defunct mask. As the mask disintegrates it leaves a void that needs to be filled, thus ensuring that the next stage of the actor's work is meaningful.

The emphasis now shifts from an awareness of inauthenticity and the possibility of existential displacement to a more instructive study of the self as apprehended. In a manner directly analogous to Stanislavskian emotional memory, the actors are asked to make comparisons between themselves and some other personage:

a) Observe a new-born baby and compare its reactions to those of one's own body.
b) Search for any vestiges of infancy in one's own behaviour. . . .
c) Find those stimuli which reawaken in one the needs of infancy.[34]

Comparison has the advantage of placing the actors outside themselves while introducing as well the need for stringent scrutiny. As the baby is not in fact a role to be played, the contrast with Stanislavsky becomes clear: whereas in Stanislavsky the self is invoked in order to bring credibility to the 'other', in Grotowski the 'other' makes possible a greater understanding of the self. In stage (c) this inversion becomes more explicit as the emphasis shifts from recognition to discovery. The locus of significance is now not the character but the self.

Once this reorientation of the actors' task is established, the actor can engage the incipient stages of characterization:

do not play a dog-like a real dog because you are not a dog. Try and find your own dog-like traits. . . . You can begin by imitating the voice of a dog . . . but later on in the development you must find your own natural self.[35]

The observation with which Stanislavsky concludes his life's work, that in mimicry lies the magic of total assimilation into a role, is now the familiar territory in which Grotowski begins his research. By somatically inhabiting their roles, Grotowski's actors learn in fact to explore themselves. In Grotowski, the actor must possess the capacity sys-tematically to inhabit an 'other' sphere but, having done so, must treat that otherness not as an end in itself as in Stanislavsky, but as a means of initiating introspection.

Finally, the actors graduate from fledgling investigations conducted on the margins of theatrical activity to potentially far more deeply revealing encounters with fully-fledged dramatic roles:

He told them to think Hamlet's monologue in their own words. . . . He told them to declaim it in the traditional way. Then he told them to shout it, all at once, but each just a little after the other had begun. . . . Then they had to think the monologue as old men, then as youths during the war period, as heroes. . . . It was forcing the actor to dredge up for himself strata of existence which he had not suspected of being within him.[36]

In so far as all acts of translation require that the text in question be accommodated within the sensibility of the mediator, the paraphrase at the start of the exercise demands that the actors adopt an attitude to the text that is analogous to that of Stanislavsky's actor: one cannot possess what one does not first understand. Then a twofold alienation occurs. First, shouting both dislocates found meaning and provides the actors with an opportunity to absorb the substance of that dislocation without the customary self-consciousness which could repress its import. We are now in the territory of Brecht but already some characteristics of Grotowski's theatre have appeared – for the temporal offset compels the actors to listen not merely to the interpretations of others but to themselves as well.

The movement away from the self/role is carried further in the next stage of the exercise. As the actors are asked to play their speeches as characters who are neither themselves nor Hamlet, they become aware that they must enter otherness twice over. They must not only view their once subjective interpretations as objects (in the manner of Brecht) but must also alter them to suit the inclinations of the other 'other' who must now speak the self/other's lines. In the person of another 'other', the actors do not merely view themselves as selves viewing text; far more importantly, they go on to discover in themselves selves they had not met before, selves broader, deeper and more substantial than they had brought to bear upon the monologue at the beginning of the exercise. Here again the emphasis is on discovery rather than recognition: the actor, placed outside the self in a role that functions as an intermediary, is witness to the resonances between the self and a series of 'others', each of which highlights some forgotten or unknown trait of character. 'The strength of great works', writes Grotowski of *Hamlet*, 'really consists in their catalystic effect: they open doors for us, set in motion the machinery of our self-awareness.'[37]

*

In the manner of the Stanislavsky of the 'middle' period, Grotowski argues at this time that, as it is impossible to be something without knowing it, self-knowledge equips actors with an enhanced capacity to be themselves and thereby to achieve wholeness. However, we remember from chapter 1 that Stanislavsky went on to change his view and held, towards the end of his life, that knowledge actually gets in the way of being. To know and to be, far from being equivalent, are actually mutually exclusive. Eventually Grotowski too comes to admit, in a statement of 1970, that 'thoughts . . . never fully encompass him who has made it' – for in thought 'one is from the start divided into thinking and acting'.[38] When applied to Grotowski's concern with 'being oneself', this leads to the conclusion – of 1976 – that 'I am myself when I do not think about myself.'[39] Again, in 1979, the actor 'accepts himself because he forgets about himself'.[40] Authentic being is congruent not with its intellection but with oblivion.

However, just as one cannot consciously try to forget something, Grotowski's actors now face the problem that any deliberate effort made by them to achieve nescience only keeps them from gaining the insight they seek. In his 1979 speech to the Kosciuszko Foundation, Grotowski acknowledges the dilemma and indicates that the solution has to come – as in Stanislavsky – through the body:

> The tree is our teacher. It does not ask itself such questions. It is itself. . . . For us, this is much more difficult.
>
> Maybe there is no way in which we can answer in words the question – how to be oneself? But without a doubt it can be found in action. . . . [I]n order that a man may forget about himself, he must be whole, within something. In what he is doing.[41]

It is the tree's lack of introspection that allows it simply to exist. In contrast, man, having plucked from the tree of knowledge, is forever under the curse of cognition. However, if thinking excludes being, it may be the case that an obverse aspect of thought will comprise at least one defining attribute of being. Thus, as actors seeking merely to be cannot consciously surrender consciousness, they must embrace the ontological opposite of thought which for Grotowski is action. The reactive structure of action has the advantage that it draws the actors' attention away from the self which then has space in which to 'be'. The activity of rehearsal must now demand physical application of an order that leaves no part of the mind free to contemplate and thus corrode the self. In effect, 'to be oneself means to be one's body.'[42]

When R. D. Laing says, 'In so far as I put myself "into" what I do, I become myself through this doing',[43] he is of course referring to the therapeutic capacity of any form of activity with which one can be wholly engaged. Yet to one interested in the theatre, his choice of words fortuitously suggests that acting in particular could be a powerful medium of such activity as it quite literally involves 'putting oneself into' a pattern of action that is 'other'. Similarly, Grotowski's insistence that it is better not to think but to act could be construed as referring not merely to the advantages of bodily activity in general but to that occurring specifically in the context of stage action:

The mind/body split, a western form of dualism, ceases to exist in this state. It is an instrument of absolute presence . . . that allows us to forget our bodies and our intellects. . . .

This is the purpose of a theatrical role: it provides the discipline through which an actor can free himself.[44]

Notice the manner in which the word 'forget' has crept in to occupy the space which once belonged to 'know'. Earlier, the role was a 'trampoline, an instrument with which to *study* what is hidden behind our everyday mask';[45] the text was a 'scalpel enabling us to open ourselves . . . to *find* what is hidden within us'.[46] Now, as a result of Grotowski's awareness of the dangerously double-edged nature of self-consciousness, the emphasis shifts to the ability of stage action to elicit 'a luminous and pure consciousness, . . . *a consciousness devoid of all calculation*'.[47] Through the role the actors now seek not to know themselves but to 'be immersed in existence . . . as a bird enters the air'.[48]

However, merely to alter the orientation of the actor in this way is not to rid the theatre of attributes which made previous and opposite conceptions practicable. In spite of the ease with which Grotowski is able to modify his views, the problem remains that the role is still 'other' and therefore continues to provoke knowledge at the expense of being.

Grotowski's solution to the problem of the inevitability of theatre's reflexivity is to neutralize the otherness of the role by placing the actor *literally* in the situation of the character. At the start of this chapter we saw, in a comparison with the cinema of Werner Herzog, how Cieslak had really to undergo the torment inflicted upon the Constant Prince. Grotowski's actor does not 'pretend' he is an 'other'. He appears in his own person to face the challenge posed by the activities undertaken by his character. For Grotowski, 'that which we do is what it is and we do not pretend it is anything else':[49]

The performance is not an illusionist copy of reality, its imitation; nor is it a set of conventions, accepted as a kind of deliberate game, playing at a separate theatrical reality. . . . The actor does not play, does not imitate, or pretend. He is himself.[50]

Note the 'not . . . but' form of the distinction. It is a characteristic of statements on and by Grotowski that they often define his art in terms of a three-point comparison with forms of theatre that are not difficult to associate with Brecht and Stanislavsky. Thus Grotowski may be seen as proposing a third realm of theatre ideology, one with its own quite distinct means of overcoming the paradox whereby the 'truth' of the theatre is that it is a 'fiction'. In the work of all three directors, actors play characters. The differences are those of emphasis. In Stanislavsky the actor plays a *role* and the result, ideally, is illusion. In Brecht, the *actor* plays a *role* and the intended effect is alienation. In Grotowski, the *actor* plays a role in order more clearly to be himself.

'Acting is simply abandoned here',[51] declares Grotowski and the implications are enormous. The tautology by which all actors are 'really' themselves on stage is no longer circular but conceals a deeper truth. The actors are themselves not because they are not also others; they are themselves because their relationship with their roles is such that they are no longer compelled to view themselves from the outside in a manner that keeps them 'wholly' from 'being'. They are themselves because their performance scores are now comprised entirely of un-mediated activity, the exclusive medium of being. The shadow of otherness has been obliterated.

*

However, that a Laboratory Theatre 'performance' now comprises a real human act is a necessary but not sufficient condition of the *social* purpose of Grotowski's theatre. To be oneself as a tree in itself may grant the actor a privately meaningful sense of wholeness, but it is unlikely to compel faith in a naturally sceptical society. This is because the act of being is inadequately charged with metatextual indicators as to the *significance* of this orientation. A good and humble Christian may find salvation, but it takes the sacrifice of Christ and the exhortation of Paul to found a religion.

It follows that Grotowski's actors cannot merely be; in order to alienate the sacrificial authenticity of their act, they must be in a manner that is inspirational:

> If the actor, by setting himself a challenge publicly challenges others, and through excess, profanation and outrageous sacrilege reveals himself by casting off his everyday mask, he makes it possible for the spectator to undertake a similar process of self-penetration.[52]

The theme of excess, of a revelational influx into being, recurs relentlessly in Grotowski's writings. The 'actor must provoke and fascinate the audience',[53] writes Grotowski; he must become 'a sorcerer who enthralls the spectator'.[54] It is only on the basis of some hard evidence of inner transcendent experience that an audience may be induced to adopt greater faith in their capacity for wholeness than they are naturally wont to have. The dramas selected by Grotowski are, as a result, physically and emotionally enormously demanding. Grotowski's intention is to provide his actors with an opportunity to be themselves in a manner sufficiently conspicuous to draw attention to the exemplary remedial capacity of their action. The actors do not act; they are. But that which they are must be utterly immoderate if it is to galvanise the spectator into a position of faith.

There is a certain ease in the manner in which Grotowski repeatedly conflates the notion of being with its transcendence which suggests that the actor's required state of being does not hold as perplexing a paradox as may at first seem to be the case. For instance, when Grotowski writes that the function of art is 'to take us *beyond our limits*, to fill our void, to overcome our disabilities, in short to *realize ourselves*',[55] the casually undifferentiated juxtaposition between authentic and elevated conditions suggests that the exalted self is synonomous with the real self where both are opposed to the unreality of social masks. If there is any knee-jerk confusion here, it is that of the cliché whereby the authentic condition of our existence is that we are inauthentic. What we really do is to conceal our real selves. Grotowski's art attempts to assist in the transcendence not of self generally but of inauthentic being. Being, it seems, *is* its sublimation.

In practical terms, the amalgamation of being and transcendence is accomplished through the somatic manipulation of a paradigm in psychology whereby one truly accepts oneself (and therefore *is* oneself) only in a condition of transcendence. It is only by constantly challenging ourselves that we gain self-respect and therefore no longer need to hide behind social masks. Thus Grotowski's technical solution to the problem of being at this stage of his career is to set the actors a series of physical challenges. These are located just outside the penumbra of their abilities so that, when they are eventually accomplished, the actors gain the somatic confidence required to accept themselves:

> there was a gymnastic element which gave them a quality of challenge. It was in confronting this challenge and being triumphant, Grotowski believed, that the actor transcended the ordinary everyday 'self'. Grotowski described this as attaining to a condition of 'primal trust', in what we are led by our natures.[56]

Notice once again the unhesitating equation of 'transcend' with 'our natures'. In a somersault an actor may learn sincerity.

The identification of authenticity with transcendence has the advantage that it allows the substitution of concrete objectives for abstract conceptions. Whereas authenticity is incorporeal, transcendence is abundantly amenable to somatic implementation. This is conducted in three stages, involving an escalation from the passing of personal barriers to overcoming more objective conceptions as to the limits of human ability. In the first stage, the actors are asked to perform routine exercises in dexterity and precision. For instance,

> Bend at the knees with arms outstretched, keeping the feet flat on the floor in the same spot all the time. . . .
>   Pick up small objects with the toes (a box of matches, a pencil, etc.)[57]

In the second stage, the actors, having acquired a certain corporeal confidence, are encouraged to approach private verges, to extend by degrees the limits of a purely personal conception of ability. Where subjective barriers are not clearly defined, the practice of past directors is construed as comprising the limits of the actors' technical ability. The transcendence of known techniques involves distilling a selected conception of the theatre into appropriately representative physical elements which must then be executed with greater virtuosity than is known to have existed within the province of any previous application. For example, Grotowski requires of his actors that they acquire the very Brechtian skill of making rapid transitions between diametrically opposed conditions – but to an extent never before deemed possible:

> Forward somersault with one shoulder touching the ground for support.
> Backward somersaults.
> 'Tiger' spring (diving forward) . . . over an obstacle into a somersault, landing on one shoulder. . . .
> 'Tiger' spring followed immediately by a backward somersault.[58]

The self, under the aspect of its ability to represent Brechtian technique, is transcended as that model is superseded. The terms of the achievement are, however, still personal.

In the third stage the levels of difficulty steepen from those sufficient to out-distance existing complexes of theory and technique to that which challenges the imagination generally. As Grotowski's actors become progressively more proficient, so too the exercises put to them become increasingly insuperable. '[U]se your voice to make a hole in the wall,'[59] demands Grotowski, 'to overturn a chair, . . . to make a picture fall.'[60] The actors must now strive to make viable the impossible. They must overcome not merely their own individual limitations but the most durable boundaries of man's finitude: flight, for instance, or that other ageless marker of humanity – visibility:

> the project has in it essential things that are not possible. For example, in order to do this the actor must be able to fly, to be invisible, things that are against nature. But to be really truthful, one must do it.[61]

Grotowski's actors, we remember, cannot resort to metaphor; they must literally realize the evidence of their transcendence. In 'Theatre Laboratory 13 Rzedow', 'Acrobatics liberate the actor from the laws of gravity.'[62] In *Towards a Poor Theatre*, there is an exercise called 'flight':

1) Squatting on the heels . . . hop and sway like a bird ready to take flight. . . .
2) Still hopping, raise yourself into an upright position, while the hands flap like wings. . . .
3) Take off in flight with successive forward movements. . . .
4) Land like a bird.[63]

Only miracles can compel the faith of an unbelieving audience.

*

Technical virtuosity of the kind achieved by the Laboratory Theatre created two problems for Grotowski. First, it became increasingly apparent that there is a contradiction between the use of skill to instil faith in an audience and Grotowski's longer-term ambition of making it possible for the spectator, on the basis of this faith, to follow the example of the actor. In 'The Theatre's New Testament', Grotowski insists, we remember, that 'if the actor, by setting himself a challenge publicly challenges others . . . he makes it possible for the spectator to undertake a similar process of self-penetration'.[64] Yet seven pages later in the same article Grotowski demands that this 'challenge' consist of 'magical acts (which the audience is incapable of reproducing)'.[65] By having the actor perform feats which are well beyond the ability of the spectator, Grotowski is in effect setting an example which the audience has no means of following. The result is either incomprehension,

> I did not learn anything about my own response to suffering through watching Cieslak suffer. One reason, perhaps, is the huge gap between these productions and any common experience.[66]

or a quite vehement refusal to listen:

Grotowski pulls us in because our envy of Cieslak's intensity and freedom forces us to look at ourselves, our limitions . . . [but] eventually you may come to resent those who make you feel inferior. . . . [T]his resentment can become a block to one's receptivity to the event, to one's search within.[67]

The coexistence of being and transcendence, lacking the cover of myth surrounding for example the Son of Man, is either irrelevant or liable to be construed as criticism rather than inspiration.

Grotowski's second problem is that, in the actors' experience, technical proficiency tends to become a mask in its own right and begins thereby to inhibit rather than facilitate the actor's revelation of self. Looking back over his work in the late 1960s, Grotowski observes that through technique one learns in fact 'how to arm oneself. We arm ourselves to conceal ourselves; sincerity begins when we are defence-less'.[68] Although technical ability provides the actors with an opportunity to be themselves, it does not compel that revelation. Rather, it tends all too easily to ossify into a spectacle in which the actors find it convenient to withhold themselves. If self-revelation requires the confidence that skill brings, that skill can also breed complacency.

Concomitant with Grotowski's growing awareness of these problems is the conviction that a complete reversal of the nature of the actor's engagement with technique would invert as well the products of that programme:

if one learns *how to do*, one does not reveal oneself; one only reveals the skill for doing. . . . This is the most difficult point. For years one works and wants to know more, to acquire more skill, but in the end one has to reject it all and not learn but unlearn, not to know how to do but how not to do.[69]

In a retrospective introduction to Barba's notes on the Actor Training methods used by the Laboratory Theatre between 1959 and 1962, Grotowski attempts to place the period of his pursuit of technical transcendence in the context of its immediate aftermath – a pull in precisely the opposite direction:

I was searching for a positive technique or . . . a certain method of training capable of objectively giving the actor a creative skill. . . . Certain elements from these exercises were retained in the training during the period that followed, but their aim has changed. . . . The actor no longer asks himself: 'How can I do

this?' Instead, he must know what **not** to do, what obstructs him.
. . . This is what I mean by **via negativa**: a process of elimination.[70]

The actors must now sacrifice their ability in spectacular fashion to make a sacrifice.

Via negativa is of course greater than the sum of all inverted attributes of transcendence. It has a relationship with wholeness that is quite independent of its logically predictable ability to de-activate the divisive effects of skill. Raymonde Temkine makes a connection between the self-denial implicit in the abrogation of technique and the wholeness thus achieved:

The more discipline and denuding of self – stripping away – are developed, the more the actor can open himself to another order. . . . A certain inner harmony and peace are acquired. It is after questioning, after this stripping away . . . that self-integration is achieved.[71]

As in some monastic orders, it is not the specific attributes of the objects relinquished as much as the act of dispossession that is significant. What is important is not that certain potentially damaging skills are abandoned but that the actors learn to let go of something that has painstakingly been acquired. The 'reward' is that this opens the self to the sublime agency of an 'other'. Writing on and by Grotowski is replete with vague but reassuringly consistent references to this 'other order'. Grotowski speaks for example of his attempt to recover 'the life giving force in the world' through which access may be had to the 'complete man'.[72] Equally inscrutibly, Osinski holds that Grotowski's work is essentially concerned with 'connecting to a force and acquiring that force'.[73] For Grotowski the product of the union of the self with this numinous presence is wholeness. The readiness is all.

It is not terribly important intellectually to pin down terms like 'force': in Grotowski these ideas always translate far more effectively as practical exercises. Thus the *via negativa* promises wholeness in proportion to the extent to which actors are able in rehearsal to obliterate internal obstacles and surrender to the synoptic benevolence of the spirit which surrounds them. In keeping with somatic injunctions, Grotowski construes as indicators of such felicity a number of physical conditions. Of these, the unfettered emission of sound is perhaps the most unambiguous. Actors must for instance learn to exhale strongly without having the column of air in their lungs come up against obstacles such as a closed larynx or insufficiently opened jaws:

95

The vocal process cannot be free without a well-functioning larynx. The larynx must first be relaxed. . . .

If the larynx does not relax and open, you must find a way to make it do so. That is why I asked the third pupil to stand on his head. If he does this, and at the same time speaks, shouts or sings, there is a good chance the larynx will open.[74]

The opening of the larynx (a physical condition) becomes in the exercise a way of opening the self to the 'force' (an abstract condition). By somatic inversion, symptoms can be treated as indistinguishable from causes: an absence of tension in the voice not only signifies the dissolution of the actors' resistance to the 'force' but creates it. As in all somatic work, one becomes open in mind by becoming open in body.

Actors schooled typically on Stanislavsky invariably find it difficult to adopt unnatural postures in a sufficiently relaxed manner without having a reason for doing so. Thus once the somatic agent of the *via negativa* is found, it may be supported by emotion-memory or some other motive-oriented reference:

He allowed one girl, for example, to walk around the room aimlessly, singing a song. . . . He then asked her to raise her left hand to her collar-bone while continuing to walk and sing as before. Somehow, that simple gesture greatly changed her voice – it became softer and fuller. He then asked what personal associations that gesture held for her, and then let her continue.[75]

Often sequences of such exercises are performed without interruption on the basis of the assumption that fatigue can break down the resistance of the actor more effectively than conscious contrivance. Anthony Abeson describes his experience of participating in a series of exercises designed not to effect the triumph of the body over the presented challenges but to enforce the submission of the body to the 'force' at the limits of its endurance:

I was meant to walk and sing like Donald Duck. . . . At other times I was meant merely to lie in certain positions saying one word over and over. . . .

After more than two hours of such work, I lay crumpled in a heap on the floor. My voice had begun to awaken in its entirety.[76]

It is not entirely fortuitous that 'fullness' of voice encompasses considerations of both vigour and totality, intensity and wholeness.

In *Towards a Poor Theatre*, the difference between this new-found quest for openness and the aims of the period of technical dexterity is clear. Grotowski is now adamant, in complete contrast to the force of his earlier position, that the actor 'must learn not to think of adding technical elements (resonators, etc.), but should aim at eliminating the concrete obstacles he comes up against (e.g. resistance in the voice)'.[77] Again, the 'aim is not a muscular development or physical perfection-ism, but a process of research leading to the annihilation of one's body's resistances'.[78] The wisdom of austerity has succeeded the naivety of accumulation and wizardry.

*

In an irony which seems predictable enough in retrospect, *via negativa* offers the actors the promise of a path to wholeness but denies them the means of attracting sufficient attention to the socially remedial capacity of their work. The devices of creative absence are exemplary but lack the irresistible elevation without which their example is unlikely to be widely followed. Without the solicitations of their quasi-messianic marvels, Grotowski's actors are not adequately persuasive. Grotowski thus faces the dilemma that while his ability to dazzle audiences in fact alienates them, his recourse to humility renders his actors devoid of explicit evidence as to the viability of personal transcendence. Neither technical ability nor the lack of it seems to be an appropriate vehicle for social regeneration through the pursuit of wholeness.

It is then not altogether surprising that the realization of *via negativa* is concomitant with Grotowski's gradual withdrawal from a commit-ment to public performance. 'The Theatre of the Thirteen Rows' of 1959 becomes in 1970 an 'Institute of Research into Acting Method – Laboratory Theatre' – with all the privacy and exclusion that such a shift in emphasis implies. As a larger proportion of rehearsal time is dedi-cated to clearing passages *within* the self, the impulse to share the fruits of wholeness with the audience seems all but to have run its course. The notion of theatre as 'encounter', which normally refers to the potential for contact between actors and spectators, now refers merely to the actors' elevated stability within the self. 'The core of the theatre is an encounter', writes Grotowski; 'The man who makes an act of self-revelation is, so to speak, one who establishes contact with himself.'[79] The implications are of course utterly damning for a project premised on the unity of the individual and the collective. Unable to reach the public, the actors turn in on themselves.

However, it gradually becomes evident to Grotowski that the isola-tion of the group must be temporary. Not only is it difficult for a group working behind closed doors to exert a remedial influence upon society but, far more pertinently, human contact itself comes to be seen as a means of achieving wholeness. In 1974 Grotowski asks,

> if we arrive at the conclusion that the change of the world should start from changing one's own life, then the next question arises: can we change our own lives without having any relation with others?[80]

It is not merely that society is denied its capacity to change by the withdrawal of the group but that the actors are themselves rendered infertile by their distance from society. The premise here is that the acceptance of one person by another leads to a situation in which both have the courage to shed their social masks and live authentically. The result of this process is therefore not merely a state of social cohesion (call it external wholeness), but internal integration as well, a resonance between what one is and what one appears to be. Thus in the 'Holiday' texts the idea of 'Man as he is, whole, so that he would not hide himself [internal wholeness] . . . is inseparable from meeting [external wholeness]'.[81]

> A living impulse can carry us towards another being to a point where we are no longer divided between consciousness and the flesh. This is a return towards the moment of wholeness, of fullness, of plenitude.[82]

The goal for the next stage of Grotowski's career is clear: to forge some means of achieving wholeness through authentic contact in the theatre.

At the time of the formulation of this objective, the only working model of quasi-epiphanic contact was the rehearsal situation. In rehearsal an 'element of warm openness . . . can enable the actor to undertake the most extreme efforts without any fear of being laughed at'.[83] The process thus meets the needs of Grotowski's definition of wholeness as contingent upon the obliteration of inhibition. 'One must get rid of fear [and] . . . mutual distrust', says Grotowski, 'get rid of the distinction between what one is doing and the reflection about what is being done; to try out – how to meet others halfway with one's whole self.'[84] Notice the link implied by the juxtaposition of the necessary conditions of contact with the defining attributes of wholeness: the ability of the workshop situation to satisfy the needs of the former implies its viability as a medium for the latter. To get rid of the gulf that divides people one from another is to get rid of the gulf that divides people internally into mind and body, thought and action.

However, Grotowski gradually realizes that the unification of consciousness in rehearsal is at best a means to an end and cannot be the sole objective of the group. 'The impulse does not exist without a partner', he says, but adds immediately, 'Not in the sense of a partner in acting, but in the sense of another human being.'[85] Grotowski must aspire to a wider sphere of influence in order to combat the irony of the solipsistic realization of a holistic ambition. Besides, the natural affinities within the group erode the challenge of otherness without which contact is not properly meaningful. It is then imperative, in the 1970s, that Grotowski seek contact in terrain less predictable than that manufactured at home.

The most obvious human agent of otherness with whom the actor may seek to achieve wholeness is of course the spectator. However, the problem with using the audience in this way is that the extent to which they are not somatically engaged in the action is a measure of the extent to which they are excluded from its benefits. As Jan Blonski observes,

> in order genuinely to transform the spectator, one had to persuade him to repeat the gesture of giving or sacrifice; otherwise he would be only a voyeur. The consummation of communication is impossible without visible, enacted reciprocity.[86]

André Gregory too maintains, at a Grotowski workshop of 1975, that 'It is not important that one creates art which is then presented to people but it *is* important that people – individuals who are relevant in life and work – are involved in the creative process.'[87] Only bodily experience can supply the assured veracity of being; all else is hearsay merely, and contingency.

The problem is clear. Grotowski is bound by the natural course of the development of his work to attempt to establish human contact with the audience. Yet the audience, through its definitional passivity, compromises the therapeutic potential of that contact. In Grotowski's writings, the dilemma translates as contradiction. In *Towards a Poor Theatre*, Grotowski seeks on the one hand to 'define the theatre as "what takes place between the spectator and actor"', emphasizing that 'All other things are supplementary'.[88] Yet in the same work, Grotowski, drawn by his commitment to somatic engagement, is led just as unequivocally to declare that the 'essence of theatre is the actor, his actions and what he can achieve'.[89] The conflict exists in the body of a single essay. In the original article, 'Towards a Poor Theatre', Grotowski writes, theatre can exist without make-up, ... without lighting and sound effects, etc. It cannot exist without the actor–spectator relationship of perceptual, direct, 'live' communion.[90]

Yet four pages earlier, Grotowski asserts, with suspect plainness, 'we consider the personal and scenic technique of the actor as the core of theatre art'.[91] In so far as wholeness is a function of contact, the essence of theatre must lie in the actor's meeting with the audience; but as that essence is unreachable without a somatic investment, the actor becomes the sole vehicle of truth in the theatre.

Grotowski seems intuitively to have glimpsed a way out of this dilemma when, very early in his career, he promised to 'create the world anew *with* the spectator [through] mutual participation in a collective act'.[92] If it is the inactivity of the audience that keeps them from realizing fully the remedial capacity of drama, Grotowski must draw them into the action – not merely psychologically, as Stanislavsky had done, but bodily. Initially it had seemed to Grotowski that the somatic involvement of the audience could be achieved by abolishing the traditional allocation of separate areas for actors and spectators. During performances the actors would walk amongst the spectators in an attempt to break down the traditional gulf between the audience and the participants. In *The Ancestors*, the actors went further: they treated the audience as fellow actors by including them in the action. In subsequent productions, situations were created in which the audience had definite roles imposed upon them. For instance, in *Cain*, the spectators were designated as the descendants of Cain; in *Shakuntala*, they were a crowd of monks and courtiers. By the time of *Kordian* far more drastic means were used to force the audience to act: an actor hummed a song and compelled the audience to sing along. Those who refused to comply were sought out and threatened with a cane.

Grotowski subsequently came to regard these early attempts at securing audience-participation as naive and manipulative:

> Years ago we tried to secure a direct participation of spectators. . . . We reached a point when we rejected these kind of proceedings, since it was clear that we were exerting pressure, tyranny of sorts. . . . And so we told ourselves: no, the spectators should simply be as they are, that is to say witnesses, witnesses of a human act.[93]

Under duress the audience had fulfilled the criteria of both otherness and somatic involvement. What was unambiguously lost however was the principal goal of the project – contact. The actors had not been able to 'meet' the spectators at all. Exploitation is incompatible with communication.

Grotowski's solution to this problem involved the creation of dramas internally requiring the act of witness as an aspect of plot or structure. The presence of the spectators could then be construed as having a specific dramatic function in spite of the fact that this required of the spectators no greater effort than that to which they were accustomed. The audience could now 'play' the 'roles' assigned to them without being put into a false position. In the Schechner–Hoffman interview, Grotowski discusses the literalization of the status of the audience:

> We did . . . plays where the actors encircled the spectators, . . . where they touched the spectators. But we saw that there was always cheating and trickery on our side. . . .
>
> We solved the problem when we did Marlow's *Dr Faustus*. For the first time we found a direct word-for-word situation. The dramatic function of the spectators and the function of the spectator as spectator were the same.[94]

In *Dr Faustus*, the central character had begun by asking the spectators to be his witnesses. A role was still 'imposed' upon the audience but it had been made congruent with their 'natural' role as observers. This was then repeated in *The Constant Prince* and *Apocalypsis Cum Figuris*: in each case the spectators were included in the action but were required to do no more than watch the drama.

However, what this achieved in terms of honesty, it lost in the relegation of the audience once again to a position of passivity in which they could not know contact somatically. The literalization of the situation of the audience had achieved participation only in name: the spectators still merely watched the action and were, to that extent, unable to make physical and active contact with the actors. It now seemed that direct contact between actor and spectator, however necessary within the therapeutic design of the work, was in fact a contradiction in terms. As Grotowski was to observe much later, 'the very word "spectator" is theatrical, dead. It excludes meeting, it excludes the relation: man–man'.[95] The unmistakable implication was that the theatre, once defined entirely in terms of contact, was in fact structured such that it was unable to accomplish that contact:

> Examining the nature of theatre . . . we came to the conclusion that its essence lies in direct contact between people. This in mind, we have decided to get beyond art to reality, since it is in real life rather than on the artistic plane that such contacts are possible.[96]

101

It is almost as if it is because theatre is synonomous with meeting that the theatre must be abandoned to achieve that meeting.

It takes an enormous capacity for lateral thinking to dissociate the existential basis of an activity from its effect. For Grotowski, this involves alienating the traditional association of theatre with contact as one of the many phenomena which exist on the basis of habit. Gradually Grotowski, trusting to the sensible and true avouch of his eyes rather than to inherited definitions, has the courage to come to the only conclusion available to him. He realizes that his failure simultaneously to have both theatre and somatic interaction is a function purely of the fallacy of the existing *a priori* equation between theatre and contact. In so far as theatre necessarily implies a distinction between action and witness, it excludes genuine somatic meeting. However, once theatre is stripped of its confused definitional identification with contact, it becomes possible for Grotowski to choose between cause and effect:

> One day we found it necessary to eliminate the notion of theatre
> (an actor in front of a spectator) and what remained was a notion
> of meeting.[97]

Grotowski's commitment is not to the theatre but to contact as a medium of wholeness. If theatre jeopardizes wholeness, then it must be abandoned. 'It is not theatre that is indispensable', he declares, 'but something quite different. To cross the frontiers between you and me'.[98]

Abandonment had of course always been the dominant theme of the 'Poor Theatre' – but it had naturally not contemplated relinquishing itself in the interest of the principal object of its poverty. However, once contact – and through contact, wholeness – was seen as being incompatible with theatre's divisive ontology, Grotowski began to think in terms of 'another, hitherto unknown, form of art beyond the traditional division of onlooker and active person, man and his product, creator and recipient'.[99] Encounters with the public now took the form of communal events in which the guests were encouraged to take the initiative:

> The essential movement and rhythm were always dictated by the
> outsiders. If they were active, the guides followed. If they were less
> active, the guides subtly 'stimulated the space, creating certain
> vibrations'. . . . Then the participants would enter. Then the
> guides would follow.[100]

This suppressed pulse of intermittent intervention and liberation is analogous to the relationship between director and actor in workshop.

Just as in Grotowski's previous theatre work, rehearsal had begun to take precedence over performance, so now, in an extension of that impulse, there is no separation between the creative process and the result. Now everything is workshop, but this no longer implies the exclusion of the outside world.

In its earliest stages, what came to be called 'active culture' borrowed the know-how of the Laboratory Theatre. It used improvizations, movement exercises and musical rhythms. However, the adaptation of old rehearsal methods had the disadvantage that they were associated with a certain degree of skill. As a result, the outsider-participants tended to be inhibited by their technical shortcomings. That Grotowski no longer demanded virtuosity did not prevent unskilled musicians, for example, from being unable comfortably to use musical instruments to make contact with actors whom they knew possessed a formidable talent that had now been discarded.

In response to this problem, Grotowski abandoned all exercises which evoked the past in favour of an entirely new medium of contact founded on actions simple enough to neutralize completely the imbalance of skill in the group. For instance, in the context of a workshop, even the most trivial everyday duties such as cleaning and adapting a space were alienated out of their customary insignificance and imbued with the agency of contact. Groups of participants would be assigned simple and familiar chores which, as they were performed together, would make for the incipient stages of contact. In keeping with the tenor of Grotowski's affinity with Herzog, all the constituent elements of these exercises were real: if water had to be fetched it was because it was required, if a fire was lit it was because it was cold. To the extent that none of these activities required a specialized talent to perform, they did not evoke disturbing memories of a divisive 'theatre'.

The cohesive function of Grotowski's communally created 'homes' would then be far more poignantly defamiliarized as participants were intermittently withdrawn from its security:

> Every person went in a different direction. The only light came out of the big fire, but it disappeared as you went deeper into the forest. . . . After some time, the forest enfolded you entirely. . . . Personally I had a very strong need to communicate with the rest of the group. . . . It felt as if the fire created a magnetic pole that drew you back to it.[101]

Solitude is created simply by walking. Conversely contact can consist, in all its warmth and welcome, in just being 'offered a drink of water from a little dish they had in their hands'.[102] As these elementary forays into contact with an unskilled public become more intense, the commitment to simplicity remains. Darkness is used, for instance, for in it inhibitions are vulnerable and the senses more alert:

> The torches disappeared somewhere. It was night, there was speed, cold breeze, wet grass. I heard shouts around me. And I shouted myself. . . . HE responded. . . . I found HIM, or HE found me. We rolled about, seemingly having forgotten we were not children any more. Again the thought struck me that I was being very silly, but so was HE.[103]

What contact has in common with wholeness is a reliance upon the obliteration of social masks. Thus, as literalization finds a new lease of life in this work, the force of its originally twofold opposition to performance (both as 'theatre' and as 'social mask') returns. The workshop is now 'a place where there is no theatre, where one man comes out to meet another, without playing any role. . . . He is what he is, complete in himself . . . he only wants to meet'.[104] Active culture is an extension of Grotowski's impulse to wholeness as a function getting away from playing a-part.

*

In 'The Art of the Beginner', Grotowski makes the connection between contact and wholeness: '*I-Thou*', he says, '*is the experience where everything is included*'.[105] One of the tests of so extreme a claim must be the extent to which it allows of infinitely diverse participation. The history of the Laboratory Theatre has in this respect been the story of a gradual widening of the range of contact. Whereas in *The Constant Prince* the so-called 'total act' was limited to just one character, in *Apocalypsis Cum Figuris* it was intended to include all the actors. The institution of active culture represents a further broadening of this sphere to include a few, select members of the public. 'We don't try to attract everyone', says Grotowski initially, 'we simply look for those close to us'.[106] Gradually, however, participation is made more accessible:

> we are working on means to *extend* the sphere of active culture. What is the privilege of a few, can also become the property of others. I am not talking about a mass production of works of art, but of a kind of personal creative experience.[107]

In complete contrast to the earlier attitude of the group, Grotowski now declares, 'If he differs from us, so much the better'.[108] By 1978 Grotowski is trying to create an environment in which 'human beings who are so different but who even if they have no common language can . . . take off towards common flight'.[109] The 'Objective Drama' project of the 1980s, conducted in the immediate aftermath of the work discussed here, seeks forms of theatre 'composed of those characteristics found to be common to the ritualistic practice of many diverse cultures, and perceptible to members of all'.[110]

For Eugenio Barba, Grotowski's attempt to rediscover forms of contact that have supposedly been 'lost in . . . civilization-cultural development'[111] may be 'compared to an anthropological expedition. It goes beyond civilised territories into virgin forest'.[112] In 1973, in pursuit of an authentic contact between diverse cultures which would affirm a theory of universal wholeness, Peter Brook travelled not to the virgin forest of Barba's metaphor but to villages in the Sahara with a group of actors who did not share a common language.

PETER BROOK

In Farid Ud-din Attar's *The Conference of the Birds* a flock of diverse species of birds together undertake to find their God Simurgh. Their quest carries them through a most daunting sequence of Valleys, those of Astonishment and Understanding, of Detachment and Unity, of Nothingness, of Love and, reflexively, the Valley of Quest itself. At the end of their travels they are rewarded with the revelation that the God they seek has always lain dormant within themselves. As Attar's fiction thus makes metaphors of its facts (the names of the valleys are those of the emotions, the external journey is an internal one), the observation 'I am Thou, Thou art I'[113] implies a further union – that between all living things in God. As the Hoopoe observes, 'Although you seem to see many beings, in reality there is only one – all make one which is complete in its unity'.[114] Attar's fable is then a story about the pursuit of wholeness: 'If you would be perfect', he declares, 'seek the whole, choose the whole, be the whole'.[115]

Given the well-nigh universal nature of Grotowski's quest taken in its most general aspect (the question 'How should one live?' and its solution in terms of wholeness), it is not entirely surprising that it should bear some resemblance to Attar's amalgamation of being and wholeness as he too attempts to arrive at a knowledge of spiritual things. Interestingly, the comparison does not stall as the principle of wholeness in

Attar is analysed in more detail. To break the idea down into its two most obvious aspects, wholeness in *The Conference of the Birds* has both an internal aspect ('When the soul was joined to the body it was a part of the all'[116]) and an external bearing ('From the back of the fish to the moon every atom is a witness to his Being . . . ; the world visible and the world invisible are only Himself'[117]). The similarity remains even if one analyses the idea further so as to bring in the particulars of practical application. In so far as Simurgh responds to the quest of the birds by declaring that 'in me you shall find yourselves',[118] the birds may be seen as seeking to slake their thirst for *self*-perfection. In keeping with the eventually somatic strain of Grotowski's approach to the problem of being oneself, Attar maintains that one must 'not ask for an explanation'[119] but contrive instead to make a physical assault upon truth. 'Submit then to trials', writes Attar, 'so that you may know yourself'.[120] If this corresponds to the failed positive period of Grotowski's schooling of his actors, the *via negativa* of the Poor Theatre also appears in Attar: 'Open the door of spiritual poverty and poverty will show you the way. . . . [Y]our body and your soul will disappear; you will then be worthy of the mysteries'.[121]

Perhaps the one aspect of Grotowski's schematic proximity to Attar which is even more surprising – because it is not as universally the concern of the mystic – is the concern with a reflexive literalism. As the *quest* of the birds leads them to the Valley of *Quest*, as they *set out* in pursuit of Truth and *arrive* at an Essence, a semantic conjunction is effected between the spheres of action and contemplation. For the much travelled Grotowski too, a journey is both an image and a reality: on the one hand, 'the actor who accomplishes an act of self-penetration is setting out on a journey',[122] but on the other hand an 'Encounter with the East, not in a theatrical, but in a wider human sense, seems to me a vital thing in itself'.[123] In both Grotowski and Attar there are somatic advantages to be had in the literal experience of a metaphor.

The implication of this for Grotowski's actors is, as we have seen, that they must forsake the cover of imitation and engage as fact the fiction of their dramas. Similarly, in Attar's story of Joseph and Zuleikha, Joseph cannot, in spite of the charity of his persecutor, pretend to be beaten: his groans must be real if they are to wield any influence. In Grotowski, the effect of the literalization of the action is that the actors, by invading the fiction of their characters, realize in fact themselves. 'Enter into yourself',[124] says Simurgh at last to the birds, and the message to the reader is unambiguous: 'this is none other than your own story'.[125]

*

One of Peter Brook's earliest talks on Shakespeare was concerned primarily with the concept of the journey, with the symbolic significance of the acts of leaving, returning and reconciliation. In December 1972, however, Brook embarked literally upon a 'long journey in search of truth'[126] through Africa. The principal component of the theatre material carried by the company was a series of improvizations based on Attar's fable. The journey carried the group to Ife, regarded by the native Yorubas as the source of harmony in the universe, the place where 'Reality becomes Whole'.[127] At Ife, John Heilpern, the writer travelling with the group, visited the local Oracle. The Oracle, with no knowledge of the sketches in the repertory of the company, said to Heilpern, 'You have travelled to Ife only to find something which is already with you'.[128]

The Oracle's insight is startling not merely because of his clairvoyant allusion to a theme in the work of the group. It is remarkable also because his attribution of that understanding to Heilpern registers the operation of a more self-conscious literalism which is also a significant feature of Brook's work in Africa: by playing the story of a journey in search of truth while literally on such a journey, Brook's actors explore both the substance of Attar's work and the specially reflexive form in which these themes are experienced in the original. Literalism in Brook is then twofold. First, his actors must learn to be what they play: they must do (both in their theatre and in real life) what the birds do. Second, in so far as their characters are themselves preoccupied with this reflexive mode of action, the actors must enact as well the literalism that is, as we have seen, a peculiar feature of Grotowski's proximity to Attar: the distinction between theatre and real life must be modified to allow a degree of interpenetration.

Thus in the first category, one would note Heilpern's choice of a title, *Conference of the Birds*, evocative both of Attar's work and of the telling recurrence of group conferences in Africa. This leads to some suggestive ambiguities:

> It's the crucial point of the Sufi fable, . . . 'Seek the trunk of the tree, and do not worry about whether the branches do or do not exist.'
>
> So Brook's actors set off to the sacred forest, to seek the trunk of the tree, as it were. They gather as birds.[129]

As birds? In the person of their characters, the birds? Or in the manner of the birds, their characters? Heilpern's awareness of the significance of

107

the literal pursuit of a principle phrased as metaphor recurs as he remarks on the uncertainty to which both groups of pilgrims are subject, the birds in their valleys, the actors in their unprepared scenarios:

> anything can go wrong for no one knows in advance what might happen. In the book of *The Conference of the Birds*, the birds who make the journey do not know what might happen to them either.[130]

Both groups are equally heterogeneous: the birds are of diverse species and the actors are from as many countries. In the case of the birds, uncertainty is a product of ignorance; in the case of the actors, it is a somatic stimulant. If the birds were to know in advance that it was in fact themselves that they were seeking, their journey would be redundant. Similarly, if the actors were to posit the self as their object directly, they would lose the practical means of exploring it.

In the second category, one would note Brook's repeated insistence that he doesn't want things 'acted'. Echoing precisely Grotowski's claim that acting is abandoned in his theatre, Brook observes that although 'Actors are prone to think: I am an actor, I have to act. It is not a matter of acting'.[131] If Grotowski's actor creates what is neither a fictional story nor a metaphor but an actual event, so also Brook's ideal performance is one in which a 'relationship had to be made – or not made – in human terms . . . because something happened *in fact*'.[132] This implies that for Brook real-life events may nominally be treated as dramas. For instance, Bruce Myers' potentially fatal disappearance in the desert generates a search which Heilpern cannot help seeing as an improvization: 'Myers had given me a terrific role to play', he writes, 'I was playing the lead'.[133] Later, a real death challenges Heilpern's conventional conviction that theatre imitates: 'The killing of the ram', Heilpern notes, 'had become a form of theatre'.[134] With its incursion into the world of irreversible action, theatre is expelled from the sanctuary of make-believe.

The complementary aspect of this 'wish to avoid the traditional trap of living in water-tight separation between work and life outside'[135] is, predictably, its obverse – Brook's tendency to treat theatre events as real-life occurrences. In practice, Brook's effort somatically to reveal to the actors the principle by which 'one starts from the basically non-theatrical notion'[136] involves, for instance, the creation of *The Walking Show*:

> In order to go back to a real beginning, Brook asked the actors literally to walk again. In such a way, no dramatic convention could be taken for granted. . . .

It's astonishing – but given the simple direction to do no more than walk, everyone was running . . . in the scramble to 'perform', show out.[137]

In order simply to walk, the actors must do no more than exist. Or, to reverse the equation in terms of somatic imperatives, the actors must act without acting in order plainly to be.

Brook's inclination to the substantive conflation of drama and real life has a somewhat confused history. On the one hand, in a manner that is consistent with Grotowskian literalism, Brook respects Jeanne Moreau because 'she doesn't characterise';[138] he admires a production of Jack Gelber's *The Connection* in which the actors 'aren't acting, they are being'.[139] On the other hand, Brook seems equally to adhere to the more traditional view that 'Everything in the theatre is an imitation of what is outside the theatre'.[140] The latter and more orthodox position has two characteristics which give it potential for conversion into the former, more radical paradigm. First, it is usually granted that the theatre of imitation is convincing in proportion to the extent of the life experience which feeds it. Second, Brook's view that 'theatre is only legitimate if it reflects a deeply committed 'search for something real' which can be carried over into life beyond the theatre'[141] anticipates and therefore admits of the fusion of fictive and existential spheres of import.

The catalyst responsible for the sublimation of this potential into a condition of literalism is a growing sense of the contextualization of drama by its location within some larger structure. In Africa, Heilpern conjectures that Brook is, at this stage of his career, 'a man in search of something more essential to him than performing'.[142] For Yoshi Oida, 'the real aim isn't physical but spiritual':[143] for him, 'Acting has become a way to find God'.[144] When drama thus comes to serve something far beyond drama, the boundaries between theatre and life, seeming now to be artificially precious, are dissolved. As Brook poses questions as to why one does theatre, performing becomes not just a vocation but a way of addressing the broader issue of what it is to be human:

For the actors, this journey in search of the miraculous wasn't only an experiment in theatre. It was about themselves. . . . Struggling to transform theatre, he [Brook] transforms himself.[145]

Ultimately, the purpose of the workshop exercise is not to create a more interesting style of theatre but to use the theatre as a way of trying to fulfil oneself. Form, staging and characterization are eventually not ends in themselves but means of making concrete what is otherwise unreachably abstract: life, truth, reality.

We have seen how literalism in Grotowski carries a more profound charge than that contained within its ability merely to secure a stunning realism. Ultimately, Grotowski is concerned less with the debate between rival 'isms' in the theatre than with the capacity of literalism to generate an existential answers to questions as to how one should live. Similarly, the fact that Brook's literalism is directed at a work which is itself related by literalism to Grotowski, suggests two things: first, that Brook is also less interested in the ontology of performance than in the quality of living; and second, that his search is likely to be directed at realizing a pure state of being as its solution.

There is a compound set of connections here, two of which interest me in particular. First, the implication of Brook's acting, consciously or coincidentally, on the dual import of Attar's proximity to Grotowski implies that Brook's relationship to Grotowski is not limited merely to the reflexive interest of *The Conference of the Birds* but embraces as well the more substantial issues of schema and technique. Brook has literalism in common with Attar, and Attar in turn has in common with Grotowski the pursuit of authenticity through transcendence and the *via negativa*. This suggests that Brook too is likely to show an interest in these methods – and indeed, although the forms Brook uses are very different to those employed by Grotowski, the impulses which animate them are, as we shall see, very similar. Second, the existentially homogenizing effects of literalism, seen as operating with an almost autonomous inevitability in Grotowski, are likely to have the same effect in Brook's theatre. Judging by our experience of Grotowski's work, the mere fact of the existence of a relationship of literalism seems logically to imply the emergence of immaculate being. If Grotowski seeks to be 'immersed in existence . . . as a bird enters the air',[146] so also Brook must infiltrate a fable about birds to achieve a 'being pure and without effort that some birds express'.[147]

*

As in Grotowski, it is incumbent upon every actor in Brook's company to train 'To become true to himself'.[148] As Vittorio Mezzogiorno acknowledges, his work as an actor consists primarily of attempting 'to free things from within myself, to give, to be myself'.[149] Occasionally, lacking the subterfuge of theatrical paraphernalia as they improvise on a carpet, Brook's actors are able to achieve this consummate transparency:

> such moments in theatre are always touching. It isn't a matter of fine acting performances. . . . It's more a question of heart. That

110

in an empty space, a group of actors simply and openly show themselves for what they are, and hope to be.[150]

The notion of 'being oneself' operates in that gulf between potential and fact which the Bible, for example, renders intelligible as being a reassuringly necessary characteristic of post-Lapsarian existence. Work on and by Brook is replete with statements which both assume the existence of this dissonance and call for its abolition. As in Grotowski, this is to be achieved through an organically constructed congruence between the inner/hidden self and the outer/displayed personality. Thus Brook's attempts to create an environment in which the actor may 'drop his normal defences' and create 'a moment of truth'[151] assume the operation of a mask which coexists with the concealed truth in an infirm and toxic dualism. When the actor is able to summon the courage to reveal himself, he achieves a condition of existence in which, for Brook, 'public truth and private truth become inseparable parts of the same essential experience'.[152] 'Perhaps you might say we are looking for passages', says Brook in his Introduction to *The Conference of the Birds*, 'passages that connect the inner and outer worlds'.[153]

It is a significant feature of the definition of being as consonance that the 'truth' in such a situation is measured not by the degree to which the substance of what is revealed resembles an external model of veracity. It is assessed instead by the extent of its attunement to an internal condition. A consequence of this is that the *nature* of the self that is revealed is irrelevant to the integrity that must accrue to the subject as a consequence merely of the *fact* of the disclosure. The highest 'virtue' to which the self can aspire is its revelation. The only condition imposed upon the quality of this achievement is that it must be comprehensive. Thus 'truly evolved human beings' are persons possessed of 'an outer casing that is a complete and sensitive reflection of the inner life'.[154] Brook's somewhat clumsy avoidance of moral terms recurs in *The Shifting Point*:

A real person is someone who is open in all parts of himself, a person who has developed himself to the point where he can open himself completely – with his body, with his intelligence, with his feelings, so that none of these channels are blocked.[155]

What reads at first as disconcertingly flabby Platonism is in fact an attempt to substitute the language of morality with a vocabulary in which value attaches instead to unity. The result is an alternative system of ethics in which 'good' and 'bad' are replaced by 'whole' and 'incomplete'.

In physical terms the lack of a time lag between thought and action is for Brook the telling symptom of somatic integration:

> A cat actually thinks visibly. If you watch him jump on a shelf, the wish to jump and the action of jumping are one and the same thing. . . . It's in exactly the same way that all Brook's exercises try to train the actor. The actor is trained to become so organically related within himself, he thinks completely with his body. He becomes one sensitive, responding whole. . . . The whole of him is one.[156]

As in Grotowski the existence of internal wholeness is detected through its manifestation as flow, that condition of felicity in which impulse and movement are one. This is the state of being to which Brook's actors must now aspire: a physical condition in which the self can *be* what it *is*.

*

Brook's synthesizing attitude to being carries the rather dubious assumption of a certain omniscience on the part of the subject, whose task is merely to align what must be the already familiar energies of all variables on the equation of truth. It is as though the problem of inauthentic being is always and completely akin to that of lying – where the individual is normally quite cannily aware of discrepancies between information held and proffered.

However, when the object in question is as mysterious an entity as the self, the subject cannot as easily be assumed knowingly to have chosen to conceal a privately well-defined identity. The problem of being oneself is then, in the incipient stages of its solution, a problem of knowing oneself. 'He will *become* more himself', writes Heilpern of Brook's actor; 'Through struggle and longing, he will have *found* himself.'[157] In so far as one cannot reveal what one is not aware of, self-knowledge is a means to an end; in so far as knowledge itself is a bridge, a means cerebrally of connecting with what is latent in oneself, self-knowledge can be synonymous with that end. The biographies of the members of Brook's expedition are replete with references to this concern with bridging the gap between outer and inner through knowledge. For François Marthouret, the actor's principal mission is to acquire 'a greater understanding of oneself'.[158] Michèle Collison confirms that Brook 'confronts you with yourself in a manner that is much stronger than what you've ever experienced before'.[159] To comprehend the self is to allow the self comprehensively to be.

112

As in Grotowski, Brook's exercises in self-awareness utilize the principle of otherness to objectify the subject. The work begins in the body. Exercises which put an unaccustomed strain on certain parts of the anatomy contrive to ensure that the body, of which one is only habitually aware, is revealed the more vividly through its efforts to enter previously unassimilated modes of being. For example, through the rigours of T'ai Chi, the defamiliarizing routine of an alien culture, the actors become more acutely aware of their bodies – and are placed outside themselves to that extent. 'A transformed understanding will liberate the muscles',[160] contends Brook, thus completing the circle of somatic cause and effect by which mind and body are supposedly unified in understanding.

To the extent that somatic theory is based on the assumption that movement and sound do not exist without distinct emotional correlatives, exercises in physical consciousness can quite easily be adapted to perform the more sensitive task of using otherness to effect psychological insights. An actor is asked to make a gesture and then repeat it exactly – after standing perfectly still for up to half an hour. The first movement is potentially a candid and therefore important manifestation of self. The second, deliberately delayed, action is in effect corporeal analysis of the first gesture: it is the product of observation, memory and the conceptual re-assemblage of the intuitive impression of the self. The demand that its execution must be accurate forces the actors to view themselves from the outside – not mechanically but in terms of meaning, of insight into the emotional content of being. In a variation of this exercise, sound is used instead of movement – and a similar reasoning applied:

> Brook observed that in exercises requiring the actor to produce a pure sound the Persians always settled on a sad dominant note. Such exercises, he believed, reveal an actor's inner activity: 'his musical pattern is the essential rorschach of the man'. The Persians' sad note was the outer form of an inner passivity. . . . Sound exercises were 'an unerring test'.[161]

Just as a study of the imagery used in a novel can tell us something about the writer, so also the sounds and movements produced in Brook's workshop can be analysed to reveal something about the actors. The only difference is that the actors participate in the process of interpretation. The exercise must therefore be conducted without the actors' having any previous understanding of its purpose. Only then can the

113

work be true to that 'emphasis by Brook on self-discovery through instinctive, improvised action'.[162]

The disadvantage of work of this kind is that the insight it generates is largely amorphous. This eventually creates the need for a more comprehensive working model of the self. Thus in a later stage of the work the actors are encouraged to consolidate their discretely acquired impressions by creating an integrated image capable of sustaining an autonomous identity. Michèle Collison describes the incipient stages of such work in the course of the preparation of *The Conference of the Birds*:

> we were going to work on birds. This meant looking for a language, a whole way of moving which was not foreign to me but which came from me. I had to find my bird. . . . We all tried different birds in different forms looking for the right one for each of us. . . . One day I did an improv and everybody just said, 'that's you'.[163]

As the exercise is conducted before roles are assigned, the actors are not limited to the specific points of resonance between self and character. They are able to realize a vision that is a poetic amalgamation of virtually every point of nature in themselves. The bird 'is' the actor, not in so far as it evinces certain predetermined characteristics but in that it resonates in a manner that is at once more general *and* concrete. One receives from the exercise not an idea but a paradigm, not a theory of the self but a trace of a region of energy.

In contrast, playing a character involves receiving an agenda by which the self must at all times comply. Whereas Collison's freedom limits her to the extent of her own inventiveness, the experience of being forced to conform to the contours of a given role has the advantage that it provides an opportunity to discover what one cannot, for all the self-transcending capacity of self-portraiture, imagine as being true of oneself. In *The Empty Space* Brook maps the projected transition, in the course of rehearsal, between these complementary approaches to self-knowledge:

> he may be allowed to discover by himself what only exists in himself; next, to force him to accept blindly external directions, so that by cocking a sensitive enough ear he could hear in himself movements he would never have detected in any other way.[164]

In the first stage, one creates an image which one feels best represents the self; in the second, the self learns to represent a given image – and in the process discovers unanticipated affinities.

In *The Conference of the Birds*, Brook's actors used masks to enter those states of being which they felt were outside their normal emotional range. The extent to which actors wearing masks are able somatically to evince unvisited realms of character suggests that these traits are not absent from their identities but latent merely, suppressed by the social mask, the personality. Thus the artistic mask, by summoning into consciousness concealed aspects of being, is for Brook far more than a conveniently concrete means of access to roles that are difficult because they are unfamiliar. The mask is as well a sensor which unearths those truant fragments of self whose discovery is a prerequisite for wholeness:

> The moment the mask absolves you in that way, the fact that it gives you something to hide behind makes it unnecessary for you to hide. This is the fundamental paradox that exists in all acting: that because you are in safety, you can go into danger, . . . because here it is *not* you, and therefore everything about you is hidden, you can let yourself appear.[165]

For Brook, 'The true mask is the expression of somebody unmasked'.[166]

The compound negative capability of the mask is best understood by dividing the effect of the mask into two distinct stages. In the first stage the mask simply obliterates the actor's social veneer by hiding it physically. The effect is comparable to that achieved in a simple exercise which involves putting a sheet of white paper over an actor's face:

> This is one of those great exercises that whoever does it for the first time counts as a great moment: suddenly to find oneself immediately for a certain time liberated from one's own subjectivity. And the awakening of the bodily awareness is immediately there with it, irresistibly; so that if you want to make an actor aware of his body, instead of explaining it to him . . . just put a bit of white paper on his face and say 'Now look around'. He can't fail to be instantly aware of everything he normally forgets.[167]

At this stage the actor is released from the obligation to perform within the constraints of his social mask. However, he cannot as yet *be* himself – for to act in his condition would still seemingly present to an external observer the question as to *who* it is that acts. This problem is solved in the second stage as the mask provides the cover of an 'other' which takes responsibility for the performance. If in the first stage the actor is not

not-himself, in the second he can be himself. In the first stage the actor's personality is suppressed, and in the second stage his individuality appears.

Grotowski, we remember, was not quite able to realize in practice this equation between truth and the 'other'. Otherness in Grotowski is an agent of knowledge which is ultimately antithetical to authentic being. Grotowski's actors were eventually able to achieve being through the intervention of literalism, through their capacity to obliterate the difference between themselves and their characters. Brook's actors, as we have seen, retain the advantages of literalism by actually living through the experience of their characters: the journey through the Sahara directly mirrors the flight of the birds through their valleys. But by using masks, Brook's actors have the additional advantage of retaining being in the presence of knowledge by having the former precede the latter. Whereas Grotowski makes the error of seeking to be as a consequence of knowing, Brook's masked actor, it turns out, knows as a consequence of being. The explicitly somatic agency of masks permits the simultaneous operation of both literalism and otherness. Indeed, it is because the mask is so physically, and therefore unambiguously, 'other' (as that more multifarious phenomenon, the role, is not), that the actors can, when they wear masks, become themselves. It is the ability of masks completely, concretely and concurrently to induce and efface otherness that allows the actors to be themselves by discovering within themselves an otherness that they had not previously had reason to imagine.

*

The otherness of the mask is a measure of the extent to which it partakes of an elevated aspect of being with which the actor is not naturally conversant. Thus masks may also be seen as generating authentic being through the common participation of themselves and truth in transcendence. The equation is the product of the juxtaposition of two quite separate observations which share the phenomenon of sublimation. First, the theatre, for Brook, is a place where a transcendent order of reality can be found: in the theatre 'an actor who lives a humdrum and confused life like everyone else in his society has a unique possibility . . . of touching at certain short moments a quite genuine but fleeting experience of what could be a higher level of evolution'.[168] For Brook all great roles have forces in them that are stronger than those to which actors normally have access. The process of assimilation into character is therefore also a process of absorbing this transcendent energy, of

116

making it one's own. Second, as in Grotowski, the self is most completely itself when it transcends itself: for Brook, 'the actor's essential self [is] . . . above their normal selves'.[169] It follows that actors can 'be themselves' by playing characters because this involves the transcendence of the self which, as in Grotowski, makes authentic being possible. It is by virtue of the exalted otherness of the character that the actor is alienated into a heightened perception of being – but not before that mode of being is itself seen as authentic because it is transcendent.

Dramatic characters, however, are not magical wands. For all their somatic leverage, great roles cannot function entirely independently of the sensitivity of the person playing them. No character can compel authenticity in spite of the inclination or ability of the actor. Characters provide at best an opportunity which actors must learn to utilize. Actors must bring to their roles questions they want answered, questions which are the products of separate searches. Roles generate authenticity through transcendence in proportion to the extent to which the actors have themselves, in some other forum, pursued truth through elevation. Thus in Brook, as in Grotowski, a major theme in rehearsal is self-transcendence through physical exercise.

Brook's model tribe, the Peulh, are supposedly 'beyond the human'[170] as a result of routines in which they 'flog and torture themselves. They push themselves to extremes. And they have gifts that no one else has.'[171] The equation of endurance with exaltation, familiar to us through Grotowski's work, is a characteristic too of the 'torture of many of the physical exercises'[172] that Yoshi Oida puts Brook's actors through. In Africa the group worked for up to nineteen hours a day on acrobatics, rhythm, timing, balance and concentration. Not the least part of their trials were, as in the case of Attar's birds, the rigours of the journey itself. Asked if he drives his actors too hard, Brook replies with studied innocence, 'I don't know what that question means.'[173]

Like Grotowski, Brook believes that 'exercising is liberating and helps you to overcome fear'.[174] The loss of fear in turn assists in the dissolution of the social mask, the cause of inauthenticity: as the actor gains confidence by passing private barriers, the need to present a façade in society becomes less pressing. As actors master the unfamiliar and prevail over formally formidable tasks, they render themselves more able to be themselves. The glow in the aftermath of their exertions, like that of athletes, is the satisfaction of those who can now accept themselves (and therefore be themselves) in this condition of self-transcendence.

Gradually, however, the hurdles to be overcome become more and more obviously insuperable. The emphasis shifts from purely personal to more objective standards of the limits of human capability. As in Grotowski, the concept of flight is central to any practical demonstration of self-transcendence. And, as in Grotowski, literalism demands that the actors strive not to imitate but to realize the transcendental import of flight. 'You know', says Lou Zeldis in Africa, 'it's getting really irritating not being able to fly.'[175] On the magic carpet he puts this urge to the test:

> Suddenly, Lou Zeldis . . . began to walk round the forest in a circle. . . .
> And very slowly began to change into a bird. . . .
> And quickened in pace. And was a bird, absolutely. And flew. He *flew*! I saw him do it. He became a bird and flew over the trees and up to the sky. . . .
> Ah, but did his feet really leave the ground?
> It was the hugest discovery for me! It doesn't matter! It doesn't matter a damn, provided you fly.[176]

*

In Grotowski, we remember, technical virtuosity was intended not merely to assist the actor to be but also to compel the credence of a faithless audience. So also for Brook the actor not only has the 'possibility of touching . . . a higher level of evolution' but 'because he touches it in public he reflects to those watching an authentic vision . . . to be attainable'.[177] However, as in Grotowski, virtuosity in Brook's theatre turns out to be as likely to convince as to alienate. As Brook observes, it is questionable whether it is 'possible for a highly trained group to meet a group at a much lower level of preparation, with all the barriers of suspicion, and envy and xenophobia'.[178] In Teheran, one of the Persian actors with whom Brook's company worked 'said he felt himself withdrawing all the time because he recognised the gaps between his technique and that of the Paris group'.[179] The disunion implicit in excellence is not merely external. In *The Empty Space*, with exactly the same reasoning as that offered by Grotowski, Brook writes,

> Easily, know-how can become a pride and an end in itself. It becomes dexterity without any other aim than the display of expertise – in other words, the art becomes insincere.[180]

As in Grotowski, a concern with technical excellence tends both to antagonize collaborators and prove inimical to the actors' revelation of self.

Brook's reply to the beleagured Persian is that 'know-how is not the most important thing in this work'.[181] This is consistent with Brook's attempts to counteract the divisive pressures of skill by adopting an approach which involves 'not a process of building but of destroying obstacles that stand in the way of the latent form'[182] – the exact equivalent, of course, of Grotowski's *via negativa*. Now 'the director's job is to say No to habits, not to instruct'.[183] Actors who seek to reach authentic being are now required not to add to their skills but to 'strip away their outward personalities, mannerisms, habits . . . until a higher state of perception is found'.[184] We are now in Attar's Valley of Poverty and Nothingness.

The impulse to a negative technique is not without a history in Brook's work. As early as 1961 Brook had sworn allegiance to a process of elimination in the theatre. In opposition to a Stanislavsky title, Brook had emphasized that

> preparing a character is the opposite of building – it is a demolish-ing, removing brick by brick everything in the actor's muscles, ideas and inhibitions that stands between him and the part, until one day, with a great rush of air, the character invades his every pore.[185]

The paradox whereby the actor must pare down the self in order to meet the inflated needs of character is remarkably similar to the manner in which, as Brook writes in *The Empty Space*, Grotowski's actor does not actively seek out a character as much as 'allows a role to "penetrate" him'.[186] *The Empty Space* was published in 1968. So was *Towards a Poor Theatre*. Both titles advocate the shedding of excess in the interest of a greater concentration of effect. In the work of both directors this applies as much to the technique of the actor as to the paraphernalia of staging. In 1962 the process of preparing *King Lear* involved for Brook the systematic elimination of scenery, costume, music and even colour. Nineteen years later, his *Tragédie de Carmen* was yet another exercise in the use of complete simplicity on the stage. Brook has for a long time hovered in the vicinity of Grotowski's 'point of emptiness'.

The *via negativa* and technical virtuosity coexist without contradic-tion because they are linked by a necessary complementarity. Just as spontaneity is meaningful only after the actor has absorbed the virtues of discipline, so also artlessness realizes its full potential only when actors start with complexity and work to conclude with simplicity. In Attar, the trials of the journey are a necessary precondition to the realization that they are not necessary. It is with a similar sense of the relevance of what is ultimately irrelevant that Brook's actor, 'having come to understand past experience and techniques, must throw them all out, strip himself naked'.[187] Skill and naivety are associated sequentially. After creating the grandeur and spectacle of Orghast, Brook's actors struggle in Africa to try to build a simple dramatic relationship through a piece of bread. Or a pair of old shoes.

In Grotowski, *via negativa* is a means of emptying the self so that it may be filled by a 'force'. In Brook too there is an attempt to partake of a mysterious power – and access to it is linked to deprivation. Through denial the actor's body becomes 'trained to open itself up to the invisible'.[188] The word 'open' recurs in Brook as an adjective which describes that condition of alert acceptance, the product of systematic dispossession, which facilitates contact with the otherwise unreachable world of the spirit. In *The Empty Space*, Brook observes of the actor that 'if he is relaxed, open and attuned, then the invisible will take possession of him; through him, it will reach us'.[189]

Part of the purpose of a trip to Africa was to make this equation available to the actor – if not in experience, at least by force of example. In Oshogbo the actors watch a group of tribal women dance:

> Without effort or apparent will, their bodies vanished and burned. . . . Human bodies became a vehicle for the spirit. . . . I received a vision of sheer existence. And God passed before our eyes.[190]

Following the example of his African model, Brook requires of his actor that he too must

> lose his ego. His body must become air. The movement must flow so irresistibly and with such awesome certainty that it seems to happen by itself. . . . [T]he whole of him will become one. Such a state, reached without effort or conscious will, . . . is called the 'artless art".[191]

In both cases wholeness is evinced as effortless and unwilled action, the somatic aspect of the union of external and interior truth. This in turn is related to the abrogation of the self: in both cases internal wholeness is achieved as a consequence of the extinction of the resistance of the self to its denial. The perceptual motor element in which this equation finds objective expression is flow – the lack of a time lag between thought and action, inner and outer.

As in Grotowski, Brook's actors must stalk this condition by working on their bodies. In workshop, Brook's means of making actors sensitive to the virtues of simplicity includes asking them to perform certain tasks while straitlaced by the severest reductions in the means available to them. For instance, the actors must communicate ideas by using fewer and fewer means until they are restricted to just one finger or just one tone of voice. The imposition of these restrictions alienates the communicative potential of each of the elements which can then be reassembled to produce in the self an instrument of greater sensitivity. In existential terms, this is truth achieved through the dismemberment of all surrogate attributes upon which the inauthentic self depends for its enervating security. The actors must reach what they are in essence by ridding themselves of what is inessential.

In Africa, the experience of playing to tribes with whom the group shared no common assumptions was itself in part an exercise designed to alienate the superfluous and provoke its abandonment. Brook's sense of the advantages to be had from playing to a radically 'other' audience dates back to the period immediately following his 1947 production of *Romeo and Juliet* when he wrote sadly that there would be no way of testing the true merits of such a performance until one had at Stratford an audience with no preconceptions about Shakespearean production.[192] At the time of *A Midsummer Night's Dream*, Brook spoke of the manner in which children, as they make for a 'lively audience with no preconceptions, . . . demand that things be clear'.[193] Whereas the imposition of drastic reductions in the means available to the actor is both artificial and vulnerable to unwitting reliance upon shared codes of theatre practice, the task of improvising before an audience of children forces actors to reconstruct the basis of their art in a manner that is more real and reliable.

However, western children are unlikely to be entirely untouched by assumptions as to the nature and conventions of the theatre event. In contrast, African audiences, as they are presumably uncontaminated by preconceptions as to the latest trends in theatre practice in the west, demand quite explicitly that Brook's actors clarify what they seek to communicate by discarding what is needlessly complex – precisely as is required of them in the *via negativa*. In an interview with Michael Gibson, Brook explains how playing to an audience for whom at best 'Adolf was a warrior who fought many battles',[194] helped strip the actors of obfuscating inessentials:

Very easily one came to the point where a barrier between oneself and the audience could be felt because one was within a form. . . .

Now since we were sometimes in places where there had never been any theatre at all meant that even that couldn't be taken for granted, because if somebody who's walking straight suddenly doubles up, he might genuinely at that moment have been taken ill. . . .

It was very interesting, really starting from zero.[195]

There is no noble-savage naivety or condescension about this. Brook is using a theory not of the inferiority of the African audience but of its otherness – which can, if true, be relied upon quite rigorously to compel the *via negativa*. The difference between the assumptions of the group and that of their African spectators compels the actors to abandon their preconceptions. As abandonment is also positively correlated with susceptibility to the 'force', the stripping away of needlessly sophisticated theatre forms is concomitant with the shedding of personal masks. The process of re-thinking theatre forms is synonymous with the re-evaluation of the self. Of the members of Brook's expedition, perhaps only Yoshi Oida has been able to find the courage to deny the self as a means of recovering it more fully: 'Over the years, he's consistently and honestly tried to take to pieces his own superstructure', writes Heilpern, 'And . . . something has opened. . . . [T]he beautifully created image of Yoshi has been replaced by something more true. He's more himself'.[196] To be is not to be. In order truly to be, the actor must learn to let be.

*

The assistance Brook's actors require from their African audiences is vulnerable to the charge that it is exploitative. To the extent that the actors use the audience to test what is finally a private state of enlightenment, Brook's work in Africa seems self-regarding and intrusive. Brook's assertion that 'there is no truth in theatre without an audience',[197] while intended to counteract the weary solipsism of the group, in fact further fuels the view that for Brook the function of the audience is to augment the personal achievement of the actor.

However, the use of contact as a means of ascertaining the extent of an actor's wholeness does not necessarily imply that communication is secondary to being. Nor does it exclude the view that the actor's felicity, however attractive in itself, is at best an indispensable stage in the pursuit of a more substantial object, a theatre of 'individuals offering their most intimate truths to individuals, . . . sharing a collective experience with them'.[198] As the Centre International de Recherche Théâtrales becomes the Centre International de Créations Théâtrales, for Brook 'personal expression ceases to be an aim and we go towards shared discovery'.[199] It is the task of theatre now to explore the significance of placing *'human being in relation to human being'*,[200] of making possible 'embryonic contacts . . . between previously sealed off souls'[201] which makes them 'slightly more alive'.[202] The actor's enlightenment is not in itself of paramount importance; its utility is related to the extent to which it can help to build bridges between people, to find forms that make exchange possible. 'What I am searching for in the theatre', declares Brook, is 'an act of communion.'[203] The otherness of the African is only derivatively a foil designed to disinter the actor's inner self. Ultimately, the African's remoteness is a distance to be travelled, an attribute to be expunged. The journey carries us into Attar's Valley of Love.

The priority thus given to contact is not irreconcilable with the use of contact to secure internal wholeness. To make contact one needs to strip away inessentials as in the *via negativa*. To the extent that the *via negativa* may be relied upon to generate internal wholeness, the effort to make contact with the African may be seen as comprising an approach to the condition of authentic being. As contact is the only externally verifiable attribute of internal wholeness, it is understandable that it should be treated as a test of internal wholeness. However, to treat contact in this way is not to demean it, nor deem it secondary to authenticity. Internal wholeness and contact are complementary in a manner that does not compromise the priority given to meeting. Failed contact is a telling guide to the nature of the imperfections that delimit the self. Success, on the other hand, is valued not for the internal wholeness it reveals but for the external wholeness of which too it is a symptom. Just as theatre is inconceivable without an audience, so also for Brook truth is meaningless without meeting.

The equations in this matrix are posited by Brook in his sociologically dubious but metaphysically interesting 'Rainbow Theory':

I scandalised an anthropologist by suggesting that we all have Africa inside us. I explained that this was based on my conviction that we are each only parts of the complete man: that the fully developed human being would contain what today is labelled African, Persian or English. . . .

Each culture expresses a different portion of the inner atlas: the complete human truth is global and the theatre is the place in which the jigsaw can be pieced together.[204]

In essence, internal wholeness and external wholeness are really one and the same thing. Which, for all its romantic sweep of unprovable assumptions, is an idea with a respectable pedigree. In the *Upanishads*, for instance, 'Brahman [the cosmic order] is all and Atman [the self] is Brahman'.[205] Thus when Brook claims that through contact you bring back the lost parts of yourself, the interaction of the group with the Africans is not subjugated to the actor's wholeness but is synonymous with it.

The fact that authenticity and contact are interchangeable implies that, just as contact can be used to test for internal wholeness, so also internal wholeness can be pursued as a means of achieving some kind of social harmony. These are not just two ways of saying the same thing: for although the process involved is the same (the journey to Africa), the orientation of the group is now much more in keeping with Grotowski's belief in the possibility of securing social remedies through internal exertions. This was the basis, we remember, of Grotowski's affinity with Tarkovsky, the point at which we began this chapter. For Brook too, the theatre, as a medium of sharing, can demonstrably 'counterbalance the fragmentation of the world'.[206] In a world of ubiquitous disaffection, the pursuit and dissemination of wholeness through contact is for Brook a return to 'the theatre's original purpose, sacred and healing'.[207] As fewer people retain the will to avail of the inspiration of traditional piety, the arts must celebrate their latent sacramental ability. If the ambition of art is to remove the randomness that characterizes the natural presence of wholeness in our lives, then the theatre, as a medium of meeting, is better able to do this than most. If theatre is to serve a society sadly 'not rooted in any form of shared and generally accepted wishes, beliefs, affirmations,'[208] it can do so by providing what people most need – companionship on the basis of their being.

*

A director seeking to unify society through a public realization of wholeness must attempt first to forge his own group into something of a community: the actors must explore in detail the situation which they wish to bring before their audience. But just as the rehearsal of a conventional drama involves not only generating sequences of events but alienating them such that their import may be properly communicated, so also Brook's group must share not just any experience but specifically the experience of meeting. This is not a tautology: the circularity of the idea comprises its defamiliarization. Brook must design exercises such that what the actors share is their common participation in the discovery of that region of energy in which authentic being and external wholeness are one.

In the earliest stages of the work, when the actors are yet to develop sufficient confidence in their ability to reach in practice a private point of wholeness, exercises posit the coexistence of internal and external truth by utilizing the suggestive force of analogy. For instance, 'a group of actors would each represent one part of a particular person, including invisible functions such as the voice or the subconscious, seeking a coherent relationship between the whole'.[209] Here the group has really to work as a team (achieve external wholeness) in order symbolically to represent that state of integration in the individual in which the visible and the invisible are one (the condition of internal wholeness). Thus the exercise not only provides the actors with an opportunity to work together so as to generate a sense of group harmony, but also suggests unambiguously the link between this condition and that required of each actor individually – a state of internal unity. The harmony between the actors comprises precisely a model of personal authenticity.

In a more complex version of the exercise,

> A needs a job . . . and is torn between ingratiating himself and venting his hostilities. The rest of the group . . . are personality-adjuncts of A. . . . They speak only as and when A replies to the Interviewer's questions, and their response is determined entirely by what A actually says and what they glean from the way he says it.[210]

Once again the collaboration between the actors externally comprises a working image of internal wholeness. However, whereas in the previous exercise internal wholeness was experienced as an idea, here it can be realized in practice. By eliminating time for thought, the exercise makes possible the inception of a state of flow in the individual. This signals a state of internal wholeness which, if it occurs, palpably assists in the creation of external wholeness between the actors. The less the actors allow their conscious minds to interfere with their responses, the more receptive they are to the rest of the group. Equally, the more attentive they are to the others, the easier it is to answer questions appropriately. The exercise is then literally able to realize the import of the metaphor proposed by its structure. The less divided the actors are between mind and body, the less fragmented the group is as a whole. And vice versa.

Brook's image for the flow of wholeness through a group is a circle. In workshop, this circle is created in a series of exercises designed to introduce actors to the array of interlocking factors which comprise the confluence of internal and external wholeness. In the first exercise, gestures are passed around a circle of actors who must modify what they receive without disturbing the integrity of the rhythm of the group.[211] Equally, the actors may pass 'words around the circle in sequence as a real phrase delivered quite naturally'.[212] In both exercises, wholeness as a product is demystified as success or failure are concretely manifested in the natural truth of the created phrase or movement. The interdependence of internal and external wholeness is established by the manner in which both conditions depend palpably for their sustenance upon a single attribute in the actor: openness. The openness of the actors to the 'force' (which makes for internal wholeness) is the very quality required of them in their working relationships with one another (which makes for external wholeness). The circle is broken if the actors either self-consciously create complex effects (undistilled by the *via negativa* into internal wholeness) or if they fail to find in themselves something that corresponds, on the terms of external wholeness, to the image presented to them.

Harmony in a company of actors as diverse as Attar's birds is significant for two reasons: first, it disciplines the interdependence of external wholeness and authenticity. The likelihood of local factors being responsible for the state of flow in the group diminishes in proportion to the heterogeneity of the company. Second, the extent to which the group is radically multilingual is a measure of the extent to which the wholeness they achieve may be said to have a universal quality. In so far as the members of the company represent not merely countries but cultures, this universality has both a geographical and a temporal dimension. Indeed, the traditions represented (Noh theatre, Yoruba drumming, etc.) are themselves, by virtue of their age, the nearest thing we have to the constants of culture. It follows that any communication between these systems strengthens further the case for the universality of the application of external wholeness.

For Brook, these traditions are particularly valuable in that they house physical indicators as to the manner in which deep currents of wholeness may be tapped. Thus when Brook uses the diversity of his actors to introduce them to the sounds, shapes and attitudes of different parts of the world, the intention is that they somatically imbibe something of the wisdom that enables these systems wholly to be:

> Everyone in the group kneels, holding short sticks or fans. Facing them, the stern and disciplined Yoshi Oida. The actors sing an ancient Japanese song, in Japanese. Occasionally, Oida stops them abruptly, corrects the sound and begins again. . . .

126

Bagayogo . . . teaches an African song. . . .
In silence . . . the group returns to T'ai Chi. . . .[213]

In workshop, the somatic transmission of these traditions generates universality in a manner that is precisely congruent with the construction of external wholeness by individuals in a state of flow:

> two actors faced each other in silence, one performing a sequence of unpatterned movements, the other seeking to mirror the movements as closely as possible, to the extent, at best, of knowing instinctively what would come next.[214]

The attunement of alien cultures one to another (an African drummer does T'ai Chi) is indistinguishable from the unerring mutual sensitivity of individuals (Bagayogo and Oida). Equally, the actors' attempts to be open to the source (to have internal wholeness as a function of *via negativa*) is inextricably associated with their ability to come together to make external wholeness. Which, if Atman and Brahman are one, is as it should be. In flow, the body and the spirit, the self and the other, the others and us, are one.

*

If Brook's exploration of contact as a medium of wholeness is to realize the promise of its therapeutic potential, it must eventually features the public at large. The equation between contact and wholeness, having been vetted and approved in workshop, must now be broadened to make space for the audience. However, as a vital feature of the contact between performers in rehearsal is that it is active, Brook must somehow contrive to ensure that his spectators engage physically in the action. Concomitant with the inclusion of the audience within the therapeutic design of the work is the obligation to harness any influence somatic elements may have on the manifestation of wholeness.

One might expect the incidence of a high degree of exclusive positive correlation between spectator-participation and external wholeness to be of some interest to a director in pursuit of epiphany as an antidote to social schism. However, virtually all occasions in which external wholeness is achieved in Africa have two features in common: the manifest ability of certain tribes to realize their openness somatically and the fact that, often fortuitously, this activity precedes Brook's performance. Brook never seems to generate in his audiences the impulse to participation: contact is made only if a tribe is naturally inclined both to perform and to countenance the subsequent involvement of the Paris group. Brook arranges an evening with the Peulh only after he has heard their sound. The success of the encounter is entirely contingent upon the Peulh being willing to make music with Brook's company. At the meeting with the Tuaregs, contact is once again associated with the fact that the tribal women just happen to perform first:

The pulse grew out of the skills of generations. . . .

Hesitantly, Swados . . . joined their music. . . .

The Tuaregs were taken by surprise now, shrieking with delight at this unexpected audience participation. . . .

The wall was down. In its place, real exchange, real and precious sharing. . . .[215]

The vitality of the work in Wuseli and Gangara is just as contingent upon the anteriority of the Africans' performance. In reports on these performances, the term 'audience' refers in turn to the Paris group and the locals – but only in that order.

The fact that Brook does not actually elicit participation in Africa, when juxtaposed with the role played by chance in furnishing situations in which the Africans just happen to perform first, leads one to infer a curious passivity in Brook's attitude to wholeness in this period. Now the energy of a communal inscape, 'this combustion, this chemical process depends very, very largely on certain elements that the audience brings'.[216] Placed beside his belief that 'an audience cannot whip itself into being "better" than it is',[217] Brook's inertness disconcertingly undermines the inspirational value of the actors' work. Brook needs the wholeness that is the product of participation, but he will not learn to draw out that somatic input if it is not already forthcoming.

Brook's failure to see the significance of the role of audience participation in the substantiation of the deep structures of concord in Africa could be an accidental oversight. I am more inclined to believe, however, that Brook deliberately de-emphasizes the reliance of wholeness upon somatic understanding. This seems to be the case because Brook is clearly not oblivious to the part played by participation in the creation of contact. When Brook observes for instance that a performance in Africa was a 'real coming together' because in it 'we were actually making something for them in exchange for what they had offered us',[218] a connection is quite clearly made between intimacy and physical exchange. If Brook is aware of this link, and it appears he is, then its exclusion from the governing parameters of the Africa experiment could only have been intentional.

The manner in which Brook urges a somatic investment from the audience in the 1960s is itself an indication of his awareness of its potency – which suggests that his subsequent abandonment of it was deliberate. The beginnings are tentative: in having the chorus working from amongst the spectators in *Oedipus*, Brook is able only symbolically to fuse actors and audience on the grounds that they occupy the same space. In *The Tempest*, the somatic contribution of the audience is thrust upon them as they are wheeled about the playing area in towers of movable scaffolding. In *A Midsummer Night's Dream*, the actors reach out to touch the spectators, but not at the audience's instigation. Each of these devices derives from a principle Brook comes subsequently to deplore:

> The fact of playing with and implicating the audience (by the actors penetrating the auditorium, for example) is an effect, and like everything else it wears itself out. It becomes something we've seen before, it loses its freshness.[219]

In 1970, the year of Grotowski's abandonment of the theatre of actors and spectators, Brook too speaks of a 'break with the past'[220] and declares that he must 'leave this theatre altogether'.[221] Like Grotowski, Brook becomes involved with 'trying to discover a form of theatre that's totally new',[222] which is 'non-result-producing'[223] and in which 'the actors come before an audience prepared to produce a dialogue, not give a demonstration'.[224] Audiences are asked to stay behind after performances to discuss the work of the group. This leads to the institution of 'Theatre Days' – workshops designed to share the group's workshop experiences with a public audience (or visiting theatre groups of which, in New York, Grotowski's company was one). As a result perhaps of Brook's association with Grotowski, and of the presence in his group of actors like Malik Bagayogo who had worked previously in the Laboratory Theatre, Brook's interest in audience participation seems at this stage very much in step with Grotowski's.

Given the extended period of Brook's continuing preoccupation with the question as to whether the audience has a role to play, one might quite reasonably assume that any positive answers accidentally provided by the experience of the group in Africa would eventually have been manipulated to cohere into a more dynamic and reliable programme for remedial performance in the future. However, this work remains secondary as Brook reverts to productions in which the actors withhold the right to control the playing space. Of course, the continuance of the actor–audience divide in Brook's theatre does not in itself imply the withdrawal of Brook's investment in participation – for Brook has been able to function in both modes concurrently. His work in local communities, in prisons, schools, drug rehabilitation centres and mental institutions does continue to derive from his commitment to the therapeutic potential of performance. Yet it seems a pity that Brook's frontal assault upon social problems should not filter through to reach the wider public to whom he has access through his stage productions. To treat members of the public who have few special requirements as though they had no need of wholeness is to be untrue to the notion that wholeness is finally a condition not of normality but of transcendence. The word 'therapy' has for too long suggested that the maladies it addresses are aberrations and therefore incompatible with the condition in which the greater mass of people typically live their lives. The study of wholeness suggests rather that it is the *norm* that is in some way pernicious and to be overcome.

Equally disconcerting is the note of equivocation that has crept into Brook's attitude to somatic sharing. On the one hand, Brook admits of the somatically active audience that 'the very fact that they participate heightens their perception'[225] – where heightened perception, we remember, is a defining feature of wholeness. Being is another characteristic of harmony and, appropriately, for Brook the substance of theatre 'can only be understood at first-hand by partaking'[226] – where 'partaking' is defined as the 'experience not of looking at another style but of being right on the inside of it'.[227] On the other hand, Brook's observation that 'there is only a practical difference between actor and audience, not a fundamental one',[228] while seeming at first to be just as positive, in fact betrays the promise of participation by failing to see that it is the practical difference that is fundamental. Participation in Brook is now defined in a manner that directly contravenes the centrality of somatic features to wholeness:

> Whether the audience participates in a way that has become fashionable, by showing it is participating because it is moving around, whether it participates by standing motionless, or whether it participates in a sitting position is only of secondary importance.[229]

Again, 'If an actor can catch the spectator's interest, thus lower his defences . . . then the audience becomes more active. This activity does not demand manifestations'.[230] Thus Brook allows himself the possibility of claiming the advantages of participation while staging plays in a manner that is consistent with the quite contrary sentiment that 'in both the cinema and theatre, the spectator is usually more or less passive, at the receiving end of impulses'.[231]

This prevarication is of less significance in Africa, where harmony is supposedly abundantly available, than in the west where audiences are divided:

> The audience brings elements of judgement that makes the actor's work partly a fight for domination over the audience. The clearest illustration of this is in the French theatre, where one finds the expression *se defendre*. . . .
> So what we wanted to do in Africa was to go to what could be considered an optimum audience . . . because it has not in any way been conditioned.[232]

Quite apart from the suspect anthropology of the distinction, Brook's statement ironically emphasizes both a need for wholeness in the west and the definitional inability of the African experience to provide the training to meet that need. Again,

> In going to Africa we didn't go in the hope of finding something that we could learn, take away, or copy. We went to Africa because in the theatre the audience is as powerful a creative element in the primal event as the actor.[233]

Audience participation is not practicable in the west – if only for the reason that it is required there. The actors will find harmony in Africa but its healing potential will not be shared with western theatre audiences who need it most *because* they need it so much. Which is ironic – not least because sharing, finally, is the remedy.

As Brook moves back into the theatre of actors and audiences, his work retains of course the implicit potential for remedy that is contained in all art. I do not have the space to discuss at length whether or not art does carry a latent spiritual capability. I believe it does; but when art fails *explicitly* to address social and political issues, it relinquishes the possible operation of a relationship of *necessity* between that potential and its realization. Artists surrender control of those factors that determine the therapeutic impact of their work. Any remedial import that does accrue to the spectator is the product of the accidental alignment of sufficient conditions. Grotowski and Brecht's consistently more overt manipulation of the variables on the equations of alienation and wholeness, while obviously not so perfectly honed as to guarantee success, nevertheless retains a greater likelihood of contributing, in however small a way, to the betterment of the world for which they work. The experience of Grotowski establishes that the forms in which these solutions are most likely to be forthcoming include the somatic involvement of the public. The ambiguity that shrouds the continuance of this undertaking in Brook is then a measure of Brook's withdrawal from a position of affinity with Grotowski.

*

The widening gulf between Brook and Grotowski is, however, not quite as damaging as may be suggested by speculation about Brook's attitude to his participation experiments. Nor is it as irresponsible as to be entirely the product of his attraction to spectacle at the expense of therapy. It is true that Brook's showmanship is a vital part of the appeal of his theatre, and that the flamboyance he favours would neither have been possible nor relevant in work with a relatively unskilled public. But Brook's temperamental inclination to theatricality is not the only reason for the marginalization of his search for a somatic role for the spectator. Brook's criticism of Grotowski hinges rather on the irony by which, for all Grotowski's claims to wholeness, his theatre explores only a narrow segment of experience:

> the very purity of their resolve, the high and serious nature of their activity inevitably brings a colour to their choices and a limitation to their field. They are unable to be both esoteric and popular at one and the same time.[234]

Brook's view that 'Along with serious, committed and probing work, there must be irresponsibility'[235] makes a case for lightness on two grounds. First, levity itself provides a unique means of access to wholeness which Grotowski's relentless intensity must necessarily forgo. The concluding phrase of *The Empty Space*, 'a play is play',[236] invokes Lila, the notion of drama/sport which, in some traditional Indian philosophy, characterizes the highest orders of enlightenment. Second, it seems to Brook inconceivable that wholeness can accrue to any construct which excludes. For Brook, the 'experience of one man's world, however fascinating . . . is not enough, because it is always incomplete'.[237] Thus while Grotowski's fidelity to his impulses is in effect restrictive, Brook must aim to cultivate a means of linking the fastidious and the capricious, the vulgar and the esoteric, which only *together* comprise wholeness. If this means exploring a range of formative influences, so much the better.

It is a characteristic of both reasons that they are premised on a commitment to wholeness. Thus Brook's impulse to multiplicity and excess, while it irrevocably disengages him from Grotowski, does not completely compromise the integrity of his theatre. Nor does this link between plenitude and harmony necessarily negate Grotowski's more spartan and exclusive attempts to reach the same end. Yoshi Oida expresses quite vividly the differences between these alternative but equally valid approaches to wholeness:

> In Japan if you wish to find a rock . . . we dig and dig and dig always in the same place. But Western people change the place if they cannot find the rock . . . Perhaps the Japanese way is silly – always the same hole, very very deep. Brook digs in many different places . . . always changing. Which is better? I'm not sure now.[238]

Oida's image may be realistic in that it attributes the discovery of the rock as much to strategy as to chance. The image of a circle, however, has the advantage of presenting with greater clarity the relationship of necessity between scrutiny and revelation upon which these approaches are founded.

Construe a circle of inanimate matter ranged about a nucleus of enormous energy. The spokes of this wheel are various disciplines, cables of exploratory activity which burrow from surface towards centre in search of the spirit which must animate the otherwise lifeless shell of physical existence. Vitality accrues to a construct in proportion to its proximity to the core. Wholeness is a condition of absolute access to all life on the circumference. This is achievable typically through the complete extension of the increasingly incandescent contact given by each discipline. At the still point of the turning world the subject gains access on all axes to the whole of creation. This is the wholeness of the Peulh who can show us the shape of all things in the resonance of a single musical note. This is the wisdom of the teacher of Bharatanatyam who will not permit his student to explore any other dance forms on the grounds that all lateral adjustment in the circle is movement away from the centre. This is the attitude I associate with Grotowski, the director who digs ever deeper, but within an infinitely narrow band of experience.

The approach to which Brook is temperamentally more inclined, on the other hand, involves travelling all the way along the circumference in an effort to absorb the import of all disciplines till a full circle is described which too is wholeness. In this, Brook's model is Shakespeare whose work evinces the whole condition of man as he is able uniquely to 'be all those things at the same time'.[239] In Brook's theatre, this translates as self-enfranchisement to move with strategic abandon between all styles and subjects, 'to synthesize', as Brook puts it, 'the self-contained achievements of the Theatre of the Absurd, the epic theatre and the naturalistic theatre. This is where our thinking must go'.[240]

Brook's earliest attempts at realizing his panoramic affinities have involved bringing together forms and materials that had earlier been independently and minutely studied. Thus for instance *The Bone*, an exuberant African farce, appeared on a double bill with the more abstract and refined theatre version of *The Conference of the Birds*. In an attempt further to highlight his disavowal of the self-enclosed vitality of single forms, Brook's company performed *The Conference of the Birds* in a number of different styles in the course of a single evening:

> The version at 8.00 p.m. was rough theatre: vulgar, comic, full of life. The one at midnight was a search for the holy: intimate, whispered, to candlelight. The final version . . . finished at sunrise – it was in the form of a chorale, everything happened through improvised song. . . . Next time we must bring all these different elements together within the same performance.[241]

This then is the Rainbow Theory not of the self but of the theatre: 'nowhere in the world is there a complete theatre', writes Brook in *The Shifting Point*, 'but only fragments of a theatre'.[242] In setting out to bring these fragments together synergically into a single edifice, Brook is trying to create in his theatre an image of the wholeness he would like to see made attainable in the world.

Brook and Grotowski have the same objectives, but the differences in the manner in which they seek to realize their aims – the one on the spoke, the other on the circumference – mean that in practice their work can coincide only briefly. Then Grotowski's territory must be left behind, as were Stanislavsky's and Brecht's, and Brook must go on to investigate other orders and formulations until at last he is able to galvanize them sufficiently to cohere. 'In *The Mahabharata* I will start the search again', writes Brook. 'Perhaps this time we will be able to bring all these elements together in one form'.[243] It is to this production, *Le Mahabharata*, that I turn in the Epilogue.

Epilogue

A MULTI-FACETED ONTOLOGY IN PERFORMANCE:

Uniting rough and holy in *Le Mahabharata*

> Usually each single project has only one aspect . . . a facet of the truth. . . . But always I've been searching for a more complete expression, a theme, and a way of expressing it that enters as many aspects as possible of living experience and that succeeds in making links between many contradictions.[1]
>
> (Peter Brook)

I would like, before relinquishing this study, briefly to follow the rehearsal methods discussed here into performance. To do so would of course be to depart substantially from the principal interest and rationale of this book. But it would also provide an opportunity to discuss the value of Brook's astutely indiscriminate amalgamation of the styles he has culled in the course of his inordinate apprenticeship. It would be unjust not to acknowledge that, although Brook has hitherto been able at best only to modify the legacy of others, the reassemblage of his borrowings in *Le Mahabharata* is arguably an achievement un-paralleled by his more independent but less prodigiously inclusive precursors. This is not to retract the contention that Brook's reputation for originality is to some extent unmerited. I seek merely to redress the balance of this book in the light of a recent revelation. Much as we may deride Brook's inexcusably prolonged inability to find a personal idiom, we must nevertheless admire the well-nigh unique facility by which he is now able to make his imitations cohere.

Brook's writings have repeatedly affirmed the virtues of coalescence. For example Brook proposed in 1965 to film *King Lear* using the old Abel Gance device of placing three screens side by side and running separate images on them simultaneously. For Brook the technique was to provide an answer to the problem of playing texts as encyclopaedic and flexible as those of Shakespeare, texts which operate on so many

135

levels that it is impossible to present them in any one style or convention. When Brook finally filmed *King Lear*, editing supplied the suppleness he had sought in Cinerama. As Brook remarked in a letter to Grigori Kozintsev, 'realism was distorted to encompass the contradictory styles of writing. . . . Now in the editing we are searching to interrupt the consistency of style, so that the many-levelled contradictions of the play can appear.'[2] The capacity of art to approach a condition of wholeness is a function of the extent to which it has unconstrained access to all available modes of representation.

In *Meetings with Remarkable Men*, there is a sequence in which a little child is imprisoned in a chalk circle drawn by his friends who mock his psychological inability to break the suggested barrier. Finally an onlooker, the young Gurdjieff, releases the boy by rubbing out a part of the circle. The lesson is that of the lateral thinking problem: the solutions of the imagination are denied us by the categories of existing thought. Brook said of his attraction to the Gurdjieff autobiography that it was the closest he had ever been to a subject that was complete and offered a very dense, multi-sided view of reality.[3] The circle in the film may then be construed as being symbolic not merely of form, style or convention but of the supposedly self-evident need for consistency which grounds these constructs and negates their iridescence. Available form is various, yet, fearing versatility, we use for our projects only a very incomplete set of codes. Plunged in plenitude, we are shy of its fullness and tell truncated truths.

Brook's achievement in *Le Mahabharata* lies in the challenge he presents to modern theatre's inhibition regarding the fusion of forms. He brings to a text which, like the complete Shakespeare, can be at once light-hearted and profound, expansive and intense, an appropriately exhaustive medley of conventions – without for a moment, in nine hours of performance, offending the audience's supposed need for coherence.

*

In theory, the notion of an unbounded semiotics is subject to the charge that it is anarchic. A performance is supposedly accredited with the status of reality only if it utilizes some prearranged system of mutual understanding. If an audience makes the assumption that once a particular mode of expression is established it will be adhered to uniformly, then directors are bound by the force of that expectation in proportion to their need for acceptance. Moreover, what is gleaned from common practice is quickly accorded the status of a virtue: as Muriel Bradbrook writes, 'the value of such a system of Rules is that it imposes consistency, and only allows one set of conventions at a time'.[4] Professor Bradbrook does not defend her equation of consistency with excellence: the merits of uniformity are for her self-evident.

For Brook, however, consistency is one of those encrustations of past practice that progressive directors must seek to eliminate. Consistency, for Brook, is a concession to mediocrity, a medium only for directors who are incapable of handling the turmoil of a naturally dispersed reality and therefore make maimed truths the norm. 'I refuse to allow a consistent style to emerge', declares Brook, 'because I dread the idea.'[5] In *The Empty Space*, Brook's analysis of the inadequacy of unidimensional vision is structured around a generic opposition between 'Rough' and 'Holy' theatres. The Rough theatre has the theoretical advantage that it allows drama to break from artificial demands for unity in style; but in practice it invariably betrays the promise of this versatility as Roughness becomes solipsistic:

> The Rough Theatre has apparently no style, no conventions, no limitations – in practice, it has all three. . . . The defiant popular theatre man can be so down-to-earth that he forbids his material to fly.[6]

Equally, while Brook admires the immaculate austerity of the Holy theatre of Samuel Beckett and Jerzy Grotowski, he finds their work too severe: like electrical musical instruments, these theatres are sterile in proportion to their purity.

Working towards a solution in uncircumscribed signification, Brook suggests that the Rough theatre is most effective when allowed to participate in the effects of that which is least itself – the Holy theatre. Similarly, the Holy theatre needs to be humanized, made to share in the warm chaos of the Rough. Neither mode is 'Immediate' outside a dialectical synthesis with the other. Similarly,

> the mask of comedy and the mask of tragedy are, in fact, arbitrary masks. In real life, tragedy and comedy intertwine. . . . If theater is a reflection of real life, then there is a place for everything. . . . Our research in Paris is directed towards trying to find a new form that can carry the same spectrum.[7]

Theatre must reflect life's peculiar cohesiveness of significance. The difference between partial truths and reality is not that of degree, that which on an equation can be read off as the sum of discrete insights. Rather, it is categorical – for encyclopaedicity has access to the *correspondences* which constitute a vital aspect of the truth. If wholeness is a condition in which all human layers are connected, then one must devise some means of depicting life which allows one 'not to be so caught up with one level that you can't hear the other.'[8]

*

In 'Everything and Nothing' Jorge Luis Borges writes of Shakespeare that 'no one has ever been so many men as this man who, like the Egyptian Proteus, could exhaust all the guises of reality.'[9] Like Richard II who plays 'in one person many people', like the figure in his fifty-third sonnet who prevails 'in every blessed shape we know', Shakespeare is, for Brook as well, 'man simultaneously in all his aspects.'[10] Shakespeare's ability to make irreconcilable elements cohere has of course been much discussed: Brook's distinction between Rough and Holy resembles what Professor Muriel Bradbrook calls 'the high road and the low road to drama proper',[11] those mutually exclusive traditions which Shakespeare's 'strength alone was capable of welding . . . fully together.'[12] A large part of Professor Bradbrook's work on Shakespeare treats the singular manner in which the courtly and the common, the cosmic and the human, coalesce in this uniquely multi-faceted drama. Robert Weimann's analysis of the Elizabethan theatre also draws attention to its capacity to 'make a Clowne companion with a Kinge',[13] to produce 'A Lamentable Tragedy Mixed full of Pleasant Mirth.'[14] Both writers at once exult in this profusion of contiguous irreconcilables and despair of its ever recurring. There is a proud pessimism about the manner in which Professor Bradbrook, for example, periodically emphasizes the ephemerality of the conditions that made possible Shakespeare's enduring transcendence:

> the especial greatness of the plays written in the last decade of Elizabeth's reign and the first decade of James' was dependent on conditions essentially *transient* – upon the *momentary* fusion of the popular and learned traditions, the *temporary* interaction of two modes which were *not permanently* compatible with each other. . . . [A]rtificial and natural, they reflected a way of life and of speech which were likewise *of the hour.*[15]

It is no wonder that successive generations of dramatists, even if deeply attracted to the hybridization of forms, should have been wary of imitating so complex an alloy.

For Brook the overbearing presence of this immensely attractive but utterly inimitable mosaic has the unfortunate effect of making attempts at producing a similar work faintly ridiculous. Perhaps it is in part this protest against the relatively perfunctory truths of western drama since, and because of, Shakespeare that has driven Brook East: for it is said of the god Krishna that if one were able to look into his mouth, as his mother once did, one would 'see there all there is to be seen'. As generations of Indian authors have observed, what is in *The Mahabharata* is everywhere to be found, but what is not in *The Mahabharata* is nowhere to be found.[16]

*

The *Mahabharata*'s name for its author – Vyasa – derives from a Sanskrit verb meaning 'to fit together'. The name is an appropriate one for the creator-figure in a work which is clearly the product of several centuries of interpolation and encompasses treatments of mythology, history, philosophy, politics and law. Through this work of 220,000 lines, eight times the length of *The Iliad* and *The Odyssey* put together, fifteen times the length of the Bible, Brook and Carrière tread a conservative path. Nine years of research has produced nine hours of carefully integrated narrative which, although drastically short by the standards of the original, is not effectively poorer – for plenitude in the *Mahabharata* is a function less of length than of density. Just as selected vertical sections of a rock would, however reductive of the length of the deposit, nevertheless discover all the layers of its constituent sediments, so also Carrière's text, although simple, explores pastiche as a medium of wholeness.

Thus a single episode in the *Mahabharata* – such as that involving the battle between the Kauravas and the Pandavas on the one hand, and Arjuna's esoteric reluctance to fight on the other – accommodates Rough and Holy as abundantly as the contrast between Hamlet's indecisive soliloquies and the nature of the events leading to the tableau of corpses in *Hamlet*. Krishna's solution to Arjuna's dilemma involves making a distinction between the Guna-self and Purusha, Rough mortality and Holy perpetuity, the unity of which is the ideal product of discipline in Yoga. The war itself, though brutal, is steeped in the context of love: Arjuna and Drona, Yudhishthira and Bhishma, must kiss before killing; Arjuna and Duryodhana, enemies but cousins, must carry their dead uncle Bhishma off the field of battle together. The attempted rape of Dhraupadi is another example: Rough, yet, in the manner of its avoidance through divine intervention, infinitely Holy.

Dhraupadi's sari unfurls, like the anthropomorphism that runs through the epic, at the point of the intersection of divinity and mortality, fallibility and perfection. In aesthetic terms, each of these amalgams sets up an axis of complicity between divergent sets of correspondences which the narrative can exploit to shift planes of significance. Vyasa, the author-figure, for example, is born of the forces of the imagination; once accorded the status of a character in and by his work, he may invade the further fiction of his creations, advise them, exhort them, even sleep with them so as to beget a line of kings without whom his story cannot run its foretold course.

In theatrical terms such shifts between orders of being necessitate a means of presentation in which form is provisional, subject always to immediate revision. The triumph of the Brook production stems from its ability effortlessly to incarnate as many traditions of telling as the rich medley of the epic demands. Gods, demons and humans present themselves to the audience simultaneously as material beings and spiritual, as actors, as performers of a story and as physical theatrical presences. Boots and trousers mingle with ghagras and dhotis, shawls with skirted battle dresses. The audience is addressed directly and totally ignored, scenes are played realistically and in mime. And all the while the production, supposedly oblivious to the novelty of its un-prepared transitions, remains inscrutably silent on the subject of this tendency. If mutability gives the production its completeness, it is the intriguing nonchalance with which it withholds concessions to the audience's preconceptions that gives the performance its bite.

From the start the audience is engaged in a whirligig of conventions. Vyasa enters but, contrary to the expectations one has of a story-teller, ignores the audience completely. He speaks at first to a little boy who questions him as to the significance of his story. Only then does he begin to dictate to Ganesha, who is both his scribe and creation. Ganesha, idea realized, god made flesh, is identified by the mask he wears. Once the symbol is established, the mask loses its function and is therefore put aside. Vyasa then introduces his characters. So powerful is his invocation, and so engaged is Ganesha, that the characters actually appear, realized by the strength of Vyasa's description. Ganesha writes on, but minutes later, his role as scribe having been established, he is trans-formed into one of the characters he inscribes. Vyasa too, his introductions having been appropriated by one of the characters he has introduced, becomes a character in his epic and debates with his creations the morality of his sleeping with them. All this and we are just fifteen minutes into the epic.

Nine hours later, the hurly-burly of business on earth and stage completed, the exhausted mortals rest – the characters in heaven, the actors on the clay. Dhritirashtra and Gandhari, now immortal, recover their sight; Cieslak, now an actor, loses his blindness. Tiny oil lamps are set afloat in the river. Biscuits are passed around. Tired actors drink from the river, others sit in groups and talk, enemies having been reconciled in heaven. Silently we recount the happenings of the world, the stage. The use of realism: Dhritirashtra's blindness as played by Cieslak. The use of alienation: the little boy's questions; the speech to the audience after Dussasana's horribly real death asking them not to avert their eyes – this is only theatre. The use of suggestion: Ganga's veil is her child as she mimes its death; swinging beds make Virata's court decadent; a musical instrument is an elephant's trunk in a wedding procession. The use of symbolism: Krishna is identified by his flute, Ganga by water, Shiva through his stance. The use of metaphor and metonymy: a wooden board is a chariot in one scene, a wheel a chariot in another. And beneath all this a reality that is not the reality of realism, a reality more fundamental than that of convention, a reality in which this diversity is anchored: water is water, earth earth, fire fire.

If the spectrum of techniques evinced thus in performance excludes those of Grotowski, it is because the work on the self is not naturally amenable to explicit presentation. However, following the publication of Garry O'Connor's *The Mahabharata: Peter Brook's Epic in the Making*, we know that Grotowskian imperatives were very much a part of the invisible underpinning of the production. For Vittorio Mezzogiorno, playing Arjuna involved 'work on yourself, a research of yourself which goes in the direction of knowing yourself.'[17] Mallika Sarabhai acknowledges that, in keeping with Brook's affinity with the existential implications of the *via negativa*, 'He taught me to peel away my character like an onion and find the nothing that is there at the centre.'[18] In Grotowski, the result of this introspective orientation is literalism; in a rehearsal of *Le Mahabharata*, Maurice Benichou observes that 'You must not act Krishna, but be present.'[19]

In an effort to draw attention to the medley of styles in performance, Brook solves recurring problems of staging in strikingly various ways. As Vyasa's narrative engages the birth of the first generation of kings, their faces light up behind self-held screens. The birth of the Kauravas, on the other hand, begins realistically but quickly shifts to farce as required by the Sanskrit original: Gandhari's pregnancy is a swollen stomach but her grotesque labour reveals only a huge black ball which has to be cracked open with a stick before the children can emerge. The Pandavas, in contrast, are born to ceremony and the peal of bells, adult presences who gather solemnly by the river as Vyasa strives with chants and fire to invoke them. Karna too is born to smoke, bow in hand, immense, divine, the Sun.

At archery class, arrows fly as they disappear in the boys' bows through sleight of hand and appear in birds that drop out of the sky. At a tournament, the act is replayed and the trick revealed: as the arrows in the bows disappear, visible extras fling pierced birds into the air. In the deaths conducted by Krishna, arrows kill as he walks across the stage with them and gently pierces those they must find. If this, like Krishna's role in the attempted rape of Dhraupadi, is metaphor realized, the real finds a metaphor as showers of arrows fall across the smoke-lit upstage wall to backstage cries of death, alarm and music. Krishna's death reverses the convention of his agency: a hunter's arrow is carried across the stage by an actor and placed gently between the toes of the sleeping god.

*

The crucial question in all this is, how does Brook get away with this versatility? How is it that we accept this irregularity, we who normally expect a production to live within its means, to adhere consistently to the conventions we allow it to set up for itself? What is it that compels us to construe as reality this farrago, this clutter of styles more various than we are accustomed to seeing? Why is it that we allow this production to snatch from us the prerogative to disbelieve, this production which concedes so little to our expectations, premisses on the basis of which, after all, *we* must grant or deny reality?

The Elizabethan model suggests little. In *Themes and Conventions of Elizabethan Tragedy*, Professor Bradbrook shows that Shakespeare's audience did not rely upon continuities of form and narrative to 'let belief take hold'. The difficulties we have in accepting anomalies just did not exist for them. On the contrary, medleys delighted their audiences 'by an unpredictable mixture of predictable items that belonged together because they had been seen together before.'[20] Robert Weimann agrees with Professor Bradbrook:

It was a multiple unity based on contradictions, and as such allowed the dramatist a flexible frame of reference that was more complex and more vital to the experience of living and feeling within the social organism than the achievement of any other theatre before or since.[21]

142

As the success of Shakespeare and his contemporaries was contingent upon factors not present today, the analysis of their theatre does not explain how Brook can get away with being so effortlessly unorthodox.

Even a study of the influence of Brecht does not help: *Le Mahabharata* not only employs a larger number of styles than Brecht had use for but invests each with an autonomous integrity as Brecht was unable to do. In Brecht the linear relationship between emotion and alienation precludes the sheer abundance of styles that characterizes Brook's work in *Le Mahabharata*. Whereas Brecht's work is largely the product of a two-point opposition (the deployment and disfigurement of emotion), *Le Mahabharata* enjoys a plethora of conventions and techniques. Thus Brechtian flexibility too cannot explain Brook's encyclopaedicity.

*

There is a curious irony in current attitudes to heterogeneity in the theatre whereby one who would question its use in a contemporary work would nevertheless revel in its operation in Shakespeare. We accept Shakespeare because his achievement is a given condition of his appeal, his work a manifest denial of the objections we must nevertheless continue to level at works as yet unborn, as yet unproven, as yet unable self-evidently to refute our claims.

A consequence of this curious double-standard is, in Brook, a hugely ambitious optimism based on his faith in the coercive capacity of skill. Theatre may through inventiveness compel admiration – and through admiration belief. Just as Shakespeare's credibility is a function of his prowess, so also for Brook adroitness is seductive: it makes the authenticity of stage action unquestionable. In *Le Mahabharata*, Ganga's children drown because Mirelle Maalouf is a skilled mime artist; Arjuna's chariot flies across the battlefield because of the deftness with which Maurice Benichou as Krishna handles a wooden wheel.

The consistent use of certain styles would erode this potential – for conventions dictate foreseeable solutions on the basis of past agreements. While this allows directors to get on with *what* they are saying, it denies their productions some of the interest of *how* it is being said. By constantly switching conventions, Brook draws attention far more vividly to the 'how' of his production. By placing real and artificial components in striking juxtaposition, Brook makes evident the limits of each in isolation. Aware of these limitations we are better able to appreciate the choice of a particular mode of representation in a particular scene; more willing, that is to say, to grant inconsistency licence on the basis of its apparent necessity.

Where there is skill, there need be no consistency; and where inconsistency has the authority of truth, drama has an existential vitality unmatched by the predictability of convention-bound reality. 'From moment to moment the new medley convinces',[22] writes Professor Bradbrook of Shakespeare's art, and the same can be said of *Le Mahabharata*. With every new scene, the performance risks discredit, throws the truths it has built into jeopardy. With every new display of directorial flamboyance, of invention and ingenuity, our belief is re-charged and the authority of the production reaffirmed. In *The Empty Space*, Brook writes of the actor that he must be 'compelled, by the honesty of his search, endlessly to shed and start again. . . . [T]his is the only way a part, instead of being built, can be born.'[23] In keeping with the sentiment, in keeping with the tenor of Brook's career as a whole, *Le Mahabharata* is prepared to discard truth before truth can lose its vitality. Brook once said of Shakespeare that his plays were not inter-pretations of reality but 'the thing itself.'[24] *Le Mahabharata* produces a similar conviction – for while art usually distils the unbounded in-coherence of life into a form, this drama brings to the discipline of form the abundance and contrariety of life. The distinction is not sentimen-tal: it stems from having participated, for nine hours, in the creation of life.

NOTES

INTRODUCTION

1 Konstantin Stanislavsky, *My Life in Art*, translated by J. J. Robbins (London, 1980), p. 214.
2 J. C. Trewin, *Peter Brook: A Biography* (London, 1971), p. 146.
3 Kenneth Tynan, 'Director as Misanthropist: On the Moral Neutrality of Peter Brook', *Theatre Quarterly*, vol. 7, no. 25 (1977), p. 22.

1 TO BE

1 Peter Brook *et al.*, *US: The Book of the Royal Shakespeare Theatre Production* (London, 1968), p. 29.
2 Konstantin Stanislavsky, *Stanislavsky's Legacy*, translated by Elizabeth Reynolds Hapgood (London, 1968), p. 11.
3 Konstantin Stanislavsky, *My Life in Art*, translated by J.J. Robbins (London, 1962), p. 24.
4 ibid.
5 Konstantin Stanislavsky, *An Actor Prepares*, translated by Elizabeth Reynolds Hapgood (London, 1967), pp. 46–9.
6 *Stanislavsky's Legacy*, pp. 188–9.
7 *An Actor Prepares*, p. 49.
8 ibid.
9 Konstantin Stanislavsky, *Stanislavsky on the Art of the Stage*, translated by David Magarshack (London, 1967), p. 193.
10 ibid.
11 Quoted in Christine Edwards, *The Stanislavsky Heritage* (London, 1966), p. 49.
12 Vasily Osipovich Toporkov, *Stanislavsky in Rehearsal: The Final Years*, translated by Christine Edwards (New York, 1979), p. 156.
13 Quoted in ibid., p. 124.
14 David Magarshack, *Stanislavsky: A Life* (London, 1950), p. 305
15 Quoted in *The Stanislavsky Heritage*, p. 49.
16 ibid.
17 Nikolai M. Gorchakov, *Stanislavsky Directs*, translated by Miriam Goldina (New York, 1954), p. 38.

18 Konstantin Stanislavsky, *Creating a Role*, translated by Elizabeth Reynolds Hapgood (London, 1983), p. 5.
19 *Creating a Role*, p. 10.
20 ibid., p. 42.
21 Quoted in *Stanislavsky Directs*, p. 22.
22 Quoted in *Stanislavsky in Rehearsal: The Final Years*, p. 44.
23 ibid., pp. 95–6.
24 ibid., pp. 126–7.
25 *Stanislavsky Directs*, p. 370
26 *Stanislavsky in Rehearsal: The Final Years*, p. 215.
27 *My Life in Art*, p. 245.
28 *An Actor Prepares*, p. 21.
29 ibid., p. 22.
30 ibid., p. 229.
31 *My Life in Art*, p. 405.
32 ibid., p. 478.
33 Quoted in *The Stanislavsky Heritage*, p. 49.
34 Quoted in Eugene Herrigel, *Zen in the Art of Archery* (London, 1953), p. 7.
35 *An Actor Prepares*, p. 283.
36 *Stanislavsky's Legacy*, p. 184. The article was written for *Encyclopaedia Brittanica* in the late 1920s. All references are to the reprinted version in *Stanislavsky's Legacy*.
37 *An Actor Prepares*, p. 21.
38 Quoted in Norman Marshall, *The Producer and the Play* (London, 1975), p. 96.
39 Quoted in *The Stanislavsky Heritage*, p. 82.
40 *My Life in Art*, p. 165.
41 Quoted in *Stanislavsky: A Life*, p. 46.
42 Konstantin Stanislavsky, *Building a Character*, translated by Elizabeth Reynolds Hapgood (London, 1968), pp. 16–17.
43 ibid., p. 19.
44 ibid., p. 30.
45 Nikolai Gorchakov, *The Theatre in Soviet Russia*, translated by E. Lehrman (New York, 1972), p. 362.
46 *Creating a Role*, p. 150.
47 Quoted in *Stanislavsky in Rehearsal: The Final Years*, pp. 160–2.
48 *Creating a Role*, p. 86.
49 *Stanislavsky Directs*, pp. 297–8.
50 *Stanislavsky: A Life*, p. 58.
51 *An Actor Prepares*, p. 27.
52 ibid., p. 44.
53 ibid., p. 40.
54 *My Life in Art*, p. 333.
55 ibid., p. 165.
56 Quoted in *Stanislavsky in Rehearsal: The Final Years*, p. 159.
57 ibid., p. 161.
58 ibid., p. 171.
59 *Creating a Role*, p. 213.
60 ibid., p. 228.
61 ibid., p. 245.

62 ibid., p. 201.
63 ibid., p. 209.
64 ibid., p. 153.
65 ibid., p. 224.
66 ibid., p. 241.
67 *Stanislavsky in Rehearsal: The Final Years*, p. 163.
68 *My Life in Art*, p. 483.
69 Charles Marowitz in 'Lear Log', in Charles Marowitz and Simon Trussler (eds), *Theatre at Work* (London, 1967), p. 141.
70 ibid.
71 ibid., p. 144.
72 Quoted in Glen Loney (ed.), *Peter Brook's Production of Shakespeare's A Midsummer Night's Dream: Authorised Acting Edition* (New York, 1974), p. 56. Hereafter merely 'Loney'.
73 'Lear Log', p. 135.
74 ibid., p. 133.
75 ibid., p. 134.
76 Jan Kott, '*King Lear*; or *Endgame*', in Jan Kott, *Shakespeare: Our Contemporary* (London, 1978).
77 'Lear Log', p. 133.
78 ibid., p. 135.
79 ibid.
80 ibid., p. 136.
81 ibid.
82 ibid.
83 ibid.
84 ibid., p. 144. My italics.
85 ibid.
86 ibid., p. 144.
87 ibid., p. 143.
88 ibid., p. 135.
89 ibid., p. 134.
90 ibid.
91 Quoted in *The Stanislavsky Heritage*, p. 47.
92 'Lear Log', p. 139.
93 Yoshi Oida, 'Shinto Training of the Actor', in Dartington *Theatre Papers*, vol. 3, no. 3 (1979), p. 12.
94 William James, 'What is an Emotion?', in *Mind*, vol. IX (1884); repr. in Dartington *Theatre Papers*, vol. 1, no. 5 (1977), p. 2.
95 Quoted in Eileen Blumenthal, *Joseph Chaikin* (London, 1984), p. 73. See also ibid., p. 83.
96 David Selbourne, *The Making of A Midsummer Night's Dream* (London, 1982), p. 31.
97 ibid., p. 85.
98 ibid., p. 175.
99 Peter Ansorge, 'Director in Interview', in *Plays and Players*, vol. 18, no. 1 (1970), p. 18.
100 Michael Crawford and John Kane, 'The Actor as Acrobat', in *Plays and Players*, vol. 18, no. 11 (1971), p. 15.
101 Loney, p. 26.

102 ibid.
103 Meyerhold, quoted in Edward Braun, *The Theatre of Meyerhold* (London, 1986), p. 166.
104 *Stanislavsky on the Art of the Stage*, p. 161.
105 *An Actor Prepares*, p. 113.
106 *The Making of A Midsummer Night's Dream*, p. 71.
107 ibid., p. 181.
108 ibid., p. 21.
109 Quoted in ibid., p. 11.
110 ibid., p. 9.
111 ibid., p. 55.
112 Loney, p. 53.
113 *Joseph Chaikin*, p. 83.
114 Quoted in *The Making of A Midsummer Night's Dream*, p. 11.
115 ibid., p. 45.
116 Quoted in J. C. Trewin, *Peter Brook: A Biography* (London, 1971), p. 180.
117 *The Making of A Midsummer Night's Dream*, p. 11.
118 ibid., p. 75.
119 Peter Brook, *The Empty Space* (London, 1968), p. 15.
120 *The Making of A Midsummer Night's Dream*, p. 99.
121 ibid., pp. 11–13.
122 ibid., p. 65.
123 ibid., p. 201.
124 ibid., p. 109.
125 *My Life in Art*, p. 262.
126 *The Making of A Midsummer Night's Dream*, p. 269.
127 ibid,, p. 171.
128 ibid., p. 51.
129 *An Actor Prepares*, p. 29.
130 Quoted in *The Making of A Midsummer Night's Dream*, p. 101.
131 ibid., p. 261.
132 ibid., pp. 109–11.
133 *Peter Brook: A Biography*, p. 184.
134 *The Empty Space*, p. 19.
135 ibid., p. 131.

2 TO BE AND NOT TO BE

1 Bertolt Brecht, 'In Praise of Doubt', in *Poems, 1913–1956* (London, 1976), p. 334.
2 Peter Brook, *The Empty Space* (London, 1968), p. 80.
3 Bertolt Brecht, 'Notes on Stanislavsky', *Tulane Drama Review*, vol. 9, no. 2 (Winter 1964), p. 155.
4 Bertolt Brecht, *Brecht on Theatre* (London, 1984), p. 78.
5 'Notes on Stanislavsky', p. 156.
6 ibid., p. 157.
7 Bertolt Brecht in a note on *Mother Courage*, in *Collected Plays*, vol. 5, no. 2, translated by John Willett (London, 1980), p. 92.
8 *Brecht on Theatre*, p. 237.

9 ibid., pp. 143–4.
10 Bertolt Brecht, *The Good Person of Szechwan, Collected Plays*, vol. 6, part 1, translated by John Willett (London, 1985), p. 109.
11 *Brecht on Theatre*, p. 201.
12 John Willett, *The Theatre of Bertolt Brecht* (London, 1959), p. 56.
13 Bertolt Brecht, 'On The Experimental Theatre', *Tulane Drama Review*, vol. 6, no. 1 (September 1961), p. 9.
14 *Brecht on Theatre*, p. 248.
15 ibid., p. 125. My italics.
16 ibid., p. 44. My italics.
17 ibid., p. 203. See also ibid., p. 85.
18 'Notes on Stanislavsky', p. 156. My italics.
19 *Brecht on Theatre*, p. 194.
20 ibid., p. 45.
21 ibid., p. 138.
22 ibid., pp. 137–8. My italics.
23 *The Theatre of Bertolt Brecht*, p. 175.
24 'Notes on Stanislavsky', p. 163.
25 *Brecht on Theatre*, p. 139.
26 ibid., p. 15.
27 ibid., p. 109.
28 Bertolt Brecht, *Collected Plays*, vol. 2, no. 2, translated by Ralph Manheim and John Willett (London, 1979), p. 102.
29 'Notes on Stanislavsky', p. 159.
30 *Brecht on Theatre*, p. 277.
31 'Notes on Stanislavsky', p. 166.
32 ibid., p. 159.
33 David Richard Jones, *Great Directors at Work* (London, 1986), p. 89.
34 Bertolt Brecht, 'On *The Caucasian Chalk Circle*', *The Drama Review*, vol. 12, no. 1 (Fall 1967), p. 91.
35 ibid., p. 92.
36 *Collected Plays*, vol. 5, no. 2, p. 93.
37 'On *The Caucasian Chalk Circle*', p. 92.
38 *Brecht on Theatre*, p. 244.
39 ibid., p. 241.
40 ibid., p. 200.
41 Quoted by Margaret Eddershaw, 'Acting Methods: Brecht and Stanislavsky', in Graham Bartram (ed.), *Brecht in Perspective* (London, 1982).
42 Quoted in Ronald Hayman, *Brecht: A Biography* (London, 1983), p. 344.
43 Carl Weber, 'Brecht as Director', *The Drama Review*, vol. 12, no. 1 (Fall 1967), p. 103.
44 Bertolt Brecht, *The Resistible Rise of Arturo Ui*, translated by Ralph Mannheim, *Collected Plays*, vol. 6, part 2 (London, 1981), p. 78.
45 'On *The Caucasian Chalk Circle*', p. 95.
46 Bertolt Brecht, quoted in Ronald Hayman, *Techniques of Acting* (London, 1969), p. 55.
47 *Brecht on Theatre*, p. 106.
48 ibid., p. 70.
49 'Notes on Stanislavsky', p. 164.

50 *Brecht on Theatre*, p. 231.
51 ibid., p. 126.
52 *Complete Plays*, vol. 2, Part 2, p. 105.
53 *Brecht on Theatre*, p. 54.
54 *The Theatre of Bertolt Brecht*, p. 178.
55 Bertolt Brecht, *Diaries 1920–1923*, edited by Herta Ramthun, translated and annotated by John Willett (London, 1979), p. 32.
56 Quoted in Martin Esslin, *Brecht: A Choice of Evils* (London, 1959), p. 123. My italics.
57 Bertolt Brecht, 'Estranging Shakespeare', *The Drama Review*, vol. 12, no. 1 (Fall 1967), p. 108.
58 *Brecht: A Choice of Evils*, p. 123.
59 Bertolt Brecht, *The Caucasian Chalk Circle*, translated by James and Tania Stern with W.H. Auden, *Collected Plays*, vol. 7 (London, 1976), p. 165.
60 *Brecht: A Choice of Evils*, p. 123.
61 'Notes on Stanislavsky', p. 166. My italics.
62 *Brecht on Theatre*, p. 129.
63 ibid., p. 137. My italics.
64 'Acting Methods: Brecht and Stanislavsky', p. 138.
65 Peter Brook, *The Shifting Point* (New York, 1987), pp. 26–7.
66 ibid., p. 42.
67 ibid., pp. 42–3.
68 Bertolt Brecht, *The Mother*, translated by Steve Gooch (London, 1978), p. 38.
69 *The Theatre of Bertolt Brecht*, p. 118.
70 *The Shifting Point*, p. 192.
71 Bertolt Brecht, *In the Jungle of the Cities*, *Collected Plays*, vol. 1 (London, 1970), p. 118.
72 Peter Brook in an interview with Don Ranvaud, 'Brook's Remarkable Men', *Framework*, issue 9 (Winter 1978–9), p. 32.
73 Peter Brook quoted in J.C. Trewin, *Peter Brook: A Biography* (London, 1971), p. 149.
74 *The Empty Space*, p. 81.
75 *Peter Brook: A Biography*, p. 153.
76 *The Shifting Point*, p. 60.
77 *Brecht on Theatre*, p. 15.
78 *Collected Plays*, vol. 5, no. 1, p. 29.
79 ibid.
80 Bertolt Brecht quoted in John Fuegi, *Bertolt Brecht: Chaos, According to Plan* (Cambridge, 1987), p. 127.
81 Bertolt Brecht, 'Theatre for Learning', *Tulane Drama Review*, vol. 6, no. 1 (September 1961), p. 25.
82 Irving Wardle quoted in *Peter Brook: A Biography*, p. 159. My italics.
83 *The Shifting Point*, p. 54.
84 Peter Brook in Frank Cox, 'Interview with Peter Brook', *Plays and Players*, vol. 15, no. 7 (April 1968), p. 50.
85 *The Shifting Point*, p. 54.
86 ibid., p. 107.
87 ibid., p. 95.
88 ibid., p. 62. My italics.

89 ibid.
90 ibid., p. 63.
91 ibid.
92 Peter Brook *et al.*, *The Book of US* (London, 1968), p. 26.
93 ibid., p. 17.
94 ibid., p. 29.
95 ibid., p. 135.
96 ibid., p. 14.
97 ibid., p. 16.
98 ibid., pp. 19–21.
99 ibid., p. 21.
100 ibid.
101 ibid., p. 27.
102 ibid., p. 53.
103 ibid., p. 15.
104 ibid., pp. 28–9.
105 ibid., pp. 137–8.
106 ibid., p. 14.
107 ibid., p. 139.
108 ibid.
109 ibid., pp. 139–40.
110 ibid., p. 140.
111 ibid.
112 ibid., p. 22.
113 ibid.
114 ibid.
115 ibid., p. 28.
116 ibid., p. 135.
117 ibid., pp. 29–30.
118 ibid., p. 150.

3 LET BE

1 A. Lechika in Zbigniew Osinski, *Grotowski and His Laboratory*, translated by Lillian Vale and Robert Findlay (New York, 1986), p. 130.
2 Peter Brook in Margaret Croyden, *The Centre: A Narrative* (New York, 1980), p. 1.
3 Jerzy Grotowski in Zbigniew Osinski and Tadeusz Burzynski, *Grotowski's Laboratory* (Warsaw, 1979), p. 55.
4 Peter Brook in A.C.H. Smith, *Orghast at Persepolis* (New York, 1972), p. 52.
5 *Grotowski's Laboratory*, p. 25. Osinski's view is not untypical. See also Eugenio Barba, 'Theatre Laboratory 13 Rzedow', *Tulane Drama Review*, vol. 9, no. 3 (Spring 1965), p. 157; and Jan Blonski, 'Grotowski and his Laboratory Theatre', *Dialog* (1970), p. 147.
6 Jerzy Grotowski, *Towards a Poor Theatre* (London, 1969), p. 213.
7 Wojciech Dzieduszycki quoted in *Grotowski and his Laboratory*, pp. 86–7.
8 Jennifer Kumeiga, *The Theatre of Grotowski* (London, 1987), p. 128.

NOTES

9 Ludwik Flaszen, 'From the Point of Emptiness', *Canadian Theatre Review* (Summer 1981), p. 10.

10 *Grotowski and his Laboratory*, pp. 19–20.

11 *Towards a Poor Theatre*, p. 167.

12 'Grotowski and his Laboratory Theatre', p. 145.

13 Jerzy Grotowski quoted in *The Theatre of Grotowski*, p. 227.

14 *Towards a Poor Theatre*, p. 93.

15 ibid., p. 91.

16 ibid.

17 ibid.

18 ibid.

19 ibid., p. 23.

20 *Grotowski and his Laboratory*, p. 130.

21 Patrick Sciaratta, 'The Polish Connection: An Encounter with Grotowski and the Theater Laboratorium', *Exchange* (Fall 1976), p. 102.

22 ibid., p. 101.

23 ibid.

24 *Towards a Poor Theatre*, p. 21.

25 ibid., p. 96.

26 R.D. Laing, *Self and Others* (London, 1969), p. 82.

27 Jerzy Grotowski in *Grotowski's Laboratory*, p. 109.

28 *Self and Others*, p. 83.

29 Jerzy Growtowski in *The Theatre of Grotowski*, p. 225.

30 Jerzy Grotowski, 'Holiday', *Theatre Quarterly*, vol. 3 no. 10 (April–June 1973), p. 22. Quotations from 'Holiday' are taken from both *The Drama Review* vol. 17, no. 2 (June 1973) and *Theatre Quarterly*, each of which covers different sections of the original talk given by Grotowski in New York. The sources of all 'Holiday' quotations below will be distinguished by 'TDR' or 'TQ' in brackets following the 'Holiday' citation.

31 *Towards a Poor Theatre*, p. 206.

32 Anthony Abeson, 'The Many Sides of Silence', *Village Voice* (9 October 1969), p. 59.

33 *Towards a Poor Theatre*, p. 170.

34 ibid., pp. 111–12.

35 ibid., p. 189. See also ibid., pp. 110–11.

36 *Grotowski and His Laboratory*, p. 104.

37 *Towards a Poor Theatre*, p. 57.

38 'Holiday', (TDR), p. 119.

39 'The Polish Connection', p. 102.

40 Jerzy Grotowski in *The Theatre of Grotowski*, p. 228.

41 ibid., p. 225. See also Eric Forsyth, 'Conversation with Ludwik Flaszen', *Educational Theatre Journal*, vol. 30, no. 3 (October 1978), pp. 312–13.

42 Tadeusz Burzynski, 'Grotowski's Laboratory – 1977/78 Season', *The Theatre in Poland*, vol. 20, no. 5 (1978), p. 19.

43 *Self and Others*, p. 127.

44 Jerzy Grotowski in Maggie Topkis, 'A Ritual Called Conference', *Theatre International*, nos. 3–4 (1981), p. 47.

45 *Towards a Poor Theatre*, p. 37. My italics.

46 ibid., p. 57. My italics.

47 Jerzy Grotowski in *The Theatre of Grotowski*, p. 151.

48 Jerzy Grotowski in Leszek Kolankiewicz, 'On the Road to Active Culture', unpublished document translated by Boleslaw Taborski (Wroclaw, 1978), p. 13.
49 Jerzy Grotowski in *Grotowski and his Laboratory*, p. 123.
50 Ludwik Flaszen, quoted in *Grotowski's Laboratory*, p. 59.
51 'Holiday' (*TDR*), p. 120.
52 *Towards a Poor Theatre*, p. 34.
53 'Theatre Laboratory 13 Rzedow', p. 164.
54 Eugenio Barba and Ludwik Flaszen, 'A Theatre of Magic and Sacrilege', *Tulane Drama Review*, vol. 9, no. 3 (Spring 1965), p. 173.
55 Raymonde Temkine, *Grotowski*, translated by Alex Szogyi (New York, 1972), p. 74. My italics.
56 *The Theatre of Grotowski*, p. 122.
57 *Towards a Poor Theatre*, p. 107.
58 ibid., p. 106.
59 ibid., p. 134.
60 ibid.
61 Richard Schechner and Theodore Hoffman, 'An Interview with Grotowski', *The Drama Review*, vol. 13, no. 1 (Fall 1968), p. 39.
62 'Theatre Laboratory 13 Rzedow', p. 162.
63 *Towards a Poor Theatre*, p. 105.
64 ibid., p. 34.
65 ibid., p. 41.
66 Irving Wardle, 'Grotowski the Evangelist', *The Times*, (4 October 1969).
67 Stefan Brecht (ed.), 'On Grotowski: A Series of Critiques', *The Drama Review*, vol. 14, no. 2 (Winter 1970), p. 195.
68 Jerzy Grotowski in *The Theatre of Grotowski*, p. 113.
69 'Holiday' (*TQ*), p. 23.
70 *Towards a Poor Theatre*, p. 101.
71 *Grotowski*, p. 102.
72 Jerzy Grotowski, 'On the Theatre of Sources', *The Theatre in Poland*, vol. 21, no. 11 (November 1979), p. 24.
73 *Grotowski's Laboratory*, p. 14.
74 *Towards a Poor Theatre*, pp. 151–2.
75 'The Many Sides of Silence', p. 48.
76 ibid., p. 59.
77 *Towards a Poor Theatre*, p. 36.
78 ibid., p. 114.
79 ibid., pp. 56–7.
80 Joseph Kelera, 'Grotowski in Free Indirect Speech', *The Theatre in Poland*, vol. 16, no. 10 (October 1974), p. 10.
81 'Holiday' (*TQ*), p. 24.
82 Jerzy Grotowski, 'We Simply Look for Those Close to Us', *International Theatre Information* (Winter 1975), p. 8.
83 *Towards a Poor Theatre*, p. 47.
84 'Grotowski in Free Indirect Speech', p. 12.
85 *The Theatre of Grotowski*, p. 135.
86 Jan Blonski, 'Holiday or Holiness', translated by Boleslaw Taborski, *Gambit*, vol. 9, no. 33 (1979), p. 68.
87 *The Theatre of Grotowski*, p. 179.

88 *Towards a Poor Theatre*, p. 32.
89 ibid., p. 143.
90 ibid., p. 19.
91 ibid., p. 15.
92 Jerzy Grotowski in *Grotowski and his Laboratory*, pp. 53–4.
93 'Holiday' (*TDR*), p. 129.
94 'An Interview with Grotowski', pp. 40–1.
95 'Holiday' (*TDR*), p. 120.
96 Leszek Kolankiewicz, 'What's Up at Grotowski's?', *The Theatre in Poland*, nos. 5–6 (1977), p. 24.
97 Jerzy Grotowski in Richard Fowler, 'The Four Theatres of Jerzy Grotowski: An Introductory Assessment', *New Theatre Quarterly*, vol. 1, no. 2 (May 1985), p. 176.
98 'Holiday' (*TDR*), p. 133.
99 'On the Road to Active Culture', p. 7.
100 *Grotowski and his Laboratory*, pp. 170–1.
101 Dan Ronen, 'A Workshop with Ryszard Cieslak', *The Drama Review*, vol. 22, no. 4 (December 1978), pp. 73–4.
102 ibid., p. 74.
103 'On the Road to Active Culture', pp. 28–9.
104 'Grotowski in Free Indirect Speech', p. 10.
105 Jerzy Grotowski, 'The Art of the Beginner', *International Theatre Information* (Spring–Summer 1978), p. 9.
106 'We Simply Look for Those Close to Us', p. 7.
107 Jerzy Grotowski in 'On the Road to Active Culture', p. 96.
108 'Holiday' (*TDR*), p. 131.
109 'The Art of the Beginner', p. 10.
110 'The Four Theatres of Jerzy Grotowski', p. 178.
111 *Grotowski's Laboratory*, p. 113
112 'A Theatre of Magic and Sacrilege', p. 174.
113 Farid Ud-din Attar, *The Conference of the Birds*, translated from de Tassey's French version of *Mantiq Uttair* (London, 1978), p. 92. Hereafter 'Attar' to distinguish the work from John Heilpern's account of Brook's work in Africa and Brook and Carrière's drama, which both carry the same title.
114 ibid., p. 115.
115 Farid Ud-din Attar in John Heilpern, *Conference of the Birds* (London, 1977), p. 41. Hereafter 'Heilpern'.
116 Attar, p. 5.
117 ibid., p. 3.
118 ibid., p. 132.
119 ibid., p. 5.
120 ibid., p. 72.
121 ibid., p. 33. See also ibid., p. 51 and p. 125.
122 *Towards a Poor Theatre*, p. 38.
123 'Holiday' (*TDR*), p. 132.
124 Attar, p. 133.
125 ibid., p. 80.
126 Heilpern, p. 49.
127 ibid., p. 251.
128 ibid., p. 275.

129 ibid., p. 295.
130 ibid., p. 238.
131 *Orghast at Persepolis*, p. 76.
132 Michael Gibson, 'Brook's Africa', *The Drama Review*, vol. 17, no. 3 (September 1973), p. 44. My italics.
133 Heilpern, p. 75.
134 ibid., p. 236.
135 ibid., p. 50.
136 *Orghast at Persepolis*, p. 141.
137 Heilpern, pp. 199–200.
138 Peter Brook in J. C. Trewin, *Peter Brook: A Biography* (London, 1971), p. 112.
139 Peter Brook quoted in Albert Hunt, '*The Ik*: A review', in David Williams (ed.), *Peter Brook: A Theatrical Casebook* (London, 1988), p. 266.
140 Peter Brook, *The Shifting Point* (New York, 1987), p. 232.
141 Peter Brook in *Peter Brook: A Theatrical Casebook*, p. 228.
142 Heilpern, p. 28.
143 ibid., p. 169.
144 ibid., p. 87.
145 Heilpern, pp. 26–7.
146 'On the Road to Active Culture', p. 13.
147 Heilpern, p. 61.
148 *The Shifting Point*, p. 238.
149 *Peter Brook: A Theatrical Casebook*, p. 376.
150 ibid., p. 299.
151 *Orghast at Persepolis*, p. 153.
152 *The Shifting Point*, p. 41. See also *The Empty Space*, p. 58 and p. 97.
153 Peter Brook and Jean-Claude Carrière, *The Conference of the Birds* (Chicago, 1982), 4th of 12 unnumbered pages. Hereafter 'Carrière and Brook'.
154 *The Shifting Point*, p. 218. My italics.
155 ibid., p. 232.
156 Heilpern, p. 137.
157 ibid., p. 249. My italics.
158 *Peter Brook: A Theatrical Casebook*, p. 237.
159 Michèle Collison, 'With Brook in Paris: Preparing for an Empty Space', *Canadian Theatre Review* (Fall 1979), p. 77. See also *Orghast at Persepolis*, p. 87, *Peter Brook: A Biography*, p. 181 and Peter Brook, 'Search for a Hunger', *Encore*, vol. 8, no. 4 (July–August 1961), p. 21.
160 Peter Brook in Heilpern, p. 93.
161 *Orghast at Persepolis*, p. 129.
162 ibid., p. 195.
163 'With Brook in Paris: Preparations for an Empty Space', p. 81.
164 *The Empty Space*, p. 127.
165 *The Shifting Point*, p. 231.
166 ibid., p. 219.
167 ibid.
168 Brook in *Orghast at Persepolis*, p. 251.
169 Brook in ibid., p. 130.
170 Heilpern, p. 130.
171 ibid., p. 139.

NOTES

172 ibid., p. 30.
173 Brook in *Orghast at Persepolis*, p. 261.
174 Georges Banu, 'Peter Brook's Six Days', *New Theatre Quarterly*, vol. 3, no. 10 (May 1987), p. 106.
175 Heilpern, p. 229.
176 ibid., p. 295.
177 *Orghast at Persepolis*, p. 251.
178 Brook in ibid., pp. 256–7.
179 ibid., p. 130.
180 *The Empty Space*, p. 130.
181 Brook in *Orghast at Persepolis*, p. 130.
182 ibid., p. 107.
183 ibid., p. 58.
184 Heilpern, p. 147.
185 *The Shifting Point*, pp. 7–8.
186 *The Empty Space*, p. 66.
187 *Orghast at Persepolis*, p. 58.
188 'Peter Brook's Six Days', p. 100.
189 *The Empty Space*, p. 47.
190 Heilpern, p. 297.
191 ibid., p. 171.
192 *The Shifting Point*, p. 72.
193 Brook in *Orghast at Persepolis*, p. 34.
194 Heilpern, p. 219. See also ibid., p. 63, p. 67, p. 96.
195 *The Shifting Point*, pp. 118–20.
196 Heilpern, p. 114.
197 *Orghast at Persepolis*, p. 205. See also Jean Richards, 'An Interview with Peter Brook at the Fifth Annual Festival of Arts, Persepolis, Iran', *Drama and Theatre*, vol. 10, no. 1 (Fall 1971), p. 5.
198 *The Shifting Point*, p. 40.
199 ibid., p. 79.
200 Malik Bowens in *Peter Brook: A Theatrical Casebook*, p. 243.
201 *The Empty Space*, p. 149.
202 ibid., p. 150.
203 Brook in *Peter Brook: A Theatrical Casebook*, p. 310.
204 *The Shifting Point*, p. 129. See also Garry O'Connor, *The Mahabharata: Peter Brook's Epic in the Making* (London, 1989), p. 68.
205 Svetasvatra Upanishad in Juan Mascaro (ed. and trans.), *The Upanishads* (London, 1965), p. 83.
206 *The Shifting Point*, p. 239.
207 *Orghast at Persepolis*, p. 19.
208 ibid., p. 52.
209 ibid., p. 33.
210 Charles Marowitz in *Peter Brook: A Theatrical Casebook*, p. 40.
211 See *Peter Brook: A Theatrical Casebook*, p. 340.
212 ibid., p. 348. See also *The Empty Space*, p. 128.
213 Heilpern, p. 56.
214 *Orghast at Persepolis*, p. 73. See also *The Empty Space*, pp. 56–7 and *Peter Brook: A Theatrical Casebook*, p. 343.
215 Heilpern, pp. 123–4.

216 'Brook's Africa', p. 47.
217 *The Empty Space*, p. 25.
218 Brook in 'Brook's Africa', p. 46.
219 *Peter Brook: A Theatrical Casebook*, p. 368.
220 Heilpern, p. 159.
221 David Selbourne, *The Making of A Midsummer Night's Dream* (London, 1982), p. 41.
222 Heilpern, p. 17.
223 *Orghast at Persepolis*, p. 260.
224 *The Shifting Point*, p. 111.
225 *The Empty Space*, p. 63.
226 *Orghast at Persepolis*, p. 254.
227 ibid., p. 255.
228 *The Empty Space*, p. 150.
229 'Brook's Africa', p. 47.
230 *The Empty Space*, p. 144.
231 *The Shifting Point*, p. 190.
232 ibid., pp. 126–8.
233 Brook in 'Brook's Africa', p. 47.
234 *The Empty Space*, p. 68
235 ibid., p. 78.
236 ibid., p. 157.
237 Brook in *Orghast at Persepolis*, p. 111.
238 Heilpern, p. 142.
239 *The Shifting Point*, p. 242.
240 ibid., p. 86.
241 ibid., p. 154.
242 ibid., p. 125.
243 ibid., p. 156.

EPILOGUE

1 Brook in James Moore, 'A Subject that is Complete', *Arts Guardian* (20 July 1976).
2 Grigori Kozintsev, *King Lear: The Space of Tragedy*, translated by Mary Mackintosh (London, 1977), pp. 240–1.
3 Brook in 'A Subject that is Complete'.
4 Muriel Bradbrook, *Themes and Conventions of Elizabethan Tragedy* (Cambridge, 1960), p. 4.
5 Don Ranvaud, 'Brook's Remarkable Men', *Framework*, issue 9 (Winter 1978–9), p. 32.
6 Peter Brook, *The Empty Space* (London, 1968), p. 80.
7 Peter Brook and Jean Claude Carrière, *The Conference of the Birds* (Chicago, 1982), 4th of 12 unnumbered pages.
8 'Brook's Remarkable Men', p. 33.
9 Jorge Luis Borges, *Labyrinths* (London, 1964), p. 285.
10 *The Empty Space*, p. 98.
11 Muriel Bradbrook, 'Shakespeare's Primitive Art', in Muriel Bradbrook, *The Artist and Society in Shakespeare's England* (New Jersey, 1982), p. 88.

12 Muriel Bradbrook, *The Growth and Structure of Elizabethan Comedy* (Cambridge, 1973), p. 5.
13 Robert Weimann, *Shakespeare and the Popular Tradition in the Theatre* (London, 1978), p. 198.
14 ibid., p. 238.
15 *The Growth and Structure of Elizabethan Comedy*, p. 7. My italics.
16 Richard Schechner, *Performative Circumstances from the Avante Garde to Ramlila* (Calcutta, 1983), p. 238.
17 Garry O'Connor, *The Mahabharata: Peter Brook's Epic in the Making* (London, 1989), p. 94.
18 ibid., p. 92.
19 ibid., p. 85.
20 'Shakespeare's Primitive Art', p. 91.
21 *Shakespeare and the Popular Tradition in the Theatre*, p. 174.
22 'Shakespeare's Primitive Art', p. 99.
23 *The Empty Space*, p. 129.
24 Ralph Berry, *On Directing Shakespeare* (London, 1977), p. 115.

BIBLIOGRAPHY

Abeson, Anthony, 'The Many Sides of Silence', *Village Voice* (9 October 1969).
Adair, Gilbert, 'A Meeting with Peter Brook', *Sight and Sound*, vol. 49, no. 1 (Winter 1979–80).
Adler, Renata, Review of *Tell Me Lies*, *New York Times* (18 December 1968).
Adler, Stella, Soloviova, Vera, and Meisner, Sanford, 'The Reality of Doing', *Tulane Drama Review*, vol. 9, no. 1 (Fall 1964).
Ansorge, Peter, Interview with Geoffrey Reeves, *Plays and Players*, vol. 16, no. 2 (November 1968).
—— 'Director in Interview', *Plays and Players*, vol. 18, no. 1 (October 1970).
Artaud, Antonin, *Collected Works*, translated by Victor Corti (London, 1971).
Attar, Farid Ud-din, *The Conference of the Birds*, translated from de Tassey's French version of *Mantiq Uttair* (London, 1978).
Balukhaty, S.D. (ed.), *The Seagull Produced by Stanislavsky*, translated by David Magarshack (London, 1952).
Banu, Georges, 'Peter Brook's Six Days', *New Theatre Quarterly*, vol. 3, no. 10 (May 1987).
Barba, Eugenio, 'Theatre Laboratory 13 Rzedow', *Tulane Drama Review*, vol. 9, no. 3 (Spring 1965).
—— 'A Sectarian Theatre', *Tulane Drama Review*, vol. 14, no. 1 (Fall 1969).
—— 'Words or Presence', *Tulane Drama Review*, vol. 16, no. 1 (March 1972).
—— *The Floating Islands* (Holstebro, 1979).
—— 'Theatre Culture 1979', Dartington *Theatre Papers*, third series, no. 7 (1979–80).
—— 'Creating the Roles', *Canadian Theatre Review* (Summer 1981).
—— *Beyond the Floating Islands* (New York, 1985).
Barba, Eugenio and Flaszen, Ludwik, 'A Theatre of Magic and Sacrilege', *Tulane Drama Review*, vol. 9, no. 3 (Spring 1965).
Barber, John, 'Magic Touch of Fairyland', *Daily Telegraph* (14 September 1970).
—— 'Real Food for Thought', *Daily Telegraph* (20 January 1975).
—— 'Down to the Bare Boards', *Daily Telegraph* (10 December 1977).
Barker, Clive, *Theatre Games* (London, 1977).
Barnard, Roger, Review of *US*, *Peace News* (21 October 1966).
Barnes, Clive, Review of *Oedipus*, *New York Times* (31 July 1968).

—— Review of *A Midsummer Night's Dream*, *New York Times* (28 August 1970).

Barrault, Jean-Louis, 'On Stanislavsky and Brecht', *Theatre Quarterly*, vol. 3, no. 10 (April/June 1973).

Barthes, Roland, 'Seven Photo Models of *Mother Courage*', *Tulane Drama Review*, vol. 12, no. 1 (Fall 1967).

Baxandall, Lee, 'Brecht in America 1935', *Tulane Drama Review*, vol. 12, no. 1 (Fall 1967).

Beck, Julian, 'How to Close a Theatre', *Tulane Drama Review*, vol. 8, no. 3 (Spring 1964).

—— 'Thoughts on Theatre from Jail', *New York Times* (21 February 1965).

—— *The Life of the Theatre* (New York, 1986).

Beckerman, Bernard, *Dynamics of Drama: Theory and Method of Analysis* (New York, 1979).

Beeman, William O., Review of *La Tragédie de Carmen*, *Performing Arts Journal*, vol. 22, no. 8 (1984).

Benedetti, Jean, *Stanislavski: An Introduction* (London, 1982).

Benjamin, Walter, *Understanding Brecht*, translated by Anna Bostok (London, 1973).

Bentley, Eric, 'A Prologue', *Tulane Drama Review*, vol. 6, no. 1 (September 1961).

—— 'Are Stanislavsky and Brecht Commensurable?', *Tulane Drama Review*, vol. 9, no. 1 (Fall 1964).

—— *The Theory of the Modern Stage: An Introduction to Modern Theatre and Drama* (London, 1968).

—— *The Brecht Commentaries* (London, 1981).

Bergman, Ingmar, *Bergman on Bergman*, translated by Paul Britten Austin (London, 1973).

Bernard, Kenneth, 'Some Observations on the Theatre of Peter Brook', *Theatre* (Fall/Winter 1980).

Berry, Cicely, *Voice and the Actor* (London, 1973).

Berry, Ralph, *On Directing Shakespeare* (London, 1977).

Billington, Michael, 'RSC in *US*', *Plays and Players*, vol. 14 (December 1966).

—— 'From Artaud to Brook and Back Again', *Guardian* (6 January 1976).

—— 'Written on the Wind: The Dramatic Art of Peter Brook', *The Listener* (21 and 28 December 1978).

—— 'Krishna Comes to the City of the Popes', *Guardian* (16 July 1985).

Biner, Pierre, *The Living Theatre* (New York, 1972).

Blonski, Jan, 'Grotowski and his Laboratory Theatre', *Dialog* (1970).

—— 'Holiday or Holiness?', translated by Boleslaw Taborski, *Gambit*, vol. 9, no. 33 (1979).

Blumenthal, Eileen, 'Joseph Chaikin: An Open Theory of Acting', *Yale Theatre*, vol. 8, no. 2/3 (Spring 1977).

—— *Joseph Chaikin* (London, 1984).

Boal, Augusto, *The Theatre of the Oppressed* (London, 1979).

Borges, Jorge Luis, *Labyrinths* (London, 1964).

Bradbrook, Muriel, *Themes and Conventions of Elizabethan Tragedy* (Cambridge, 1960).

—— *The Growth and Structure of Elizabethan Comedy* (Cambridge, 1973).

—— 'Shakespeare's Primitive Art', in Muriel Bradbrook, *The Artist and Society in Shakespeare's England* (New Jersey, 1982).

Bradby, David (ed.), *Performance and Politics in Popular Drama* (Cambridge, 1980).

Brahms, Caryl, 'Toddling on to Triumph', *Guardian* (9 September 1970).

Braun, Edward, *The Director and the Stage: From Naturalism to Grotowski* (London, 1982).

—— *The Theatre of Meyerhold* (London, 1986).

Brecht, Bertolt, 'An Expression of Faith in Wedekind', *Tulane Drama Review*, vol. 6, no. 1 (September 1961).

—— 'On Chinese Acting', *Tulane Drama Review*, vol. 6, no. 1 (September 1961).

—— 'On The Experimental Theatre', *Tulane Drama Review*, vol. 6, no. 1 (September 1961).

—— 'Theatre for Learning', *Tulane Drama Review*, vol. 6, no. 1 (September 1961).

—— 'To Those Born Afterwards', *Tulane Drama Review*, vol. 6, no. 1 (September 1961).

—— 'On Theatre 1920', *Tulane Drama Review*, vol. 7, no. 1 (Fall 1962).

—— 'Notes on Stanislavsky', *Tulane Drama Review*, vol. 9, no. 2 (Winter 1964).

—— 'Notes to *Mother Courage and her Children*', *Encore*, vol. 12, no. 3 (May/June 1965).

—— 'Estranging Shakespeare', *The Drama Review*, vol. 12, no. 1 (Fall 1967).

—— 'Dialogue: Berliner Ensemble', *Tulane Drama Review*, vol. 12, no. 1 (Fall 1967).

—— 'On *The Caucasian Chalk Circle*', *The Drama Review*, vol. 12, no. 1 (Fall 1967).

—— *Collected Plays* (London, 1970, 1976, 1977, 1979, 1980, 1981, 1983, 1985).

—— *Poems, 1913–1956* (London, 1976).

—— *The Mother*, translated by Steve Gooch (London, 1978).

—— *Diaries 1920–1923*, edited by Herta Ramthun, translated and annotated by John Willett (London, 1979).

—— *Brecht on Theatre* (London, 1984).

Brecht, Stefan (ed.), 'On Grotowski: A Series of Critiques', *The Drama Review*, vol. 14, no. 2 (Winter 1970).

Bresson, Robert, *Notes on the Cinematographer*, translated by Jonathan Griffin (London, 1986).

Brook, Peter, 'The Prospect Before Us', *Theatre Newsletters* (13 December 1947).

—— 'Oh for Empty Seats', *Encore*, (January 1959).

—— 'From Zero to the Infinite', *Encore* (November 1960).

—— 'The Cuban Enterprise', *Sight and Sound* (Spring 1961).

—— 'Search for a Hunger', *Encore*, vol. 8, no. 4 (July–August 1961).

—— 'Happy Days and Marienbad', *Encore* (January 1962).

—— 'Lear: Can it be Staged?', *Plays and Players*, vol. 10, no. 3 (December 1962).

—— 'Filming a Masterpiece', *Observer* (26 July 1964).

—— 'The Road to *Marat/Sade*', *New York Herald Tribune* (26 December 1964).

—— 'Endgame as King Lear', *Encore*, (January/February 1965).

—— 'The Influence of Gordon Craig in Theory and Practice', *Drama*, New Series, no. 37 (Summer 1965).

—— 'False Gods', *Flourish* (Winter 1965).

—— Introduction to Peter Weiss, *Marat/Sade* (London, 1965).

—— 'Comments', *Flourish* (Spring 1966).

—— 'Finding Shakespeare on Film', *Tulane Drama Review*, vol. 11, no. 1 (Fall 1966).

—— 'Is MacBird pro American?' *New York Times* (19 March 1967).

—— '*Tell Me Lies* in America', *The Times* (17 February 1968).

—— 'We are all Menaced', *Flourish* (Autumn, 1968).

—— Introduction to Michael Warre's *Designing and Making Stage Scenery* (London, 1968).

—— Preface to Jerzy Grotowski, *Towards a Poor Theatre* (London, 1968).

—— *The Empty Space* (London, 1968).

—— World Theatre Day Message, *The Stage in Canada*, vol. 5, no. 1 (April 1969).

—— Preface to Cicely Berry, *Voice and the Actor* (London, 1973).

—— 'The Complete Truth is Global', *New York Times* (20 January 1974).

—— 'The Three Cultures of Modern Man', *Cultures*, vol. 3, no. 4 (1976).

—— Preface to Grigory Kozintsev, *The Space of Tragedy* (London, 1978).

—— 'The Living Theatre of the Outback', *The Sunday Times* (17 August 1980).

—— *The Shifting Point* (New York, 1987).

Brook, Peter and Carrière, Jean Claude, *The Conference of the Birds* (Chicago, 1982).

Brook, Peter, Hall, Peter, Saint-Denis, Michel and Shaffer, Peter, 'Artaud for Artaud's Sake', *Encore* (May/June 1967).

—— *US: The Book of US* (London, 1968).

Brook, Peter and Marowitz,Charles, 'A Theatre of Nerve Ends', *The Sunday Times* (21 January 1964).

Brook, Peter and Reeves, Geoffrey, 'Shakespeare on Three Screens', *Sight and Sound*, vol. 34, no. 2 (Spring 1965).

Brown, John Russell, *Effective Theatre* (London, 1969).

—— *Free Shakespeare* (London, 1974).

Bryden, Ronald, 'Oedipus Newly Born', *Observer* (24 March 1968).

Burzynski, Tadeusz, 'Grotowski's Laboratory – 1977/78 Season', *The Theatre in Poland*, vol. 20, no. 5 (1978).

Bzowska, Angnieszka, 'A Somewhat Different Account of the Beehives', *Dialog*, no. 3/239 (1976).

Calvino, Italo, *Invisible Cities*, translated by William Weaver (London, 1972).

Canaan, Denis and Higgins, Colin, *The Ik* (Chicago, 1984).

Cashman, Daniel E., 'Grotowski: His Twentieth Anniversary', *Theatre Journal* (December 1969).

Chaikin, Joseph, *The Presence of the Actor* (New York, 1972).

—— 'Exiled Emotions', *Canadian Theatre Review* (Summer 1981).

—— 'Breathing in a Different Zone', *Tulane Drama Review*, vol. 25, no. 3 (Fall 1981).

—— 'Continuing Work', Dartington *Theatre Papers*, fourth series, no. 1 (1981–2).

Chekhov, Michael, *To the Actor* (New York, 1953).

Clurman, Harold, *On Directing* (New York, 1972).

Coger, Leslie Irene, 'Stanislavsky Changes his Mind', *Tulane Drama Review*, vol. 9, no. 1 (Fall 1964).

Cole, Toby, *Acting: A Handbook of the Stanislavsky System* (New York, 1955).

Cole, Toby and Chinoy, Helen K. (eds), *Directors on Directing* (New York, 1963).

―― *Actors on Acting* (New York, 1970).

Collison, Michèle, 'With Brook in Paris: Preparing for an Empty Space', *Canadian Theatre Review* (Fall 1979).

―― 'With Collison in Toronto: Emptying the Space', *Canadian Theatre Review* (Fall 1979).

Conze, Edward (ed. and trans.), *Buddhist Scriptures* (London, 1979).

Cook, Judith, *Director's Theatre* (London, 1974).

Copeland, Roger, 'The Politics of "I" and "We"', *Yale Theatre*, vol. 4, no. 2 (Spring 1979).

Corrigon, Robert W., 'Stanislavsky and the Playwright', *Tulane Drama Review*, vol. 2, no. 7 (February 1962).

Coveney, Michael, Review of *Ubu*, *Plays and Players*, vol. 25, no. 8 (May 1978).

Cox, Frank, 'Interview with Peter Brook', *Plays and Players*, vol. 15, no. 7 (April 1968).

Crawford, Michael and Kane, John, 'The Actor as Acrobat', *Plays and Players*, vol. 18, no. 11 (1971).

Croyden, Margaret, 'Peter Brook's *Tempest*', *Tulane Drama Review*, vol. 13, no. 3 (Spring 1969).

―― 'A Grotowski Seminar', *Tulane Drama Review*, vol. 14, no. 1 (Fall 1969).

―― 'A Hidden Dream of Sex and Love', *New York Times* (17 January 1971).

―― 'Peter Brook Learns to Speak Orghast', *New York Times* (2 October 1971).

―― 'Peter Brook's "Birds" Fly to Africa', *New York Times* (21 January 1973).

―― *Lunatics, Lovers and Poets: The Contemporary Experimental Theatre* (New York, 1975).

―― 'Filming the Saga of a Sage with Peter Brook', *New York Times* (26 February 1978).

―― 'Getting in Touch with Gurdjieff', *New York Times* (29 July 1979).

―― 'Whatever Happened to Jerzy Grotowski?', *New York Times* (24 February 1980).

―― 'Peter Brook's Search for Essentials', *New York Times* (4 May 1980).

―― 'Comedy, Tragedy and Mystical Fantasy: Peter Brook's New Trilogy', *New York Times* (25 May 1980).

―― *The Centre: A Narrative*, (New York, 1980).

Cushman, Robert, Review of *The Ik*, *Observer* (18 January 1976).

David, Richard, *Shakespeare in the Theatre* (Cambridge, 1979).

Davidson, John-Paul, 'Grotowski in Poland', *Plays and Players* (March 1976).

Davis, Victor, 'Brook's Fresh Tide of Ideas', *Daily Express* (22 July 1977).

Dawson, Helen, 'Peter Brook Goes Backwards', *Observer* (21 January 1968).

―― 'Doubling Up for a Triumph', *Observer* (30 August 1970).

Delza, Sophia, 'T'ai Chi Chuan: the Integrated Exercise', *Tulane Drama Review*, vol. 16, no. 1 (March 1972).

Deshpande, C.R., *Transmission of the Mahabharata Tradition* (Simla, 1978).

Dewey, Ken, 'An Odyssey Out of the Theatre', Dartington *Theatre Papers*, first series, no. 9 (1977).

Dutt, Ramesh C., *The Great Epics of India* (Delhi, 1976).

Eagleton, Terry, *Literary Theory: An Introduction* (Oxford, 1983).

Eddershaw, Margaret, 'Acting Methods: Brecht and Stanislavsky' in Graham Bartram (ed.), *Brecht in Perspective* (London, 1982).

Eddy, Bill, 'Four Directors on Criticism', *Tulane Drama Review*, vol. 18, no. 3 (September 1983).

Edwards, Christine, *The Stanislavsky Heritage* (London, 1966).

Eisenstein, Sergei, *The Film Sense*, translated by Jay Leyda (London, 1986).

Elam, Kier, *The Semiotics of Theatre and Drama* (London, 1980).

Eliot, T.S., *Collected Poems, 1909–1962* (London, 1964).

Elsom, John, *Post-War British Theatre* (London, 1979).

—— 'Brook's Latest', *Plays International* (September 1985).

Esslin, Martin, *Brecht: A Choice of Evils* (London, 1959).

—— 'The Theatre of Cruelty', *New York Times* (6 March 1966).

—— 'Are We to Blame for *US*?' *New York Times* (6 October 1966).

—— 'Brecht at Seventy', *Tulane Drama Review*, vol. 12, no. 1 (Fall 1967).

—— 'Oedipus Complex', *Plays and Players*, vol. 15, no. 8 (May 1968).

—— *The Theatre of the Absurd* (London, 1968).

—— *Artaud* (London, 1976).

—— *The Anatomy of Drama* (London, 1976).

Evans, James Roose, *Experimental Theatre* (London, 1970).

Fay, Stephen, 'A Stage for Three Carmens', *Sunday Times Magazine* (4 December 1983).

Feldenkrais, Moshe, *Awareness through Movement* (London, 1980).

Feldman, Peter, 'The Sound and Movement Exercise as Developed by the Open Theatre', Dartington *Theatre Papers*, first series, no. 1 (1977).

Feldschuh, David, 'Zen and the Actor', *Tulane Drama Review*, vol. 20, no. 1 (March 1976).

Fellini, Frederico, *Fellini on Fellini*, translated by Isabel Quigley (London, 1976).

Fergusson, Francis, 'The Notion of Action', *Tulane Drama Review*, vol. 9, no. 1 (Fall 1964).

Findlater, Richard, 'Myth and Magic Among the Persians', *Observer* (12 September 1971).

Findlay, Robert, 'Grotowski's Cultural Explorations Bordering on Art, Especially Theatre', *Theatre Journal*, vol. 32, no. 3 (October 1980).

—— 'Grotowski's *Akropolis*: A Retrospective View', *Modern Drama*, vol. 27, no. 1 (March 1984).

Flaszen, Ludwik, 'The Theatre with Thirteen Rows', *The Theatre in Poland*, no. 12 (1961).

—— 'From the Point of Emptiness', *Canadian Theatre Review* (Summer 1981).

Forsythe, Eric, 'Conversation with Ludwik Flaszen', *Educational Theatre Journal*, vol. 30, no. 3 (October 1978).

Fowler, Richard, 'The Four Theatres of Jerzy Grotowski: An Introductory Assessment', *New Theatre Quarterly*, vol. 1, no. 2 (May 1985).

Frisch, Max, 'On the Nature of Theatre', *Tulane Drama Review*, vol. 6, no. 3 (March 1962).

Fuegi, John, *The Essential Brecht* (Los Angeles, 1972).

—— *Bertolt Brecht: Chaos According to Plan* (Cambridge, 1987).

BIBLIOGRAPHY

Gaggi, Silvio, 'Brecht, Pirandello and Two Traditions of Self-Critical Art', *Theatre Quarterly*, vol. 8, no. 32 (Winter 1979).

Gardner, Sally, 'Brook at the Brooklyn Academy of Music' (September/October 1973), unpublished.

Gaskill, William, *A Sense of Direction: Life at the Royal Court* (London, 1988).

Gibson, Michael, 'Brook's Africa', *The Drama Review*, vol. 17, no. 3 (September 1973).

Gieraczynski, Bogdan, 'The No Acting Theatre of Ryszard Cieslak', *Theatre International*, no. 9 (January 1983).

Gilliat, Penelope, 'Thug in the Cradle', *Observer* (2 August 1964).

Glade, Henry, 'The Death of Mother Courage', *Tulane Drama Review*, vol. 12, no. 1 (Fall 1967).

Gorchakov, Nikolai, *Stanislavsky Directs*, translated by Miriam Goldina (New York, 1954).

—— *The Theatre in Soviet Russia*, translated by E. Lehrman (New York, 1972).

Gordon, Mel, 'Gurdjieff's Movement Demonstrations: the Theatre of the Miraculous', *Tulane Drama Review*, vol. 22, no. 2 (June 1978).

Gorelik, Mordecai, *New Theatres for Old* (London, 1940).

Grimes, Ron, 'The Theatre of Sources', *Tulane Drama Review*, vol. 25, no. 3 (Fall 1981).

Grimus, Reinhold, 'Brecht's Beginnings', *Tulane Drama Review*, vol. 12, no. 1 (Fall 1967).

Grotowski, Jerzy, '*Dr. Faustus* in Poland', *Tulane Drama Review*, vol. 8, no. 4 (Summer 1964).

—— 'For a Total Interpretation', *World Theatre*, vol. 15, no. 1 (1966).

—— 'Contemporary Perspectives', *The Theatre in Poland*, vol. 9, nos 2–3 (February–March 1967).

—— 'External Order, Internal Intimacy', *Tulane Drama Review*, vol. 14, no. 1 (Fall 1968).

—— 'Institute for the Study of Acting Methods', *The Theatre in Poland*, nos. 7–8 (1968).

—— *Towards a Poor Theatre* (London, 1969).

—— 'All Writers Seem to be Menaced Except the Great Ones', *Dramatists' Guild Quarterly* (Winter 1970).

—— 'Holiday', *Theatre Quarterly*, vol. 3, no. 10 (April–June 1973).

—— 'Holiday', *The Drama Review*, vol. 17, no. 2 (June 1973).

—— 'How One Could Live', *The Theatre in Poland*, nos. 4–5 (1975).

—— 'We Simply Look for Those Close to Us', *International Theatre Information* (Winter 1975).

—— 'The Art of the Beginner', *International Theatre Information* (Spring–Summer 1978).

—— 'Theatre of Sources 1977–80', *International Theatre Information* (Winter 1978).

—— 'On the Theatre of Sources', *The Theatre in Poland*, vol. 21, no. 11 (November 1979).

—— 'The Laboratory Theatre: Twenty Years After – A Working Hypothesis', *Polish Perspectives* (May 1980).

Hapgood, Elizabeth Reynolds, 'Stanislavsky in America', *Tulane Drama Review*, vol. 9, no. 1 (Fall 1964).

BIBLIOGRAPHY

Harris, Laurilyn J., 'Peter Brook's *King Lear*: Aesthetic Achievement or Far Side of the Moon?', *Theatre Research International*, vol. 11, no. 3 (Autumn, 1986).

Hayman, Ronald, *Techniques of Acting* (London, 1969).

—— 'Life and Joy', *The Times* (29 August 1970).

—— *Playback* (London, 1973).

—— *Theatre and Anti-Theatre* (London, 1979).

—— *Brecht: A Biography* (London, 1983).

Hecht, Werner, 'The Development of Brecht's Theory of Epic Theatre 1918–1933', *Tulane Drama Review*, vol. 6, no. 1 (September 1961).

Heilpern, John, 'Session Based on Voice', unpublished (Paris, 1972).

—— 'Peter Brook: the Grand Inquisitor', *Observer* (18 January 1976).

—— *Conference of the Birds* (London, 1977).

Hentoff, Nat, 'Yes, Let's Be Emotional About Vietnam', *New York Times* (25 February 1968).

Herrigel, Eugen, *Zen in the Art of Archery* (London, 1953).

Higgins, John, Review of *Antony and Cleopatra*, *The Times* (18 0october, 1978).

Hodgson, John (ed.), *The Uses of Drama* (London, 1985).

Hofmansthal, Hugo, 'A Prologue to Brecht's *Baal*', *Tulane Drama Review*, vol. 6, no. 1 (September 1961).

Holden, Joan, 'Collective Playmaking: the Why and the How', *Theatre Quarterly*, vol. 5, no. 18 (June/August 1975).

Holland, Peter, 'Brecht, Bond, Gaskill and the Practice of Political Theatre', *Theatre Quarterly*, vol. 8, no. 30 (1978).

Hornby, Richard, *Script into Performance* (London, 1977).

Houghton, Norris, *Moscow Rehearsals* (London, 1938).

Houston, Penelope and Tom Milne, 'Interview with Peter Brook', *Sight and Sound*, vol. 32, no. 3 (Summer 1963).

Huang, Al Chung-Liang, *Embrace Tiger, Return to Mountain: The Essence of T'ai Chi* (Utah, 1973).

Hughes, Ted, 'Talking Without Words', *Vogue* (December 1971).

Hunt, Albert, 'On Joan Littlewood and Peter Brook', *International Theatre Information* (Summer 1973).

—— 'Acting and Being', *New Society* (20 February 1979).

—— 'The Trials of Working With a Master Magician', *New Society* (26 August 1982).

—— '*The Ik*: A Review', in David Williams (ed.), *Peter Brook: A Theatrical Casebook* (London, 1988).

Hunt, Hugh, *The Director in the Theatre* (London, 1954).

Ikanowicz, Andrezj, 'On the Jerzy Grotowski Laboratory Theatre', *The Theatre in Poland*, vol. 13, no. 5 (May 1971).

Innes, Christopher, *Holy Theatre: Ritual and the Avante Garde* (Cambridge, 1981).

—— *Edward Gordon Craig* (Cambridge, 1983).

Ionesco, Eugene, 'The Avante-Garde Theatre', *Tulane Drama Review*, vol. 5, no. 2 (December 1960).

James, William, 'What is an Emotion?', *Mind*, vol. IX (1884), pp. 188–205; repr. in Dartington *Theatre Papers*, vol. 1, no. 5 (1977).

Janni, Nicholas, 'Training, Research and Performance', Dartington *Theatre Papers*, fifth series, no. 5 (1985).

Johnstone, Keith, *Impro* (London, 1985).

Jones, David Richard, *Great Directors at Work* (London, 1986).
Jung, C.G., *The Undiscovered Self*, translated by R.F.C. Hull (London, 1958).
—— *On the Nature of the Psyche*, translated by R.F.C. Hull (London, 1960).
Kane, John, 'When My Cue Comes, Call Me and I Will Answer', *Sunday Times* (13 June 1971).
Kaplan, Donald, M., 'Character and Theatre: Psychoanalytic Notes on Modern Realism', *Tulane Drama Review*, vol. 10, no. 4 (Summer 1966).
Kauffman, Stanley and Irving Drutman, 'The Provocative *Marat/Sade*: Was Peter Brook its Brain?', *New York Times* (9 January 1966).
Kelera, Joseph, 'Grotowski in Free Indirect Speech', *The Theatre in Poland*, vol. 16, no. 10 (October 1974).
Kerr, Walter, 'The Play is Scanted in the Scurry', *New York Times* (31 January 1971).
Kirby, Michael (ed.), *The New Theatre: Performance Documentation* (New York, 1974).
Kisselgoff, Anna, 'Grotowski Stresses Need for System', *New York Times* (25 November 1969).
Klossowicz, Jan, 'Grotowski in Poland', *The Theatre in Poland* (May 1971).
Knebel, Mario O., 'Stanislavsky's Method of Physical Analysis', *Theatre International*, nos. 3–4 (1981).
Kolankiewicz, Leszek, 'What's Up at Grotowski's?', *The Theatre in Poland*, nos. 5–6 (1977).
—— 'On the Road to Active Culture', unpublished document translated by Boleslaw Taborski (Wroclaw, 1978).
Komisarjevsky, Theodore, *The Theatre* (London, 1935).
Kothari, Sunil, 'Peter Brook's *Mahabharata*', *The Sunday Statesman* (28 July 1985).
Kott, Jan, *Theatre Notebook, 1947–1967*, translated by Boleslaw Taborski (London, 1968).
—— *Shakespeare: Our Contemporary* (London, 1978).
—— *The Theatre of Essence* (Evanston, 1984).
Kozintsev, Grigori, *King Lear: The Space of Tragedy*, translated by Mary Mackintosh (London, 1977).
Kroll, Jack, 'Placing the Living Shakespeare Before Us', *New York Times* (7 February 1971).
Kumeiga, Jennifer, *The Theatre of Grotowski* (London, 1987).
Labeille, Daniel, 'The Formless Hunch', *Modern Drama*, vol. 23, no. 3 (September 1980).
Labelle, Maurice H., 'Artaud's Use of Language, Sound and Tone', *Modern Drama*, vol. 15, no. 4 (March 1973).
Lahr, John, 'Knowing What to Celebrate', *Plays and Players*, vol. 23, no. 6 (March 1976).
Laing, R.D., *Self and Others* (London, 1969).
Lawson, Stephen R., Interview with Peter Brook, *Yale/Theatre*, vol. 7, no. 1 (Fall 1975).
Leonard, Hugh, 'Blue Murder', *Plays and Players*, vol. 12 (October 1964).
Levi-Strauss, Claude, *Myth and Meaning* (New York, 1978).
Levin, Bernard, Review of *A Midsummer Night's Dream* (30 September 1971).
—— 'The Seeds of Genius: Watch Them Grow', *The Times* (3 April 1980).
—— 'Two Remarkable Men on Journeys', *The Times* (26 June 1980).

Lewis, Anthony, 'Peter Brook's Theatre is a Living Event', *New York Times* (15 January 1971).

Lewis, Robert, 'Emotional Memory', *Tulane Drama Review*, vol. 6, no. 4 (June 1962).

Liehm, A.J., 'The Politics of Sclerosis: Stalin and Lear', *Theatre Quarterly*, vol. 3, no. 10 (April/June 1973).

Loney, Glen (ed.), *Peter Brook's Production of A Midsummer Night's Dream: Authorised Acting Edition* (New York, 1974).

McDowell, W. Stuart, 'Actors on Brecht', *Tulane Drama Review*, vol. 20, no. 3 (September 1976).

Magarshack, David, *Stanislavsky: A Life* (London, 1950).

Malina, Judith, *'Paradise Now* Notebook', *Yale Theatre*, vol. 2, no. 1 (1969).

—— *The Enormous Despair* (New York, 1972).

Manvell, Roger, *Shakespeare and the Film* (New York, 1971).

Marcus, Frank, 'The Future of Tempests', *Sunday Telegraph* (21 July 1968).

Marker, Lise-Lone and Marker, Frederick J., *Ingmar Bergman: Four Decades in the Theatre* (Cambridge, 1982).

Marowitz, Charles, *The Method as Means* (London, 1961).

—— 'Experiment', *The Encore Reader* (London, 1965).

—— 'Notes on the Theatre of Cruelty', *Tulane Drama Review*, vol. 11, no. 2 (Winter 1966).

—— 'Lear Log' in Charles Marowitz and Simon Trussler (eds), *Theatre at Work* (London, 1967).

—— 'From Prodigy to Professional, Directed and Acted by Peter Brook', *New York Times* (24 October 1968).

—— 'Brook: from *Marat/Sade* to *Midsummer Night's Dream*', *New York Times* (13 September 1970).

—— *Confessions of a Counterfeit Critic* (London, 1973).

—— *Artaud at Rodez* (London, 1977).

—— *The Act of Being* (London, 1978).

—— 'Emperor's New Wardrobe', *The Times* (20 June 1988).

—— *Burnt Bridges* (London, 1990).

Marowitz, Charles and Simon Trussler (eds), *Theatre at Work* (London, 1967).

Marshall, Norman, *The Producer and the Play* (London, 1975).

Mascaro, Juan (ed. and trans.), *The Upanishads*, (London, 1965).

—— (ed. and trans.) *The Dhammapada*, (London, 1984).

Mennen, Richard, 'Grotowski's Paratheatrical Projects', *The Drama Review*, vol. 19, no. 4 (December 1975).

Meyerhold, Vsevolod, 'Meyerhold to Chekhov', *Tulane Drama Review*, vol. 9, no. 1 (Fall 1964).

—— 'The 225th Studio', *Tulane Drama Review*, vol. 9, no. 1 (Fall 1964).

Milne, Tom, 'And the Time of the Great Taking Over: An Interview with William Gaskill', *Encore*, vol. 9, no. 4 (1962).

—— 'Cruelty, Cruelty', *Encore*, vol. 11, no. 2 (March/April 1964).

—— 'Reflections on *The Screens*', *Encore*, vol. 11, no. 4 (July/August 1964).

Molik, Zygmunt, 'Acting Therapy and the Voice', *Project Voice* (Cardiff, 1982).

Moore, James, 'A Subject that is Complete', *Arts Guardian* (20 July 1976).

Moore, Sonia, *The Stanislavsky System* (London, 1966).

Morgan, Joyce, *Stanislavsky's Encounters with Shakespeare* (London, 1984).

Morgenstern, Joe, 'The Great Collaborator', *New York Times Magazine* (17 April 1988).

Morley, Sheridan, 'Peter Brook: Quarrying Theatre in Australia', *The Times* (7 April 1980).

Munk, Erica, 'Looking for a New Language', *Performance*, vol. 1, no. 1 (1971).

—— 'The Way's the Thing', *Village Voice* (12 May 1980).

Needle, Jan and Peter Thomson, *Brecht* (Oxford, 1981).

Neff, Renfreu, *The Living Theatre: U.S.A.* (New York, 1970).

Neil, Boyd, 'Peter Brook: Larger than Life', *Scene Changes* (13 June 1979).

Nightingale, Benedict, 'Dream 2001 A.D.', *New Statesman* (4 September 1970).

Norwich, Julian of, *Revelations of Divine Love*, translated by Clifton Wolters (London, 1986).

Oakes, Philip, 'Something New Out of Africa', *The Sunday Times* (4 January 1976).

O'Connor, Garry, *The Mahabharata: Peter Brook's Epic in the Making* (London, 1989).

Oida, Yoshi, 'Shinto Training of the Actor', Dartington *Theatre Papers*, vol. 3, no. 3 (1979).

Osinski, Zbigniew, *Grotowski and his Laboratory*, translated by Lillian Vale and Robert Findlay (New York, 1986).

Osinski, Zbigniew and Burzynski, Tadeusz, *Grotowski's Laboratory* (Warsaw, 1979).

Pasolli, Robert, *A Book of the Open Theatre* (New York, 1970).

Patterson, Michael, *Peter Stein: Germany's Leading Theatre Director* (Cambridge, 1981).

Pitt-Rivers, Julian, 'Peter Brook and *The Ik*', *Times Literary Supplement* (31 January 1975).

Poggi, Jack, 'The Stanislavsky System in Russia', *Tulane Drama Review*, vol. 17, no. 1 (March 1973).

Polyakova, Elena, *Stanislavsky* (Moscow, 1977).

Porter, Andrew, 'In Triumph Through Persepolis', *Financial Times* (11, 14 and 16 September 1971).

Puzyna, Konstanty, 'A Myth Vivisected – Grotowski's Apocalypse', *Tulane Drama Review*, vol. 15, no. 4 (Fall 1971).

Rajagopalachari, C. (ed. and trans.), *Mahabharata* (Bombay, 1976).

Ramanujan, A.K. (ed. and trans.), *Speaking of Siva* (London, 1973).

Ranvaud, Don, 'Brook's Remarkable Men', *Framework*, issue 9 (Winter 1978–9).

Ratcliffe, Michael, 'Hindu Magic in Provence', *Observer Review* (14 July 1985).

Redgrave, Michael, *The Actor's Ways and Means* (London, 1953).

Reeves, Geoffrey, 'The Persepolis Follies of 1971', *Performance*, vol. 1, no. 1 (1971).

Rich, Frank, 'Lust and Bloodlust', *New York Times* (18 November 1983).

Richards, Jean, 'An Interview with Peter Brook at the Fifth Annual Festival of Arts, Persepolis, Iran', *Drama and Theatre*, vol. 10, no. 1 (Fall 1971).

Richie, Donald, Review of *A Midsummer Night's Dream*, *Tulane Drama Review*, vol. 15, no. 3 (Spring 1971).

Roberts, Peter, '*King Lear*: Can it be Staged?', *Plays and Players*, vol. 10, no. 3 (1962).

—— Review of *A Midsummer Night's Dream*, *Plays and Players*, vol. 18 (October 1970).

Robertson, Nan, 'Making Way for the *Mahabharata*', *The New York Times* (30 September 1987).

Rolle, Richard, *The Fire of Love*, translated by Clifton Wolters (London, 1972).

Ronen, Dan, 'A Workshop with Ryszard Cieslak', *The Drama Review*, vol. 22, no. 4 (December 1978).

Rowe, Kenneth Thorpe, *A Theatre in Your Head* (New York, 1960).

Sainer, Arthur, *The Radical Theatre Notebook* (New York, 1975).

Saint-Denis, Michel, 'Stanislavsky and Shakespeare', *Tulane Drama Review* vol. 9, no. 1 (Fall 1964).

—— *Training for the Theatre* (London, 1982).

St. John of the Cross, *The Dark Night of the Soul*, translated by Benedict Zimmerman (Cambridge, 1973).

Sarlos, Robert K., 'Performance Reconstruction: The Vital Link', *The Drama Review*, vol. 28, no. 3 (Fall 1984).

Schechner, Richard (ed.), *Dionysus in '69* (New York, 1970).

—— 'The Polish Laboratory Theatre: Towards Jerzy Grotowski', *Village Voice* (8 January 1970).

—— 'Actuals: Primitive Ritual and Performance Theory', *Theatre Quarterly*, vol. 1, no. 2 (April/June 1971).

—— 'Audience Participation', *Tulane Drama Review*, vol. 15, no. 3a (Summer 1971).

—— *Environmental Theatre* (New York, 1973).

—— 'A Critical Evaluation of Kirby's Criticism of Criticism', *Tulane Drama Review*, vol. 18, no. 4 (December 1974).

—— *Essays on Performance Theory 1970–1976* (New York, 1977).

—— *Performative Circumstances from the Avant Garde to Ramlila* (Calcutta, 1983).

—— *Between Theatre and Anthropology* (Philadelphia, 1985).

Schechner, Richard and Hoffman, Theodore, 'Stanislavsky Triumphant', *Tulane Drama Review*, vol. 9, no. 1 (Fall 1964).

—— 'An Interview with Grotowski', *The Drama Review*, vol. 13, no. 1 (Fall 1968).

Schevell, James, 'Bertolt Brecht in New York', *Tulane Drama Review*, vol. 6, no. 1 (September 1961).

Sciaratta, Patrick, 'The Polish Connection: An Encounter with Grotowski and the Theater Laboratorium', *Exchange* (Fall 1976).

Selbourne, David, 'Brook's *Dream*' in *Culture and Agitation – Theatre Documents* (London, 1972).

—— *The Making of A Midsummer Night's Dream* (London, 1982).

Sellin, Eric, *The Dramatic Concepts of Antonin Artaud* (London, 1968).

Serban, Andrei, 'The Life in a Sound', *Tulane Drama Review*, vol. 20, no. 4 (December 1976).

Sethi, Sunil, 'Stage Presence', *India Today* (15 March 1982).

Sethi, Sunil and Kothari, Sunil, 'An Epic Endeavour', *India Today* (31 July 1985).

Shorter, Eric, Review of *Marat/Sade*, *Daily Telegraph* (21 August 1964).

—— 'Lost Man of British Theatre', *Daily Telegraph* (17 October 1974).

—— 'Timon of Paris', *Drama*, no. 115 (Winter 1974).

—— 'Gamlets, Gimmick, Snooks and Puppets in Paris', *Drama*, no. 127 (Winter 1977–8).

—— 'Off the Cuff with Peter Brook and Company', *Drama*, no. 129 (Summer 1978).

—— 'False Prophet?', *Daily Telegraph* (12 January 1979).

—— 'Brook and Others in Avignon', *Drama*, no. 134 (Autumn 1979).

—— 'Chekhov through English Eyes in French', *Drama*, no. 141 (Autumn 1981).

Siciliano, Enzo, *Pasolini: A Biography*, translated by John Shepley (New York, 1982).

Sjoberg, Alf, 'Sensuality in Brecht', *Tulane Drama Review*, vol. 12, no. 1 (Fall 1967).

Smith, A.C.H., *Orghast at Persepolis* (New York, 1972).

Spolin, Viola, *Improvisation for the Theatre* (Evanston, 1983).

Stanislavsky, Konstantin, *Stanislavsky Produces Othello* (London, 1948).

—— 'Director's Diary, 1905', *Tulane Drama Review*, vol. 9, no. 1 (Fall 1964).

—— 'Director and Actor at Work', *Tulane Drama Review*, vol. 9, no. 1 (Fall 1964).

—— *An Actor Prepares*, translated by Elizabeth Reynolds Hapgood (London, 1967).

—— *Stanislavsky on the Art of the Stage*, translated by David Magarshack (London, 1967).

—— *Stanislavsky's Legacy*, translated by Elizabeth Reynolds Hapgood (London, 1968).

——*Building a Character*, translated by Elizabeth Reynolds Hapgood (London, 1968).

—— *My Life in Art*, translated by J.J. Robbins (London, 1980).

—— *Creating a Role*, translated by Elizabeth Reynolds Hapgood (London, 1983).

Steiner, George, *Language and Silence* (London, 1979).

Stoppard, Tom, Review of *Orghast*, *Times Literary Supplement* (1 October 1971).

Strasberg, Lee, 'Working with Live Material', *Tulane Drama Review*, vol. 9, no. 1 (Fall 1964).

—— 'Stanislavsky and the Actor's Studio', *Theatre Quarterly*, vol. 8, no. 29 (Spring 1978).

Styan, J.L., Review of Theatre of Cruelty Season, *Plays and Players*, vol. 11 (March 1964).

—— *Drama, Stage and Audience* (Cambridge, 1975).

—— *The Elements of Drama* (Cambridge, 1976).

—— *Modern Drama in Theory and Practice* (3 vols) (Cambridge, 1981).

—— *Max Reinhardt* (London, 1982).

Styroyeva, M.N., 'The Three Sisters at the M.A.T.', *Tulane Drama Review*, vol. 9, no. 1 (Fall 1964).

Sullivan, Dan, 'Called on the Carpet by a Theatre Guru', *Los Angeles Times* (2 September 1973).

Sullivan, John J., 'Stanislavsky and Freud', *Tulane Drama Review*, vol. 9, no. 1 (Fall 1964).

Summers, Sue, Interview with Peter Brook, *Screen International* (27 August 1977).

Suvin, Darko, 'The Mirror and the Dynamo', *Tulane Drama Review*, vol. 12, no. 1 (Fall 1967).

Suzuki, Daisetz Teitaro, *Zen and Japanese Culture* (London, 1959).

—— *Living by Zen* (London, 1972).

Suzuki, Tadashi, 'The Word is an Act of the Body', *Performing Arts Journal*, vol. 6, no. 2 (1982).

—— *The Way of Acting*, translated by J. Thomas Rimer (New York, 1986).

Talukdar-Stanchina, Kanta, 'Magnificent Obsessions', *The Illustrated Weekly of India* (18 August 1985).

Tarkovsky, Andrey, *Sculpting in Time: Reflections on the Cinema*, translated by Kitty Hunter Blair (London, 1986).

Taylor, Desmond Shaw, 'Brook's Triumph in the Bullring', *The Sunday Times* (22 November 1981).

Taylor, John Russel, 'Peter Brook, or the Limits of Intelligence', *Sight and Sound*, vol. 36, no. 2 (Spring 1967).

Temkine, Raymonde, *Grotowski*, translated by Alex Szogyi (New York, 1972).

Terayama, Shiyi, 'Farewell to Grotowski', *Tulane Drama Review*, vol. 17, no. 4 (December 1973).

Thomson, Peter, 'A Necessary Theatre', *Shakespeare Survey* (1971).

Topkis, Maggie, 'A Ritual Called Conference', *Theatre International*, nos. 3–4 (1981).

Toporkov, Vasily Osipovich, *Stanislavsky in Rehearsal: The Final Years*, translated by Christine Edwards (New York, 1979).

Trewin, J.C., *Peter Brook: A Biography* (London, 1971).

Trilling, Ossia, 'Playing with Words at Persepolis', *Theatre Quarterly*, vol. 2, no. 5 (January/March 1975).

Trussler, Simon, 'Private Experiment – in Public', *Plays and Players*, vol. 11 (February 1964).

Turnbull, Colin, *The Mountain People* (London, 1974).

Tynan, Kenneth, 'Director as Misanthropist: On the Moral Neutrality of Peter Brook', *Theatre Quarterly*, vol. 7, no. 25 (1977).

Volker, Klaus, *Brecht: A Biography*, translated by John Nowell (New York, 1978).

Waldman, Max, 'The Constant Prince', *Tulane Drama Review*, vol. 14, no. 2 (Winter 1970).

Wardle, Irving, 'Complex Simplicity', *Plays and Players* (January 1963).

—— 'Second Thoughts on Brook', *The Times* (23 March 1968).

—— 'Actors at their New Exercise', *The Times* (19 July 1968).

—— 'The Saint and the Sybarite', *The Times* (14 September 1968).

—— 'Grotowski the Evangelist', *The Times* (4 October 1969).

—— 'To the Heights on a Trapeze', *The Times* (28 August 1970).

—— 'Conjuring Buried Music Out of the Earth', *The Times* (10 and 14 September 1971).

—— 'Rituals in the Desert: the Shiraz Festival 1970', *Gambit*, vol. 5, nos. 18–19 (1971).

—— 'Paying the Price of Survival', *The Times* (16 January 1976).

—— 'The Indian Pilgrimage of Peter Brook', *The Times* (5 May 1982).

—— 'Images of Tenderness, Triumph and Death', *The Times* (13 July 1985).

Watts, Alan, *The Way of Zen* (London, 1978).

Weber, Carl, 'Brecht as Director', *The Drama Review*, vol. 12, no. 1 (Fall 1967).

—— 'Brecht in Eclipse', *The Drama Review*, vol. 24, no. 1 (March 1980).

Weill, Kurt, 'Gesture in Music', *Tulane Drama Review*, vol. 6, no. 1 (September 1961).

Weimann, Robert, *Shakespeare and the Popular Tradition in the Theatre* (London, 1978).

Weinraub, Bernard, 'Recording the *Marat/Sade* Madness', *New York Times* (13 February 1966).

—— Review of *The Ik*, *New York Times* (28 January 1976).

Weiss, Peter, *Marat/Sade* (London, 1986).

Wekwerth, Manfred, 'Brecht Today', *Tulane Drama Review*, vol. 12, no. 1 (Fall 1967).

Wesker, Arnold, 'An Open Letter to Peter Brook', *Flourish* (Spring 1966).

Wiles, Timothy J., *The Theatre Event: Modern Theories of Performance* (Chicago, 1980).

Willett, John, *The Theatre of Bertolt Brecht* (London, 1959).

—— *The Theatre of Erwin Piscator* (London, 1978).

Williams, David, 'A Place Marked by Life: Peter Brook at the Bouffes du Nord', *New Theatre Quarterly*, vol. 1, no. 1 (February 1985).

—— (ed.), *Peter Brook: A Theatrical Casebook* (London, 1988).

Willis, Ronald A., 'The American Lab Theatre', *Tulane Drama Review*, vol. 9, no. 1 (Fall 1964).

Wilson, David, Review of *Tell Me Lies*, *Sight and Sound*, vol. 37, no. 2 (Spring 1968).

Wilson, Glen, *The Psychology of the Performing Arts* (London, 1985).

Wolters, Clifton (ed. and trans.), *The Cloud of Unknowing and Other Works* (London, 1978).

INDEX

Abeson, Anthony 84
Absurd, Theatre of the 134
active culture 103–4
Actor Prepares, An 3, 7, 14–16, 22, 51
Africa 107, 109, 117, 120–4, 127–9, 131
Akropolis 79
Albany 28
Alexeyev, Konstantin 6
alienation 44–7, 49–50, 54–6, 59, 61–3, 69, 71, 74–5, 80, 87, 102, 117, 141, *see also* defamiliarization
Amazonia 79
Ancestors, The 100
Andreyev, Leonid 14
Apocalypsis Cum Figuris 79, 101, 104
Apollo 1
Arjuna 139, 141, 143
Artaud 81–2
'Art of the Beginner, The' 104
Atman 124
Attar, Farid Ud-din 105–7, 110, 117–20, 119, 123, 126
audience-participation 99–101, 128–32

Bagayogo, Malik 127, 129
Barba, Eugenio 94, 105
Battle of Life, The 21
Beckerman, Bernard 1
Beckett, Samuel 27, 137
being oneself 82–3, 87–91, 98, 106, 109–12, 117, 123, 125, 141, *see also* self-realization
Benechou, Maurice 141, 143
Berliner Ensemble 61
Bharatanatyam 133
Bhishma 139
Bible 111
bio-mechanics 32
Blonski, Jan 80, 99
Bone, The 134
Borges, Jorge Luis 138
Bottom 33, 38
Bradbrook, Muriel 136–8, 142–4
Brahman 124, 127
Brecht, Bertolt 2–3, 5, 32, 41, **42–77**, 80, 89–90, 92, 131, 143; alienation 44–7, 49–50, 54–7, 59, 61–3, 71; *Caucasian Chalk Circle, The* 46, 52, 57; dialectical theatre 50; distance between actor and role 46–9, 57–8; epic 44–6, 50, 53, 55, 64; *Galileo* 47, 64; gestus 48; given circumstances exercise 43–5, 51, 53; *In the Jungle of the Cities* 62; justification 51; *Measures Taken, The* 59; metatextuality 45–7, 49, 53–8, 63–5, 67; *Mother Courage* 61, 64; *Mother, The* 52; music 46, 49;'not . . . but' 60; parody 55–7; *Resistible Rise of Arturo Ui, The* 52; *Round Heads and Pointed Heads* 55; sequential defamiliarization 59; *Short*

174

Organum for the Theatre 47;
simultaneous defamiliarization
59–60; somatics 52, 54;
Stanislavsky, affinity with 49–52;
Stanislavsky, criticism of 42–5,
49; time 54–5; titles and
projections 46; units and
objectives exercise 51, 53
Britain 65
Brook, Peter 1–3, 5, **25–41**, 42,
61–77, 80–1, **105–34**, 135–44;
alienation 61–3, 69, 74–5, 141;
audience-participation 127–32;
being-dead exercise 72–3; *Bone,
The* 134; on Brecht 61–4;
cerebral approach to
characterization 26–9; Chaikin
chord exercise 30; *Conference of
the Birds, The* 111, 114–15;
contact 122–32; defamiliarization,
modification of, 65–6, 75, 125;
Empty Space, The 36, 41, 63, 114,
118–20, 132, 137, 144;
ephemerality of meaning 41; epic
53, 55; given circumstances
exercise 28–9, 67–9;
identification of actor and
character 40–1; John Kane on
31–2; *King Lear* 25–9, 30–1, 33,
83, 119, 135–6; language 33, 36;
Lila 132; literalism 106–10;
Mahabharata, Le 5, 134–44;
manipulation of actors' emotions
39–40; masks 114–15; *Meetings
with Remarkable Men* 136;
mendacity 64–6, 70–2; metatext
64–5; *Midsummer Night's Dream,
A* 4, 26, 29–41, 121, 129;
non-naturalistic theatre 62;
Oedipus 129; originality as a
director 3–5; rhythm 32–35,
37–9; *Romeo and Juliet* 121;
rough and holy theatre 137, 139;
self-knowledge 110, 112–16;
self-realization 110–12, 117, 125;
self-transcendence 110, 116–20;
sequential defamiliarization 73–6;
set-design 38; on Shakespeare 36;
Shifting Point, The 61, 111, 134;

simultaneous defamiliarization
76; somatics 29–41, 68–70; song
36; sound 33, 37; sound and
movement exercise 34; sticks as
words exercise 35; synthesis of
styles 1, 133–44; *Tell Me Lies* 63;
Tempest, The 29, 129; *Tragédie
de Carmen* 119; units and
objectives exercise 27; *US* 63,
65–77, 80–1; via negativa
119–122, 141; *Walking Show,
The* 108; wholeness 78, 107,
111–12, 124–7, 133, 137
Brueghel, Pieter 52
Buddhism 68, 75
Building a Character 18, 22
Bulgakov, Mikhail 13

Cain 79, 100
Canan, Denis 71
Carrière, Jean-Claude 139
Caruso 74, 76
Caucasian Chalk Circle, The 46, 52,
57
Centre Internationale de Créations
Théâtrales 123
Centre Internationale de Recherche
Théâtrales 123
Chaikin, Joseph 30–1, 34, 68
characterization, cerebral 14–17, 21,
26–9 , 51, 53, 67–8
characterization, somatic 17–25,
29–41, 52–3, 68–9, 113
Chatski 20
Chicago 62
China 59
Christ, Jesus 90, 94
Cieslak, Ryszard 79, 89, 93–4, 141
Cinerama 136
Claudius 56
Collison, Michèle 112, 114
Conference of the Birds (Heilpern)
107
Conference of the Birds, The (Attar)
105, 110
Conference of the Birds, The
(Brook/Carrière) 111, 114–15,
134
Connection, The 109